From News to Talk

From News to Talk

The Expansion of Opinion and Commentary in US Journalism

KIMBERLY MELTZER

Cover: iStock by Getty Images

Published by State University of New York Press, Albany

© 2019 Kimberly Meltzer

All rights reserved

No part of this book may be used or reproduced in any manner whatsoever without written permission. No part of this book may be stored in a retrieval system or transmitted in any form or by any means including electronic, electrostatic, magnetic tape, mechanical, photocopying, recording, or otherwise without the prior permission in writing of the publisher.

For information, contact State University of New York Press, Albany, NY
www.sunypress.edu

Library of Congress Cataloging-in-Publication Data

Name: Meltzer, Kimberly, author.
Title: From news to talk : the expansion of opinion and commentary in US journalism / Kimberly Meltzer.
Description: Albany : State University of New York Press, [2019] | Includes bibliographical references and index.
Identifiers: LCCN 2018020074 | ISBN 9781438473499 (hardcover) | ISBN 9781438473482 (pbk.) | ISBN 9781438473505 (ebook)
Subjects: LCSH: Journalism—Objectivity—United States. | Journalists—United States—Attitudes.
Classification: LCC PN4888.O25 M455 2019 | DDC 302.23—dc23
LC record available at https://lccn.loc.gov/2018020074

10 9 8 7 6 5 4 3 2 1

For Evan, Natalie, and Jocelyn

Contents

PREFACE	xi
ACKNOWLEDGMENTS	xv
LIST OF INTERVIEWS CONDUCTED WITH JOURNALISTS	xvii

CHAPTER 1
Journalism in the Current Era ... 1
   How Journalists Dealt with the Rhetoric of Trump and Others
      during the 2016 Election Cycle ... 2
   What Journalists Said after the 2016 Election ... 3
   Why Examine Journalistic Discourse? ... 11
   Journalists as Communities of Practice ... 13

CHAPTER 2
The Increase in Talk in News ... 27
   Journalistic Models ... 28
   Has Opinion in News Increased? ... 32
   Opinion Journalism Is Increasing through
   Journalists' Social Media Use ... 40
   Why Has Opinion in News Increased? ... 45
   CNN's (Jeff Zucker's) Strategy to "Diversify" Programming ... 59
   Journalists Starting Their Own Self-Branded Sites ... 66

CHAPTER 3
Journalists' Perspectives on Incivility and Opinion in Digital
News Media ... 75
   Definitions of Civility ... 77
   Research about Civility, Politics, and Journalism ... 79

Method	81
Analysis	82
Discussion	92

CHAPTER 4
Journalists' Perspectives on Opinion, Commentary, and Incivility in All Types of News — 95

Reasons for the Increase in Incivility, Uncivil Tone of Political Discourse in Media	97
Differences in Opinion and Commentary According to Medium	103
Increases in Opinion and Commentary Are Positive or Neutral	105
Opinion and Commentary from Regular People/Bloggers/Citizen Journalists through Social Media Are More Important than What's Coming From, or Through the Filter of, Legacy/Big Media	109
Not Concerned for the Audience because of Opinion in News	110
Concerned for the Audience because of Incivility in News	117
Not Concerned about Incivility	122
Concern about Incivility *from/perpetuated by* Audiences, Regular People	124
Not Concerned with Uncivil Comments from Users/Audience	128
Whether Bad or Good, the Heated and Uncivil Expression of Opinion Has Been Around for a Long Time	129
Lack of Labeling Content as Opinion Can Be Concerning for Audiences	131
Increases in Opinion and Commentary Have Negative Impacts	133
A Generational Difference?	139
Calling It "Point-of-View Journalism" or Similar, rather than Opinion or Commentary	140
How Journalists Who Provide Opinionated Content Think of Themselves and Their Own Work	144

CHAPTER 5
Opinion ≠ Incivility: The Case of PBS's Brooks and Shields — 155

Mediated Political Discourse	156
Method	157
Findings	158
Discussion: How Do We Account for Civility?	163
Conclusion	165

CHAPTER 6
Symbolic or Just Coincidence: How Journalists Made Sense of
Katie's, Anderson's, and Brian's Talk Show Experiments   167
  Analysis   169
  Why Didn't Katie's, Anderson's, and Brian's New Programs Work? 176
  The Brian Williams Scandal   179

CHAPTER 7
Journalists' Thoughts about the Future of News   183
  Opinion Is Here to Stay   183
  Personalization of News Will Continue   186
  The Notoriety and Brand of Individual Journalists   191
  The Success and Survival of Different News Mediums   195
  Predictions about the Future of Newspapers   205

CHAPTER 8
Where We Go from Here   209
Avenues for Future Research, and Implications   212

NOTES   217

BIBLIOGRAPHY   221

INDEX   245

Preface

Over the past ten years, news organizations of all types have been producing more commentary and opinion—what I construe as "talk." Professional punditry has proliferated on television in the past decade. It is a less expensive alternative to scripted news and it still attracts viewers. The talking heads found across television news are more than readily available and often participate without financial compensation (Farhi, 2016). The move toward talk within TV news programs, and the increase in opinion and commentary in other types of news, is also an attempt to provide the "value added" for audience members who have many sources of the same news to choose from. The additional personalities, opinions, debate of viewpoints, and expertise can distinguish an outlet's news coverage of a story from its competitors'. The movement toward talk also feeds the cycle of individual brand creation and management by big-name journalists (Farhi, 2014). As audiences for traditional TV news broadcasts continue to dwindle, cannibalized by newer information venues and technologies, the movement of some of the most well-known news personalities from news programs to talk shows represents a shift in the prestige of televised news and talk. It also affirms the blending of news and entertainment and the fluidity and transferability of individual TV personalities. The increasing presence of presidents, political candidates, and others regarded as authority figures, on television talk shows also helps to elevate the format's status. A media environment which will increasingly contain automated news—news stories generated and written by computer algorithms—is another reason why "talk" will be increasingly present; it could be one of the only things distinguishing robot journalists from human ones (Keohane, 2017; Levy, 2012).

Recent years have also seen the strategy by some news networks to expand the definition of news by adding other types of programs. We have also seen the creation of many online news sites started by star journalists who made a name for themselves at more traditional news organizations before leaving to begin their own enterprises. Another aspect of the increase in opinion and commentary in news is how journalists are dealing with the ability of news consumers to talk back to their stories in the form of comments on news websites and elsewhere.

As a journalism scholar who once worked in TV news in New York and Atlanta, and for local and regional newspapers, I have observed the movement toward "talk" in news. This book follows logically from my previous book (Meltzer, 2010) which tracked journalistic adaptation to television technology from the 1950s through 2009 and which left off with suggestions for predicting how journalism and television news would continue to evolve. It is also an outgrowth of ideas that have percolated through discussions in the courses I have taught over the past ten years in the Washington, DC area at Marymount University and Georgetown University.

In this book, *From News to Talk*, the technological, economic, cultural, and political forces affecting the movement toward opinion, commentary, and talk in television, online, print, and radio news are examined. This is accomplished through interviews with over 30 journalists and other industry professionals, and analysis of popular, trade, and organizational publications and proceedings about opinion, commentary, and talk in news. The interviews include key figures in journalism. The analysis centers around several key case studies of this movement toward opinion and commentary in news, including on TV with the increase in opinionated talking heads and the ushering in of a new era of talk and entertainment programs, the strategy by CNN to broaden its definition of news by adding non-news programs, and online and mobile news with the bevy of star journalists starting their own self-branded sites.

While this book focuses on contemporary cases of moves toward talk, it necessarily provides an historical tracing of opinion and commentary in television, print, radio, and online news. TV news even in its purest form was fundamentally based on "talk." The news anchors and reporters tell us the story. They talk to us at home. According to Scannell (1996, in Thornborrow and Montgomery, 2010):

> Sociability is the most fundamental characteristic of broadcasting's communicative ethos [. . .] To describe the communicative manner and style of radio and television as conversational means more than chatty mannerisms and a personalized idiom. It means orienting to the normative values of ordinary talk in which participants have equal status and equal discursive rights [. . .] The communicative task that broadcasters faced was to find forms of talk that spoke to listeners, modes of address which disclosed that listeners were taken into account in the form of the utterance

itself [. . .] [R]adio and television's communicative style was first found in the development of friendlier forms of address, a more informal discursive style as markers of a general sociable intent that showed itself in most areas of programme output. (1996: 23–24)

Thornborrow and Montgomery (2010: 101) write that "The very fact that, in broadcasting, audiences may easily disengage from the message places a considerable onus on the broadcaster to sustain their interest."

Therefore, in the shift from news to talk, the delivery of information through the spoken word is not what varies, but it is a shift in what the talk is about, and the manner in which it is delivered. It is also not as though talk and other non-news elements did not always exist to some extent within television news. Katz has argued that television has long included opinion and interpretation, and it was when television news "far eclipsed newspaper news as the main source of daily information, causing the newspapers to respond, as tabloids do, by becoming more like television . . . through the highlighting of opinion and interpretation" (Katz, 2009: 12). Ben-Porath (2007) refers to the increase in conversational news as a rise in "dialogical" news, and Cushion (2015) views it through the lenses of mediatization and journalistic interventionism, marking a shift from edited to live reporting, focusing on "the two-way convention in political coverage and the more interpretive approach to journalism it promotes."

This book argues that in the past decade, the proportion of news that talk comprises has increased. It has become amplified across television, and this may parallel a larger cultural shift toward talk. Existing reported data show that there is more "talk" content within news programs now than in the past (Wemple, 2013; Pew Research Center, 2013). Until now, evidence of journalists' own perceptions of the shift from news to talk is mostly anecdotal. A good deal of communication research in recent years has focused on the effects of televised political opinion, soft news, and satire on viewer learning, recall, and engagement (i.e., Vraga et al., 2012; Feldman, 2011; Stroud, 2011; McChesney & Pickard, 2011; Williams & Delli Carpini, 2011; Baum, 2002; 2003; 2006; Moy, 2005; Prior, 2003; and Mutz, 2007), and other research has investigated through fieldwork how journalists and users are adapting to new technologies (Bivens, 2014; Boczkowski, 2010; Usher, 2012; 2012b; 2016; Anderson, 2013). Some believe that a movement back toward opinionated news could be positive (St. John & Johnson, 2012). Some of this research has found that people can learn as much from opinionated or unconventional TV formats as from traditional, objective news. Still other studies have centered on incivility in news discourse (Mutz, 2015; York, 2013; Ben-Porath, 2007), with some findings showing a discrepancy between journalists' justification of overly aggressive—or uncivil—interviewing techniques as exemplifying their democratic watchdog role, and the audience's perception of these techniques as distasteful, leading to less regard for journalists in general.

Some scholars and activists believe that alternative venues and modes of funding are needed to foster and sustain certain forms of news. These thinkers have proposed new ways of structuring, funding, and regulating news media which include education modules in schools, professional training for media employees, and legislative action.

But to date, few studies have explored what the people working in journalism think about the movement toward often opinionated, sometimes uncivil, talk in news. This book provides an important intervention in the debates about the future of news by investigating what journalists think about the increase in opinion, commentary and talk in news, what they perceive as the forces affecting this movement, what their perceptions are of the effects of this shift on audiences and political culture, and, in their view, how the movement from news to talk affects journalists' roles and authority in society.

The title of the book, *From News to Talk*, describes two phenomena in news: the first, a spectrum ranging from news to talk, gradients in formats, content, and delivery/hosts; the second, a movement from news to talk (aka news to entertainment, "objective"/traditional to opinion/commentary).

How the Book Is Organized

Chapter 1 begins by discussing journalism in the current era—pre- and post-2016 election. The theoretical and methodological approaches are laid out. Chapter 2 traces the perspectives of journalists with regard to the increase in talk in news across all types of media. Chapter 3 examines journalists' views of the increase in opinion and incivility in political news discourse through digital media since the 1990s. Chapter 4 provides the contemporary perspectives of journalists shared through interviews about opinion and incivility in all types of news. Chapter 5 provides a case study analysis of the exchanges between Mark Shields and David Brooks on the PBS NewsHour in order to illustrate how two hosts with differing political views model productive opinionated discourse. In Chapter 6, the programming moves by Katie Couric, Anderson Cooper, and Brian Williams are explored through journalistic discourse as a means to uncovering the nature of the news/talk landscape. Journalists' predictions about the future of news are discussed in Chapter 7.

Acknowledgments

Thank you to my three great loves, Evan, Natalie, and Jocelyn, for your love, cuteness, motivation, patience, and understanding. If it weren't for my incredibly supportive husband, parents, and parents-in-law, this book would never have been written. I am indebted to my daughters' grandparents—especially Helene and Richard Meltzer, and Audrey Jones—for the countless babysitting hours, and I am thankful for the confidence in my work from my entire family.

I am also grateful to the journalists who made this book possible through their willingness to spend their valuable time talking with me about their thoughts and experiences.

At SUNY Press, I'd like to thank Senior Editor Michael Rinella, Co-Director James Peltz, and Rafael Chaiken for their interest in the book and seeing it, and me, through the publication process. I'd also like to thank Diane Ganeles, Fran Keneston, and Kate Seburyamo at SUNY Press. I wish to thank the anonymous reviewers of the manuscript for their generous and constructive reviews that strengthened the book.

The research for this book, which still took a long time, would have taken even longer had it not been for my smart and dedicated graduate research assistants on the project at CCT at Georgetown: Layan Jawdat, Emily Martik, Andrew Postal, Angela Hart, and Cecilia Daizovi Weiland. I'd also like to thank my undergraduate assistant at Marymount University, Janine Cusseaux.

I also wish to acknowledge the contributions of co-authors on two previously published articles that are included in the book: Emily Martik, my co-author of "Journalists as Communities of Practice: Advancing a theoretical framework for understanding journalism." *Journal of Communication Inquiry*, July 2017, 41(3): 207–226; and Judith Hoover, my co-author on "Civility in News Discourse: The Case of PBS' Brooks and Shields." *Electronic News*, December 2014, 8(3): 216–235. Thank you, Emily and Judith.

SAGE Journals has permitted the republishing of the following articles in the book:

Meltzer, K., and Hoover, J. "Civility in News Discourse: The Case of PBS's Brooks and Shields." *Electronic News*, December 2014, 8(3): 216–235. The final, definitive version of this paper has been published by SAGE Publishing, All rights reserved. doi: 10.1177/1931243114557598

Meltzer, K., and Martik, E. "Journalists as Communities of Practice: Advancing a theoretical framework for understanding journalism." *Journal of Communication Inquiry*, 41(3): 207–226. July 2017. The final, definitive version of this paper has been published by SAGE Publishing, All rights reserved. doi: 10.1177/0196859917706158

Meltzer, K. "Journalistic Concern about Uncivil Political Talk in Digital News Media: Responsibility, Credibility and Academic Influence." *The International Journal of Press/Politics*, January 2015, 20 (1), 85–107. The final, definitive version of this paper has been published by SAGE Publishing, All rights reserved. doi: 10.1177/1940161214558748

I am very appreciative of the Marymount University Faculty Development Grant I was awarded for summer research support, and the support of my work by Dean Christina Clark, and my colleagues in Communication and Media Design and the School of Design, Arts, and Humanities. I also wish to thank the many students in my courses at CCT and Marymount for helping to generate ideas and entertaining discussion on these topics. Additionally, Carole Sargent in the Office of Scholarly Publications at Georgetown, and the members of the writing groups I was part of, provided great ideas and spurred me on. Some of the research for the book was also supported by a Junior Faculty Research Fellowship from Georgetown. There, I wish to thank David Lightfoot and my CCT colleagues. Thank you also to Barbie Zelizer, Michael DelliCarpini, and Linda Steiner for your advice.

List of Interviews and Original Exchanges with Journalists and Industry Professionals

Most interviewees agreed to have their names used. Interviewees who wished to have their identity remain confidential were given pseudonyms or referred to in general terms, per the interview consent agreement.

Jon Allen, head of community and content for *Sidewire*; national political reporter (detailed to the White House) for NBC News Digital; formerly *Bloomberg News* Washington Bureau Chief; formerly Vox senior political correspondent (6/9/14 by phone). Also formerly worked for *Politico and Congressional Quarterly*. Has worked in print, online, mobile, and TV journalism. Is also co-author of *Shattered* and *HRC* published by Random House.

Joshua Altman, formerly of *The Hill* (7/16/14 in person).

Maria Bartiromo, Anchor, Fox Business Network (6/19/14 by phone); formerly at CNBC, CNN.

Richard Benedetto, White House Correspondent, *USA Today* (ret.) (3/26/14 in person).

Michael Calderone, Senior Media Reporter, *Huffington Post* (7/2/14 by phone). Was previously at Yahoo News, *Politico*, *New York Observer*. Has MA in Journalism from NYU and is now an adjunct professor there teaching a course on media criticism.

Tim Carney, *Washington Examiner* (remarks made at Institute on Political Journalism board meeting 3/16/15).

Paul Farhi, *The Washington Post* (6/4/14 in person at *Washington Post* old/original headquarters).

List of Interviews and Original Exchanges

Jim Henderson, formerly Money Editor of *USA Today* (12/10/14 in person).

Stephanie Lambidakis, long time CBS justice reporter (7/3/14 by phone).

Rick Massimo, WTOP, previously at *Providence Journal* (RI). (6/10/14) in person).

Dave Mastio, Forum Editor, *USA Today* (8/7/14 in person at *USA Today*, McLean, VA) The day before I interviewed Dave Mastio at *USA Today* headquarters in McLean, Gannett, their parent company, had announced a split up of the company (see *USA Today* article from Money section on 8/6/14).

Liza Mundy, New America Foundation, formerly of *The Washington Post*; contributor to *The Atlantic* and other publications; book author (7/30/14 by phone).

Bruce Perlmutter, Senior Vice President at *Conde Nast*; previously RevoltTV, E! News, CNN (8/7/14 by phone, follow-up by email 3/26/18).

Amber Phillips, staff writer at The Fix, *The Washington Post*; formerly *Las Vegas Sun* Washington Correspondent. (7/23/14 by phone). Prior to that, worked for Digital First (which has since folded) covering Congress.

Rem Rieder, former long-time editor of *American Journalism Review* (for 22 years); media columnist and editor-at-large, *USA Today*. (1/20/15 in person at *USA Today* headquarters, McLean, VA, and phone follow-up on 1/29/15). Rieder made the move to *USA Today* in July 2013. *AJR* folded in summer 2015. Before *AJR*, he was at *The Washington Post*, *Miami Herald*, *Milwaukee Journal*, and *States News Service*.

Chris Satullo, former VP News and Civic Engagement, WHYY; former editorial page editor at *Philadelphia Inquirer*; former Professional in Residence at APPC, now a media and civic engagement consultant. 3/14/16 spoke with my Journalism & Politics course at Georgetown.

Frank Sesno, former CNN Washington Bureau Chief; currently dean of George Washington University's School of Media and Public Affairs (Phone interview 10/9/14. Follow-up email correspondence 10/12/14).

Jack Shafer, *Politico* (formerly of Reuters and Slate) (2/11/15 by phone).

Brian Stelter, Host, CNN's Reliable Sources, founder of TVNewser (8/18/14 by phone).

Erik Wemple, *The Washington Post* (6/12/14 by phone), The Erik Wemple Blog, a reported opinion blog on news media. Previously editor at *Washington City Paper*; previously editor of TBD.

Referred to as "veteran TV reporter" (7/3/14).

List of Interviews and Original Exchanges   xix

Referred to as "CNN digital employee/CNN employee who works on digital/web content" (4/14/15 by phone; follow-up to remarks made in person 3/16/15).

Referred to as "confidential source who formerly worked in TV news."

Referred to in book as "confidential source who works in TV news." (8/10/14 in person).

Referred to in book as "TV journalist in Washington" (6/18/14 in person).

Referred to as "former news producer" (6/16/14).

Referred to as "former radio and online journalist" (in person 12/15).

Referred to as "television news correspondent" (2/9/17 in person).

2014 Journalism/Interactive Conference, University of Maryland, Philip Merrill College of Journalism. In-person attendance. April 4–5, 2014.

Comments from Council on Foundations Nonprofit news event at the Newseum (9/9/15): Tom Glaisyer, Managing Director, Public Square Program at the Democracy Fund; and Peter Bale, former CEO, Center for Public Integrity; currently Launch Editor, WikiTribune and President of the Global Editors Network.

Comments from Monash University session at Dirksen Senate Office Building (12/7/15): Mike McCurry, former Co-Chairman of the Commission on Presidential Debates (now a member of the CPD) and former White House press secretary under President Bill Clinton; and Angela Greiling Keane, formerly *Bloomberg News* White House correspondent who was President of the National Press Club (now at *Politico*).

All job titles and positions were accurate as of the date the interview took place. Journalists may have different or additional titles or roles at present.

1

Journalism in the Current Era

The actions of journalists today point to a different conclusion than previously arrived at (Meltzer, 2010). In my first book, I tracked how, across the decades, journalists have been initially resistant to change, slow to adapt, but eventually come around out of necessity. But now, we are in an era of hacker journalists and computer scientists, engineers, tech gurus and pioneers doing journalism, so it seems that the historical behavior patterns of journalists are changing. Journalists are doing the evolving, pushing the envelope, coming up with the new formats and technologies (Usher, 2016). One of the ways journalists have been adapting recently is in their coverage and behavior with regard to politics and government.

While the recent increase in opinion, commentary, and incivility was underway before the last election cycle, in the lead up to the 2016 election, and since his election to the presidency, Donald J. Trump has wielded inflammatory rhetoric in speeches, tweets, and debates. But as Nancy Gibbs observed, and Trump has acknowledged himself, "Conflict commands attention, attention equals influence" (Gibbs, 2017). Gibbs has observed that "[Trump] is a human algorithm, perfectly engineered to say or do whatever we are most likely to watch . . . Donald Trump is not at war with the press, nor it with him. This is a much more complex relationship. His presidency has been great for ratings, in ways that are bad for journalism and bad for the country." As Jameel Jaffer (2017) said, "President Obama's transparency record was not what we had hoped it would be, but unexpectedly it now seems relevant that President Obama didn't routinely question the value of the First Amendment, demonize the press, or deliberately undermine the public's confidence in it."

How Journalists Dealt with the Rhetoric of Trump and Others during the 2016 Election Cycle

Words matter. They can wound. They can heal. And they are what we hold our elected officials accountable to. At least that was the conventional wisdom prior to the 2016 Presidential election. But millions of voters showed that words, Trump's in this case, either did not matter to them, or expressed their own shared thoughts. Uncivil, divisive, and—at times—violence-inciting words. Trump's words were directed at his opponents, journalists, and members of the public.

How journalists dealt with Donald Trump and his competitors in the 2016 election cycle leading up to the primaries is an important subject for discussion in this book about opinion and civility in public media discourse. Throughout his run, up to the presidential final election, Trump dodged and refused to answer journalists' questions, and fought in interviews only to stay on message and further his own agenda. This prompted many critics to call out the press for being too easy on Trump and responsible for giving him free coverage which aided his rise to become a contender. In a *Washington Post* article, "Donald Trump's secret for avoiding hard questions: too many interviewers aren't asking the follow-up," media scholar Todd Gitlin wrote about what he believed journalists needed to do (Gitlin, 2016). In March 2016, after Trump's Super Tuesday wins, Ted Koppel, while a guest on "The O'Reilly Factor," publicly decried the lack of "substance" in the news coverage of the then-presidential primary winner and told Bill O'Reilly he was partly responsible (Moyer, 2016). Koppel said:

> You have changed the television landscape over the past 20 years—you took it from being objective and dull to being subjective and entertaining. And in this current climate, it doesn't matter what the interviewer asks him. Mr. Trump is going to say whatever he wants to say, as outrageous as it may be.

Journalists who did try to ask Trump serious questions and hold him accountable incurred Trump's wrath. In August 2015, then-presidential candidate Trump publicly criticized Fox News anchor Megyn Kelly through Twitter and other venues for what he claimed was unfair questioning at the presidential primary debate (Chavez, Stracqualursi, & Keneally, 2016). That began a feud with Kelly that would last throughout the remainder of the election season, and which elevated Kelly's public status. Although Kelly attempted to strike a conciliatory tone with Trump in a subsequent interview, she posed more challenging questions to him in a later debate. In December

2015, when Trump tried to avoid answering Joe Scarborough's questions on his live MSNBC program "Morning Joe" about Trump's call for "a moratorium on Muslim immigrants," Scarborough responded by announcing to viewers that he would go to commercial break rather than allow Trump to prevaricate (Borchers, 2015). Scarborough followed through by cutting Trump off and ordering producers to cut to commercials, and when the show came back on, Trump was still on the phone line, now more willing to answer Scarborough's questions. Callum Borchers (2015), a *Washington Post* reporter writing about the incident concluded,

> The lesson for the press is that this might be the most effective way of dealing with Trump. He seems to respect—and actually respond to—a level of pushback that journalists would generally consider overly assertive or even rude.

Borchers suggested that journalists must rise to the occasion with interviewees who are either uncivil or refuse to engage the issues and questions in a substantive way, and match the toughness of their interview subjects or shut them down.

But by March 2017, much had changed. In a *Washington Post* column, Margaret Sullivan discussed Scott Pelley of CBS not being neutral in reporting about President Trump anymore (Sullivan, 2017a). Pelley was taken off of the CBS Evening News broadcast in spring 2017, but CBS said it was due to low ratings and not Pelley's critical reporting on President Trump (Koblin & Rutenberg, 2017).

What Journalists Said after the 2016 Election

If almost half of Americans (minus roughly two million) voted for Trump, that is a strong indicator of those voters' feelings about civility. That journalists and news organizations got their election predictions wrong and were totally surprised by the election outcome has been attributed to several reasons, including tunnel vision, insularity, and echo chambers on the part of the press, bias, lack of restraint, and faulty poll results. Or, as others have suggested, perhaps the press and polls didn't actually get it wrong, and the surprising results were a product of a flawed electoral college and gerrymandering of voting districts (Barnes, 2017), or Russian hacking of the election (Jamieson, 2018).

On November 9, 2016, the day after the election, in his televised address to the nation, President Obama said, "That presumption of good faith is essential to a vibrant and functioning democracy."

Throughout his campaign, and into his presidency, Trump has attacked the news media, going so far as to call them the "enemy of the American people" (Grynbaum, 2017a), and brought into common conversation the term "fake news" to refer to any unfavorable coverage he receives from even long-standing reputable news outlets. The term "fake news" has morphed to mean anything that is critical or in opposition (Sullivan, 2017b; Gertz, 2017). Two other terms, "post-truth," and "alternative facts," the latter coined by Trump advisor Kellyanne Conway, have emerged as destructive forces to the information environment (Wang, 2016; Todd, 2017). At a February 24, 2017 press briefing, Trump's administration barred selected media outlets who had not covered Trump favorably from participating in the briefing (Fabian, 2017; Borchers, 2017) leading many to compare his actions to those of authoritarian regimes elsewhere in the world, and in direct conflict with the First Amendment. Trump's attempts to discredit the press and make them the enemy are strategies that can be traced to well-known propaganda techniques from decades past. Leading many to draw a comparison with the Nixon administration, these general and widespread attacks on the press undermine the foundational role of the press as the Fourth Estate and the fundamental rights of citizens and the press enshrined in the First Amendment to the Constitution of the United States.

"These are moves that governments around the world make when they are less sophisticated and they want to block the press from doing its job, and it's sad to see that it's a tactic that the Trump White House is employing," CNN Worldwide President Jeff Zucker told NPR (Folkenflik, 2017), "[i]t has no impact on our commitment to reporting and the story. If anything it only further motivates us to make sure we ferret out all the facts."

Well-known journalists and leaders of news organizations have publicly responded to Trump's attacks on American news outlets. Some of these responses included those of Marty Baron, editor of *The Washington Post*, Jeff Zucker, CNN Worldwide president, and Christiane Amanpour of CNN, in the weeks leading up to Trump's inauguration through the first few months of his presidency between January and April 2017. During this span of time, Baron, Zucker, and other prominent journalists gave interviews and spoke on the record at events about the President's assault on journalists and how their organizations will continue to operate in this era. Baron (2016) said,

> This is a time we are compelled to fight for free expression and a free press—rights granted us under the Constitution, yes, but also the very qualities that have long set us apart from other nations.
>
> We will have a new president soon. He was elected after waging an outright assault on the press. Animosity toward the media was a centerpiece of his campaign. He described the press

as "disgusting," "scum," "lowlifes." He called journalists the "lowest form of humanity." That apparently wasn't enough. So he called us "the lowest form of life." In the final weeks of the campaign he labeled us "the enemies." . . .

Donald Trump said he wanted to "open up" libel laws. And he proposed to harass unfriendly media outlets by suing them, driving up their legal expenses with a goal of weakening them financially.

With respect to *The Washington Post*, he ordered our press credentials revoked during the campaign, barring us from routine press access to him and his events, because our coverage didn't meet with his approval. Even before we were subjected to his months-long blacklist, Donald Trump falsely alleged that our owner, Jeff Bezos, was orchestrating that coverage. And he openly hinted that, if he became president, he would retaliate. . . .

The ultimate defense of press freedom lies in our daily work.

Many journalists wonder with considerable weariness what it is going to be like for us during the next four—perhaps eight—years. Will we be incessantly harassed and vilified? Will the new administration seize on opportunities to try intimidating us? Will we face obstruction at every turn?

If so, what do we do? The answer, I believe, is pretty simple. Just do our job. Do it as it's supposed to be done.

Christiane Amanpour received the Committee to Project Journalists' Burton Benjamin Memorial Award for "extraordinary and sustained achievement in the cause of press freedom." In the speech she gave after accepting the honor, Amanpour (2016) said,

> I never in a million years thought I would be up here on stage appealing for the freedom and safety of American journalists at home.
>
> Ladies and gentlemen, I added the bits from candidate Trump as a reminder of the peril we face. I actually hoped that once President-elect, all that would change, and I still do. But I was chilled when the first tweet after the election was about "professional protesters incited by the media."
>
> But postcard from the world: This is how it goes with authoritarians like Sisi, Erdoğan, Putin, the Ayatollahs, Duterte, et al.
>
> As all the international journalists we honor in this room tonight and every year know only too well: First the media is accused of inciting, then sympathizing, then associating—until

they suddenly find themselves accused of being full-fledged terrorists and subversives. Then they end up in handcuffs, in cages, in kangaroo courts, in prison—and then who knows?

A great America requires a great and free and safe press. So this above all is an appeal to protect journalism itself.

Recommit to robust fact-based reporting without fear nor favor—on the issues. Don't stand for being labeled crooked or lying or failing. Do stand up together—for divided we will all fall.

Jeff Zucker actually had a close relationship with Trump in the past. He was the head of NBC entertainment who was responsible for putting Trump's show "The Apprentice" on the air, which some have argued paved the way for his presidential run. When asked about the President calling CNN "fake news," Zucker said, "It's just unfortunate that the most powerful person in the world is trying to delegitimize journalism and an organization that plays such a vital role in our democracy. I think he's entitled to his opinion, but it's—to use one of his favorite words—sad." (Sherman, 2017).

Chris Satullo (3/14/16), former Vice President of News and Civic Engagement, WHYY; former editorial page editor at the Philadelphia Inquirer, now a media and civic engagement consultant, said, "journalists are now thought of as lower than used car salesmen." Satullo said there have been people for 40 years like Richard Mellon Scaife and the Koch brothers today, trying to discredit mainstream journalism. Since most journalists don't go into it to make money, most are ideologically liberal, he said, but he believes most do try sincerely (if not always effectively) to keep that from affecting their work. Satullo also said that after Iraq, liberal critics of the media sprang up saying the media were asleep at the switch and in bed with corporate interests. So now the media are squeezed from both sides and trust declines.

Two critical intertwined issues that have emerged since the 2016 election cycle are conservative political party-sponsored organizations being credentialed as press by the new administration, and attacks on credible journalism organizations as "fake news." In March 2017, the conservative Heritage Foundation-sponsored *Daily Signal* was chosen to have its reporter represent the entire White House Press Corp as the press pool reporter (Farhi, 2017), and controversial and conservative outlet Infowars, whose host Alex Jones has questioned the occurrence of the Sandy Hook shootings, was given a temporary press credential in May 2017 (Andrews, 2017). While partisan outlets are being credentialed, long-standing reputable news organizations are denigrated as providing "fake news."

Perhaps "fake news" is opinion and commentary taken to the extreme. It's been weaponized and used strategically, like propaganda. Dr. Claire Wardle

(2017) has created a typology she and First Draft News use for identifying different types of misinformation and disinformation online and through social media (Wardle, 2016a; 2016b). There are important differences between misinformation and disinformation. Misinformation comes from ignorance, not possessing the knowledge or accurate information, and mistakes. Disinformation is disseminated deliberately and knowingly with the intent to deceive. Disinformation is a propaganda strategy that can be traced back to WWI and WWII and even earlier. The motivation of the information-provider is a significant factor to consider in cases of "fake news."

Before and after the election, experts from several sectors (policy, journalism, etc.) have affirmed the crucial roles of journalists amidst changes. Tom Glaisyer, Managing Director, Public Square Program at the Democracy Fund (9/9/15, Council on Foundations Nonprofit Media event) said, "We're in a moment of profound transition in media." Peter Bale, then-CEO, Center for Public Integrity (9/9/15, Nonprofit Media Discussion at Newseum) discussed making connections across the traditional boundary between journalism and advocacy in the form of "solutions journalism." Chris Satullo (3/14/16) also sees the need for solutions journalism, as a corrective to reporters' tendency to dump complex problems in the lap of their audience, shrug, and walk away.

Mike McCurry, former Co-Chairman of the Commission on Presidential Debates (now a member of the CPD) and former White House press secretary under President Bill Clinton (12/7/15, session with Monash University at Dirksen Senate Office Building) said, "the press's questions and even the anticipation of questions, drives policy forward." At the same event, Angela Greiling Keane, formerly *Bloomberg News* White House correspondent who was President of the National Press Club (now at *Politico*), said that asking critical questions is an important defining factor of journalism.

Even after being attacked and called fake news by the Trump administration, a television news correspondent (2/9/17) said journalists must "keep doing their work," and that "the nature of my job is not to have too much opinion."

These quotes from journalists illustrate that in response to Trump's attacks on the press, journalists plan to hold steadfast and continue to carry out their critical roles, while some feel journalists need to invoke more aggressive tactics—even crossing the boundary into advocacy. In August 2018, more than 300 news organizations published editorials reaffirming the role of a free press in our democracy. Jacobs (2017) categorizes these statements by journalists as articulating strategies to move forward. However, Gibbs's (2017) point that covering Trump's rhetoric has been good for ratings but bad for democracy and the country, has proven to be a difficult dilemma for the press to solve. Perhaps the press shouldn't constantly cover everything that Trump tweets or says, but isn't everything the President says and does newsworthy? While journalists are quick to criticize Trump's treatment of them, they are slow to call attention to the ways in which they have benefitted.

Less than ten years ago, the political and news landscape looked drastically different from today. Back in 2008, there were other reasons to be concerned about the news. Newspapers had declined and many news organizations had cut back their operations due to financial constraints largely brought about by Internet news.

Throughout 2009 and 2010, the FCC, FTC, and New America Foundation held sessions in Washington, DC, about the future of news. The focus at these sessions was on the decline of newspapers, rise of Internet news sites and citizen journalists, and concern about the ability to provide information that the public needs. The sessions brought together thinkers from several walks of life: news executives, government agency officials, academics, and interested others. Considering the shake-up of the newspaper industry, the focus was reasonably on newspaper and Internet journalism. Throughout those particular discussions, TV news and the shifting formats and qualities of news on television were hardly mentioned in more than passing. TV news was not raised as a potential antidote or safety zone for journalism, nor as a cause for concern on par with that of newspapers. Only the IFC's Make Media Matter Panel at the Newseum in May 2009 included TV journalists such as Greta Van Susteren, John King, George Stephanopolous, Tucker Carlson, and Juan Williams. And they did talk about what was happening on TV (Meltzer, 2010: 113).

However, elsewhere, discussion was growing about the increasing number of political talking heads on TV news programs, and the opinionation of news on TV. The backdrop to all of this was the mortgage and banking crisis-caused economic recession and the political gridlock in Congress. Amidst all of this, Oprah Winfrey decided to end her syndicated talk show in May 2011, and a slew of TV personalities rushed to try to take her place. Then, in 2012, the focus on TV news formats reached a fever pitch with the shooting of Congresswoman Gabrielle Giffords in Tucson, Arizona, which was largely related through public figures and the media to uncivil discourse and polarized politics. The shooting, and subsequent coverage, then spurred the founding of dozens of civility initiatives across the country.

On the "Colbert Report" on April 9, 2014, Andrew Sullivan, founder of The Dish, said that people need to be able to get along with people with whom they disagree. Sullivan said that the founder of Mozilla shouldn't have lost his job. This was in regard to the Mozilla founder who was forced to resign after it was found that he donated money to support an anti-gay marriage proposition in California in 2008. By the winter of 2014, the four most high-profile news/talk shows on TV that had been launched since 2011 had all failed and been canceled. Still, other personalities were being tapped to launch new shows.

Few of the people in those sessions between 2008 and 2010 could have imagined the ways the news ecosystem would change and how quickly that change would occur over the next eight years. What it means to watch "television" in today's informational and technological environment has changed over the past decade with the development of "second screen" usage—simultaneously using television and another information device—and social media, which may actually be reinvigorating the TV experience in some ways. "TV" content, including news video, also became available online, streaming live to devices of the user's choosing, for a fee in some cases (Kirsner, 2014; Alvarez-Monzoncillo, 2013). According to Pew Research Center data, "momentum around digital news video picked up in 2013. More than six in ten U.S. adults now watch videos online—and roughly half of those, 36% of all U.S. adults, watch news videos" (Olmstead, Mitchell, Holcomb & Vogt, 2014). The growth of digital videos online—both professionally- and user-generated—was made possible by technological developments, including mobile devices, and major investments in digital news production on the part of news organizations, including local news (Olmstead, Mitchell, Holcomb & Vogt, 2014). Non-television news organizations, such as the *The Washington Post, Huffington Post* (HuffPost Live), and *New York Times*, have been among those making these investments to compete (Adler, 2014). Other inventions, such as Amazon's Fire TV, made it possible to view online content through the television (Tsukayama, 2014). Since "TV" can be viewed through many types of devices, some question whether there still are defining qualities of television, but a television screen is still the platform that the largest number of Americans turn to for news and prefer (Mitchell, Gottfried, Barthel & Shearer, 2016).

Pressured by the abundance of information providers, the Tow Center for Digital Journalism's report on Post-Industrial Journalism called on journalists to change "not just tactics, but also self-conception" (Sonderman, 2012):

> The authors can foresee a world where 90 percent of news reports are written by computer algorithms that convert data into narrative structures and where many newsworthy events are first described by connected citizens rather than journalists.
>
> The result: The journalist has not been replaced but displaced, moved higher up the editorial chain from the production of initial observations to a role that emphasizes verification and interpretation. . . . Working between the crowd and the algorithm in the information ecosystem is where a journalist is able to have most effect, by serving as an investigator, a translator, a storyteller.

This sounded much like what Jeremy Bowers, news application developer for NPR, said at the panel on "Data-Driven Storytelling: Present and Future," at the 2014 Journalism/Interactive Conference. Bowers said journalists should use and program robots to automatically track data and notify the human journalists of things worthy of reporting, and that journalists who are not using robots will be scooped by journalists who are using them. Robots do well what humans don't, which is tracking data 24-7, all night long, and detecting deviations from the norm. He gave an example of a robot that monitors the U.S. Geological Survey and sends automatic messages to human journalists of significant activity using templates written by editors and programmers.

Hybridity

Another way of thinking about the transitions in the format and content of news is through hybridity. Baym (2005; 2010) and others have written about the blurring of genres into hybrid ones. This view proves useful for thinking about the blurring of elements of reality and fiction, the scripted and unscripted, and news and entertainment. We may also think about the blending of news and talk into a hybrid mode that can be scripted, unscripted, or both, and results in more talk in news and news in talk. Or rather than viewing these blendings or blurrings as novel phenomena, we might take the approach that all media, and things in culture for that matter, are combinatorial and generative, in a postmodern, pastiche-like way (Jameson, 1983).

Over the past decade, I have observed five trends in journalism and technology: 1. Initial resistance to change by journalists and news organizations, and eventual adaptation; 2. Blurring of genres, hybridization; 3. Moving away from objectivity; 4. Remixing, collective production, multiple contributors; and 5. Flattening of the hierarchy of journalistic authority (Meltzer, 2009). The issues of chief concern in journalism today are many. They include:

- Opinion, partisanship, polarization, lack of objectivity, lack of accuracy/facts, transparency, the public good, media literacy
- Incivility
- Echo-chambers, selective exposure, attention and retention; lack of common ground, partisan gridlock; inability to have productive deliberations; confirmation bias
- Cult of personality/focus on individual notoriety/celebrity/brand of individual journalists
- Diluting/broadening of definition of news to include talk shows, entertainment

- Vetting of information and sources; fact-checking; fake news, misinformation, disinformation
- All of this could lead to loss of credibility/authority of journalists.

With the proliferation and rise in popularity of niche media outlets and online news sites (Stroud, 2011), this new mediascape has been hailed as liberating with news that caters to individuals' interests, but there is also concern that this climate of hyper-fragmentation means that people can selectively attend to only the versions of news that are consistent with their existing ways of thinking, therefore never having to be exposed to divergent views (Chalif, 2011; Katz, 1996). Some believe this latter situation taken to the nth degree leads to the "Echo Chamber" (Jamieson & Capella, 2008)—the polarized political and media environment we see in some ways today.

However, the dissatisfaction with journalism and politics today should come as no surprise. People have almost always been dissatisfied with the state of the news media and politics. We tend to think that eras that have come before were better—such as the golden era of television news between the 1950s and 1990s. But research I and others have done has found that there have always been criticisms of news. However, the character of the criticisms in each era reflects the unique context of the media and political environment at that time. This is true today.

This book is neither prescriptive nor normative. It describes and analyzes journalists' perspectives to understand how the people within the field who are enmeshed in the craft and controversy think about the situation from the inside. My analysis of journalistic discourse takes up all of the issues mentioned above.

Why Examine Journalistic Discourse?

Focusing on the perspectives of actual working journalists enables us to understand the ways that journalists think about the work that they do. This is an established approach that has been employed since the 1950s with seminal sociology of news studies (Tuchman, 1978; Breed, 1955; Fishman, 1980; Gans, 1980). Contemporary scholars (Jarvis & Han, 2018; Boczkowski, 2010; Usher, 2012, 2016; Anderson, 2013; Ekdale et al., 2015; Hellmueller, 2014) have reinvigorated this subfield with new research and advances in methodology that have evolved from these earlier works from the 1950s through the 1980s.

Continuing in this methodological tradition, this study collected and analyzed two types of data: Semi-structured, in-depth, in-person and phone interviews conducted with journalists, and published journalistic discourse including popular, trade, organizational publications and proceedings, and broadcast transcripts. I conducted interviews with journalists from March 2014 through March 2016. Additional interviews and content from journalists were collected in-person and face-to-face at events through April 2017. I employed purposive and snowball sampling, making use of preexisting contacts I had. In total, original material from interactions with over 30 journalists is included. The published journalistic discourse analyzed spanned January 2004–June 2017, and farther back in some cases. Like Serazio (2014: 746) and Kreiss (2009: 282, in Serazio), I "conducted interviews with key actors complemented by press articles and online material." I used a grounded theory approach to analysis to identify themes present in the discourse (Lindlof and Taylor 2011: 250–252; Glaser and Strauss 1967, as discussed in Holton 2008).

The data and analysis capture journalists' thinking prior to, and after, the 2016 election, and also consider changes over time in journalistic thinking, both through the interviews and published discourse (since 2004).

The rationale for the two main research methods used in the book—qualitative textual analysis of media discourse and personal interviews with journalists—also responds to the words of former FCC commissioner Michael Copps who implored journalists to make their ideas and voices heard in policy conversations that affect news. In February 2014, Copps wrote a letter to journalists that was published on the Columbia Journalism Review website (Copps, 2014). In it, Copps said:

> I have heard the arguments about the need to keep reporters from becoming part of the story and being tainted by involvement in public policy formation. But journalism, like government, is not a purist's redoubt. . . .
>
> An old axiom has it that decisions without you are usually decisions against you. Journalists can refuse to be part of the story, but that means they won't be part of the solution either.

The rationale for the research methods used in the book also comes naturally from the underlying theoretical framework. My previous book and much other work have employed Zelizer's (1993) theoretical framework of viewing journalists as interpretive communities. In light of changes in the structure of how journalism works due to technological, economic, cultural, and political shifts, in this book I advance the similar but distinct framework of communities of practice and apply it to journalists. In doing so, I also consider whether looking at different journalistic communities, or subcommunities, as "communities of practice" could be useful (Wenger, 1998). For the people who are the subjects of the case studies in this book, it is of particular use and interest to see which subcommunities each looks to and is regarded as being part of. Because American journalists tend to engage in conversations about their norms, values and boundaries through articles published in the popular and trade press, at organizational proceedings and organizational blogs and on their broadcasts, these are the materials that are analyzed for evidence of their thoughts about the move toward talk. This is investigated in the interviews with journalists as well.

Journalists as Communities of Practice*

Over the past decade, journalism has experienced significant changes, including the rise of news through social media, citizen journalism, opinion and niche journalism, and data journalism, and the decline of legacy journalism outlets. That is why I considered the usefulness of looking at different journalistic communities, or subcommunities, as communities of practice (Wenger, 1998). Originally coined by Jean Lave and Etienne Wenger in 1991, "communities of practice are groups of people who share a concern or a passion for something they do and learn how to do it better as they interact regularly" (Wenger, 2006). A community of practice is constituted by "a domain of knowledge, which defines a set of issues; a community of people who care about this domain; and the shared practice that they are developing to be effective in their domain" (Wenger & McDermott, 2002). In evaluating the feasibility of applying communities of practice to journalism, I considered other theoretical frameworks that have been used for examining journalistic groups, including interpretive communities, professions, and organizations, and I discuss how all of these groups take part in boundary work and metajournalistic discourse. Whereas community is often attached to the idea of discourse communities or interpretive communities, I find that focusing on the collaborative learning aspect and development of shared practice through the lens of communities of practice enables us to more fully understand the nature of skill- and practice-building among specific subgroups of journalistic practitioners. I also find the concept of boundary work useful in this exploration. Because journalism is a wide and varied field with unstable boundaries, some journalists explicitly address their identification with the community by developing and maintaining boundaries of practice, while others maintain and police interpretive rules.

Applying community models to professions with unstable or fluid boundaries—such as journalism—may assist rather than hamper scholarly thought

---

*Passages in this section included with permission from SAGE Journals. doi: 10.1177/0196850 9917706158.

on that profession. The widespread emphasis on community as a renewed way of thinking about what collections of people do largely began in the late 1980s and early 1990s, following the publication of various articles on the topic.

Until the early 1990s, consistent with the reigning Piagetian, constructivist, and information processing paradigms, the individual learner was the essential unit of instruction and analytic concern in research. This slowly changed when, following publications such as *Cognition in Practice* (Lave, 1988) and *Situated Learning* (Lave & Wenger, 1991), many educational researchers and practitioners "switched to the idea that knowing and knowledgeability are better thought of as cultural practices that are exhibited by practitioners belonging to various communities" (Roth & Lee, 2006). An even earlier example of this paradigm was exhibited by Stanley Fish in 1976, when he introduced his theory on interpretive communities.

In his article "Interpreting the Variorum," Fish (1976) first defines interpretive communities as entities "made up of those who share interpretive strategies not for reading (in the conventional sense) but for writing texts, for constituting their properties and assigning their intentions." It was originally conceived as a theoretical concept in the field of literary studies as a way to explain variances in reader-response criticism. Essentially, Fish argues that readers, or people in general, group themselves into unique communities based on their internal schema, collectively interpreting a text or the world around them in a loosely structured way. The boundaries of these interpretive communities are fluid, growing and declining as members move from one to the other. However, determining the exact size of any given community is nearly impossible, as any evidence of membership would itself be an interpretation; according to Fish, "The only 'proof' of membership is fellowship, the nod of recognition from someone in the same community, someone who says to you what neither of us could ever prove to a third party: 'we know.' "

This origin in literary studies markedly differs from that of communities of practice, which began as a framework for studying professional organizations. The term community of practice became popular following the 1991 publication of Situated Learning by scholars Etienne Wenger and Jean Lave, where it was first defined as a set of relations among persons, activity, and world, over time and in relation with other tangential and overlapping communities of practice. A community of practice is an intrinsic condition for the existence of knowledge, not least because it provides the interpretive support necessary for making sense of its heritage (Lave & Wenger, 1991). It was developed as a framework to explain channels of learning outside the classroom environment (e.g., apprenticeships; Weiss & Domingo, 2010). It became popular among scholars of anthropology and the other social sciences before exploding onto the business and management scene (Weiss & Domingo, 2010). "The number of companies launching initiatives on communities of practice is increasing so rapidly, we have no way of keeping track," wrote Wenger and co-author Richard McDermott in their application-minded book *Cultivating Communities of Practice* (2002). They are quick to point out, however, that a community of practice is not a recent development in the academic or professional world:

> They were our first knowledge-based social structures, back when we lived in caves and gathered around the fire to discuss strategies for cornering prey, the shape of arrowheads, or which roots were edible. In ancient Rome, "corporations'" of metalworkers, potters, masons, and other craftsmen had both a social aspect (members worshipped common deities and celebrated holidays together) and a business function (training apprentices and spreading innovations). (Wenger & McDermott, 2002)

With such a wide range of applications—from the schoolroom to the boardroom—it is not surprising that definitions or explanations on what constitutes a community of practice are so varied. According to John Seely Brown, a former VP and Chief Scientist at Parc Xerox, a community of practice consists of "peers in the execution of real work. What holds them together is a common sense of purpose and a real need to know what each other knows" (Allee, 2000). Communities can be small or large—ranging from a few specialists to global membership numbering in the hundreds or thousands—and "regular" interaction among their members could mean weekly face-to-face meetings or scattered phone and email conversations (Wenger & McDermott, 2002).

Despite the wide variety of forms a community of practice can take, and the differing professional opinions on what defines such a community, one basic structure of three central elements is universally agreed upon: "a domain of knowledge, which defines a set of issues; a community of people who care about this domain; and the shared practice that they are developing to be effective in their domain" (Wenger & McDermott, 2002). Organization around a clear domain creates group accountability to a body of knowledge and the development of a practice; a domain is not a fixed set of problems that can be addressed and dismissed, but a key issue that evolves with the growth of the community (Wenger & McDermott, 2002). Likewise, the community element of a community of practice "is not just a Web site, a database, or a collection of best practices. It is a group of people who interact, learn together, build relationships, and in the process develop a sense of belonging and mutual commitment" (Wenger & McDermott, 2002). As for practice, Wenger and McDermott define this element as "a set of socially defined ways of doing things in a specific domain: a set of common approaches and shared standards that create a basis for action, communication, problem solving, performance, and accountability" (Wenger & McDermott, 2002).

In addition to this basic structure, communities of practice generally follow five development stages, which include the following: Potential, Coalescing, Maturing, Active, and Dispersing (Allee, 2000). These stages define a community of practice at every level of its existence, from its beginning as a "loose network of people with similar issues and needs" to its inevitable end as a function that has "outlived its usefulness" (Allee, 2000). Of course, no stage has a set time limit, meaning that it is more than possible for a community to stall in the Potential stage or idle at its height in the Active stage, which is characterized by its creation of a new way to sustain community energy, educate novices, and gain influence (Allee, 2000).

Not all communities or practices fit the description of a community of practice—regardless of how wide that description may be. Project teams or working groups, for example, are too strictly focused on a particular task to qualify as a community of practice, which has looser bonds between members and focuses on overall development in a field of expertise (Allee, 2000). Furthermore, communities of practice are completely self-selecting, with members participating because they personally identify with the enterprise of the community and not because they were assigned to a task (Allee, 2000). Considerable "stretching" of the basic structure is permitted, however, as demonstrated by the "distributed community," which is essentially any community that cannot rely on face-to-face interaction between its members as a primary connector; ". . . in an era of globalization and worldwide communication networks, distributed communities are increasingly the norm" (Wenger & McDermott, 2002).

Boundary Work and Journalists as Interpretive Communities, Professions, and Organizations

Journalists have alternately been viewed as members of interpretive communities, professions, and organizations, all of whom monitor and maintain their group's boundaries. An international collection of scholars has recently applied boundary work in case studies of journalistic struggles (Carlson & Lewis, 2015). With boundary maintenance (Gieryn, 1983; Lewis, 2012), the journalistic community works to demarcate good from bad practices and content, and legitimate versus illegitimate members and contributions. I view the framework of boundary work as a compatible, complementary conceptualization to communities of practice and interpretive communities. As discussed in Carlson and Lewis's edited volume (2015, p. 9), the communities framework is useful for understanding how journalists interact while they are engaged in the process of newswork, while the boundaries framework helps us see how, when, and why journalists feel the need to demarcate "journalism norms, practices and participants." Journalists in interpretive communities and communities of practice can and do engage in boundary work.

Much research about journalists to date has employed Zelizer's (1993) theoretical framework of viewing journalists as interpretive communities. Conceptualizations of journalists as interpretive communities tend to envision one all-encompassing community of journalists who discursively articulate, negotiate, and maintain the norms, values, and boundaries of their craft. But given that the actual work of people said to be doing journalism can vary to such a great degree today, the interpretive communities framework is flexible enough to be adapted to consider different kinds of journalists into subcommunities, in the same way that Fraser devised the idea of subpublics (Fraser, 1999). In her 1990 dissertation and later work, Zelizer developed a particular notion of how journalists are tied together as a collective through which they discursively articulate, negotiate, and defend their identity and authority as purveyors of news.

This is in contrast to other scholars who have conceived of journalists through the formal organizations by which they are employed (Blau & Scott, 1962; Born, 2004; Epstein, 1973; Weber, 1947), or as members of a profession (Becker, Fruit, & Caudill, 1987; Freidson, 1984; Henningham, 1985). Other scholars have used the lens of occupations to consider journalistic work (Breed, 1955; Fishman, 1980/1999; Gans, 1979; Klaidman & Beauchamp, 1987; Tuchman, 1978; Tunstall, 1971; Underwood & Stamm, 2001; Weaver & Wilhoit, 1986; White, 1950). All of these conceptualizations sought to address how journalists maintain their collective autonomy and authority through self-evaluation, adaptation, and self-control against changing external circumstances.

Viewing these other conceptualizations of journalists as unable to completely capture the nature of the journalistic collective, Zelizer observed their insufficiencies. While journalists do behave like formal organizations by developing and voluntarily obeying procedures of conduct, there are no official rules or designs of a formal organization from which these procedures are derived (other than external government regulation). The formal organizations framework neglects the fact that the journalistic collective establishes and follows norms and practices precisely because of its lack of a recognized governing, rule-making body, and its need for legitimacy. The characterization of journalism as a profession is similarly flawed, according to Zelizer. Journalism does not seem to fit the professional framework's emphases on training, education, and credentialing. The professional framework also ignores the relevance of journalistic discourse in determining what members of the journalistic community do and restricts our understanding of journalistic practice to those aspects of journalism emphasized by its particular view. Although Gans (2003) characterized journalism as a service-oriented field with a certain amount of independence and a mission to serve its "clients" who are thought to be the American public, these characteristics are not sufficient to achieve professional status. While "professionalizing" journalism may serve to lend status to the journalistic community and give its members a sense of control over their work, "offsetting the dangers inherent in the subjectivity of reporting," the professional and occupational frameworks neglect to recognize the means by which reporters arrive at shared constructions of reality, informally network and depend on narrative and storytelling practices (Zelizer, 1993; Lule, 2001).

Rather than conceptualizing a community as a profession, Zelizer (1993) borrowed from anthropology, folklore, and literary studies in suggesting that a more fruitful way to conceptualize some groups may be as interpretive communities, "united through . . . shared discourse and collective interpretations of key public events" that help members determine what is appropriate practice. Although these organizations may be bureaucratic or corporate by typology, their members still behave as folkloric communities that use their own talk about themselves to keep themselves in line. Although the idea of interpretive communities was originally developed in reference to audience groups and consumers (Fish, 1980; Lindlof, 1988), it has since been applied to other types of groups including producers of cultural products such as news. Interpretive communities are characterized by common modes of interpretation of their social worlds. Interpretive communities act as cultural sites where meanings are constructed, shared, and reconstructed by members of social groups in the course of everyday life (Berkowitz & TerKuest, 1999).

Other studies (Meltzer, 2013; 2010; Berkowitz, 2000; Berkowitz & TerKuerst, 1999; Brewin, 1999; Cecil, 2002; Fish, 1980; Kitch, 2003; Lindlof, 1988; Meyers, 2003) have employed the interpretive community framework, exploring the ways in which journalists have understood and articulated their professional and social roles over the years through stories that they tell about their own work, its significance, and its relevance to larger cultural and social narratives. At the heart of such stories is an ongoing process of establishing and maintaining the collective.

Comparing Interpretive Communities to Communities of Practice

The clear contrast between communities of practice and interpretive communities is that communities of practice are focused on learning from others in the domain community and developing and evolving specific practices through interaction, while interpretive communities are chiefly concerned with interpreting news events through discourse, and maintaining and asserting identity and authority through self-criticism. In their own ways, each type of community engages in boundary work.

Both community models are similar in that they began in academia as theories and worked their way into the practical sphere. But while both can be credited with popularizing the professional community framework, their conceptual origins differ widely. It has been suggested that Lave and Wenger's framework deals with practice or action, whereas the interpretive communities framework deals more with interpretation. While the two theories developed roughly around the same time, Zelizer's notion of the community was taken from her dissertation (finished in 1990), so it was a bit earlier and draws on Stanley Fish's (1976) work in literary studies. According to Wenger (2012), himself, the concept of community of practice "has its roots in attempts to develop accounts of the social nature of human learning inspired by anthropology and social theory (Bourdieu, 1977; Foucault, 1980; Giddens, 1984; Lave, 1988; Vygostsky, 1978)" (p. 1). It is interesting that a focus on community would have developed in both journalism and education around the same time, drawing on earlier work produced in the late '70s and early '80s in literary studies, and anthropology and social theory, but we are not able to offer any obvious connections with political or cultural events as the catalysts.

That being said, there are obvious parallels between the two frameworks. One such parallel is communication, which is a necessary element within both interpretive communities and communities of practice. Communication defines the boundaries of a community and brings its members together. The ways in which this communication is apparent, however, differ slightly. Communities of practice largely favor direct communication, with members discussing in person the implications of their practice. Interpretive communities can technically include this type of communication—members undoubtedly speak to each other—but they mostly seem to operate through indirect communication, or by contributing to a body of work that "speaks" for their thoughts on their practice. The use of storytelling as a form of communication and as a tool for learning within the community is a notable exception to the general differences of discourse between the two frameworks; both communities of practice and interpretive communities use stories to understand or articulate their values to new members and to an outside audience.

Another trait the two frameworks share is a tendency toward change. Neither interpretive communities nor communities of practice are static entities. The boundaries and definitions of each change to fit the interests of their members in conjunction with external circumstances. For interpretive communities, this might mean a collective change in how to view the world, or how to view the role of journalism in society. Similarly, for communities of practice, this might mean a change in how work is completed, or a reconsideration of the community's goals. Membership in either community is constantly in flux, though judging membership in an interpretive community is largely impossible due to the subjectivity of its determining factors. In contrast to the unknowable membership of an interpretive community, membership in a community of practice is more concrete and tethered to the physical world by a specific practice. This disparity in determining an accurate member count is indicative of a larger divergence in community boundary rigidity in the two community models. Communities of practice require a very specific set of qualifications to earn the name, while interpretive communities exist with almost no qualifications. Ultimately, communities of practice present a framework on how we learn, while interpretive communities present a framework on how we view the world.

For what I am calling journalistic communities of practice, Meyers and Davidson (2016) recently came up with a similar conceptualization of "tribes of professionalism:" "We conclude that journalism has lost some of its cohesion and fragmented into tribes of professionalism practiced by a diverse set of actors."

Other work has been done on the news media's self-criticism, but it has not been talked about in the context or framework of interpretive community discussion that discursively maintains and reasserts norms and boundaries. Instead, it is discussed as "self-reflexive news media reporting" (Bishop, 2001, p. 23; Haas, 2006, p. 351), "journalistic metacoverage" (Haas, 2006, p. 352), or "boundary work" and "self-coverage" (Bishop, 1999, 2001). Bishop (2001, p. 23) and Zelizer (1997, p. 17) have contended that journalistic self-reflection is a kind of ritual sacrifice, performed to persuade audiences to have faith in journalism, to sustain ratings and readership, and to deflect potential external criticism. As Schudson (1982) wrote, the talk of journalists is a critical process of consensus-formation. "The group becomes a brotherhood that influences and colors, beyond any individual resistance to prejudice or individual devotion to fact, all of what [journalists] write" (p. 111). Current and recent work continues to employ the interpretive community framework for examining journalistic discourse. Some of that work talks about it in terms of paradigm repair and critical incidents.

In paradigm repair (Bennett, Gressett, & Haltom, 1985; Berkowitz, 2000; Hindman, 2005; Reese, 1990), a specific breach of good and normal practice necessitates action on behalf of the news organization, and the larger journalistic community, to demonstrate that the paradigm is being restored and can remain intact. This is in contrast to a "critical incident" (Zelizer, 1992), a singular event or evolution leads to the reexamination of journalistic practices.

Carlson (2015) most recently proposed pulling together all of the variations in theoretical frameworks involving discursive activities in and around journalism under the umbrella framework of "metajournalistic discourse." While it hearkens to an earlier suggestion made by Haas (2006) to focus on journalistic metacoverage, Carlson's (2015) proposition goes far beyond the applications of discursive theory to discrete events and phenomena that reside either within journalism or outside it, to instead encompass all discourse in which journalism is the object of discussion itself, or in which journalists discursively negotiate their interpretation and coverage of outside objects. It also includes discourse which involves both of those realms. Both journalistic and other external actors and sites are considered in the metajournalistic discourse theory. The new theory also delineates the different characteristics and contexts of metajournalistic discourse. In this way, the theory seeks to unify and evolve our thinking about journalism in the present day. Advancing the communities of practice framework for understanding journalism, and comparing it to interpretive communities, boundaries, and professions, then fits within and further fleshes out connections between the various individual theoretical discursive frameworks that may be said to fall under "metajournalistic discourse." The metajournalistic discourse framework moves closer toward a holistic systems theory approach or media ecology approach that considers all other parts of the system in which journalism operates.

Although Wenger (2012) wrote that "the concept of community of practice was not born in the systems theory tradition," he also wrote that the concept of community of practice is well aligned with the perspective of the systems tradition. A community of practice itself can be viewed as a simple social system. And a complex social system can be viewed as constituted by interrelated communities of practice. Further, Wenger (2012) writes that "A community of practice can be viewed as a social learning system. Arising out of learning, it exhibits many characteristics of systems more generally: emergent structure, complex relationships, self-organization, dynamic boundaries, ongoing negotiation of identity and cultural meaning, to mention a few. In a sense it is the simplest social unit that has the characteristics of a social learning system" (p. 1). This also seems an apt description of communities of journalists.

Journalists as Communities of Practice

A community of practice is a meta-theoretical approach that describes how a group communicates, learns, participates, and transforms at the same time as their practice evolves. At a basic level, it is a way of understanding how knowledge and learning are intertwined and how this occurs naturally within a social group, in this case the news organization and its journalists (Weiss & Domingo, 2010). As a framework for knowledge-sharing, communities of practice are most often applied to the areas of business management, communication studies, and education; however, "journalists and newsroom organization can be considered a form of a community of practice depending on the circumstances" (Weiss & Domingo, 2010). While this specific application has not been addressed to any great extent, certain aspects of journalism seem to fit the description of a community of practice (Weiss & Domingo, 2010). Matsaganis and Katz (2013), following Husband (2005, as cited in Matsaganis & Katz), look at ethnic media producers as communities of practice. A recent study by researchers Weiss and Domingo sought to describe specific journalist communities (e.g., online news teams) as communities of practice through their innovation practices; but while their findings technically draw associations between the two concepts, they did not seem to fully utilize relevant facets of a community of practice. For example, a section discussing the abrupt creation of a night shift at one of the observed papers to cover the Iraq War did not specify whether the decision grew organically from the community of journalists at the paper, as it would in a true community of practice, or whether it was dictated to them by management. The authors also do not make a distinction between workplace collaboration and an established community of practice.

Further research in the study of journalism implies a connection between journalism and the community of practice organizational framework, but a direct relationship is never explicitly stated. For example, in his article "The Two Professionalisms of Journalism: Updating Journalism Research for the 21st Century," researcher Henrik Ornebring defines one of two competing discourses of journalism in the following way:

> . . . occupational professionalism . . . is operationalized and controlled by practitioners themselves and is based on shared education and training, a strong socialization process, work culture and occupational identity, and codes of ethics that are monitored and operationalized by professional institutes and associations. (Ornebring, 2008)

This description of occupational journalism shares many characteristics of a community of practice—self-management, shared learning experiences, and community standards, among other things—but an explicit connection between the two concepts is never fully realized in the article. The Tow Center's blog entry about their report on Sensor Journalism (2014) mentions the need for building a "community of practice" for sensor journalism, but neither the blog entry nor the report discuss communities of practice in a way that relates to any formal definitions or conceptualizations. Similarly, a number of other journalism-related organizations and authors have used the term community of practice in relation to the work of journalists or media producers, but all use it implicitly without substantive explanation (i.e., a blog and course assignment by Paul Bradshaw at Birmingham City University (2011), a report on Fair Use and Journalism by American University's Center for Media & Social Impact (2013), the report on the future of journalism education from the Knight Foundation (Lynch, 2015), the "Journalism That Matters" conference (2015).

Additional research pertaining to the connection between journalism and communities of practice (Baumard, 1999; Macaulay, 1999) identifies the "source" (i.e., a person, publication, or record that provides information for a specific news story) as a unifying artifact in the journalism community, "where different colleagues must work together to validate the information that feeds into the creation of a news item" (Davenport & Hall, 2002). Again, a connection to the community of practice framework is implied through the suggestion of shared domain, community, and practice in the collection and verification of sources but never explicitly discussed. Each of these articles comes close but ultimately misses the chance to push the understanding of journalism as a community of practice.

The difficulty in defining "journalism" as any one thing is that the practice itself is too varied and unregulated—too loose with professional and academic requirements and standards to be a true profession, but also too structured to be a simple community. Some journalists go to school for years to work in the field; some do not have a degree at all. Some work for multimillion-dollar news networks, and some manage entire news enterprises from their homes. And still, despite this disparity, this collection of scattered and diverse practitioners constitutes a defined group that overwhelmingly follows a set of rules and standards that have survived through tradition. Understanding journalists as communities of practice helps us reconcile these characteristics that are seemingly at odds and gives them a recognizable, comprehensible shape and form.

In broad terms, journalism meets the definition of a community of practice: it is most certainly a community, with specific practices. But how can something so broad (a potentially global network of people), so multifaceted (e.g., diverse mediums and job duties), and so untraceable be considered a community of practice? Breaking the whole community down into smaller parts—groups of journalists within a single news organization, or even the organization itself—could invalidate the argument that "journalism" is one whole community, but considering the entire practice to be a single community over-simplifies its multitude of working parts and stretches the definition of a community of practice. Looking at the regular interaction among members of the journalism community—a basic necessity of any community of practice—journalism qualifies as a distributed community, especially in terms of knitting organizations together. Journalists, at times, collaborate to problem solve or discuss aspects of their domain and also interact in a remote way through criticism and acknowledgment of each other's works.

Examples of Journalistic Communities of Practice

I find that there are many vibrant examples of journalism groups and activities that fit and exemplify communities of practice. As has been suggested, journalism may be seen as a distributed community, with diverse and scattered subgroups. Although the literature on communities of practice seems to indicate that they grow out of organizations, for journalism, it could go either way: when communities of journalists become more organized over the time in which they interact over their practices in a domain, they may begin to take on the qualities of more formal organizations and can just as easily disband from any formal association. In this way, a particular group of journalists in a community of practice may be momentary and fleeting or endure for a number of years.

Among the more informal types of communities of practice are journalists providing news through social media, citizen journalists, opinion and niche journalists, and data journalists. Groups of news bloggers, political bloggers/columnists/analysts, fashion bloggers, celebrity bloggers, and media critics may similarly comprise communities of practice. These are loose collections of people in the same domain—at the coalescing stage (Allee, 2000). Each group has "a domain of knowledge, which defines a set of issues; a community of people who care about this domain; and the shared practice that they are developing to be effective in their domain" (Wenger & McDermott, 2002).

Once a group of journalists sharing a domain moves from coalescing to maturing and active, it may eventually form a more formal organization such as Andy Carvin's former site for curated citizen journalism through social media, reported.ly. The movement of a broader community of digital journalists from coalescing to maturing and active led to the invention of a more formal organization, the Online News Association. Conversely, some professional journalism organizations have changed or dissolved, such as the reformulated Association of Opinion Journalists which is merging with the American Society of News Editors (AOP, 2016) and was formerly the National Conference of Editorial Writers until 2012. Its evolution reflects changes in its community's practices, including the decreasing relevance of editorial writers amidst the ascendance of opinion journalism. Similarly, the American Press Institute was reinvented in 2012, merged with the Newspaper Association of America Foundation, amidst the turmoil in the newspaper industry (American Press Institute, 2016; Winter, 2012). The RTDNA which stands for

Radio Television Digital News Association used to be RTNDA and stand for Radio-Television News Directors Association.

The journalism community, then, could be characterized as a distributed community of practice, or many subcommunities of practice, that constantly cycle between the Potential, Coalescing, Maturing, Active, and Dispersing stages, as new technologies or models go in and out of popularity. These groups behave as, and engage in the work of, interpretive communities, policing, and negotiating boundaries, but they also act as, and constitute, communities of practice.

In applying a theoretical framework from a different disciplinary area to journalism, it was important to consider the appropriateness of doing so and the fit. Wenger (2012) wrote that when he and Jean Lave coined the term community of practice in the late 1980s, "we could not have predicted the career the concept would have." Wenger writes that their concept "has influenced theory and practice in a wide variety of fields in academe, business, government, education, health, and the civil sector," and that "New technologies, in particular the rise of social media, have triggered much interest in communities of practice. Indeed, these technologies are well aligned with the peer-to-peer learning processes typical of communities of practice" (p. 7). Wenger noted "the shift from an analytical concept to an instrumental one" and the fact that "the concept has been adopted and used in ways that are not always consistent with its origins and the diversity of adoption means that the concept is in some sense 'out of control.'" But in the end, he says, "But for myself, I find the combination of analytical and instrumental perspectives particularly productive." We find communities of practice a productive lens through which to view journalists.

Viewing Journalists as Communities of Practice around Opinion and Commentary

Thinking in terms of communities is useful for trying to understand how journalism works today, particularly as a constantly changing entity. As Carlson and Peifer (2013) have found, journalists are being forced to reckon with "new—and largely uncomfortable—modes of public discourse operating contra traditional journalism's institutionalized norms," and "journalists' responses confronted the emerging heterogeneity of mediated voices participating in the public sphere" (p. 334). Journalists of all stripes are grappling with the rapidly changing information environment and the new forms and participants that accompany it. Journalists are engaging in not just image restoration (Benoit, 1995, 1997), but in image creation, defense, protection, and maintenance (Carlson & Lewis, 2015). They are using new and old strategies to develop and maintain relationships with audiences, sources, technologies, and critics that support their place of authority (Carlson, 2017). Journalists as members of an interpretive community engage in frequent reevaluation of the journalistic collective, while journalists as members of a community of practice are tasked with constantly and faithfully redefining their domain as their practice evolves.

In analyzing the perspectives of journalists through discourse about opinion and commentary in news, I developed and adapted the communities of practice framework to journalists because they are varied and diverse and can best be understood as operating within these communities of practice.

2

The Increase in Talk in News

Brian Carroll (2014: 37) writes: "Geneva Overholser, professor at the University of Missouri School of Journalism, told the authors of *blog!* that 2005 would be remembered as the year 'when it finally became unmistakably clear that 'objectivity' has outlived its usefulness as an ethical touchstone of journalism'" (Kline and Burstein, 2005, p. 9, in Carroll).

That was in 2005. In December 2015, almost a full year before the world knew that Donald J. Trump would become President, Amber Phillips of *The Washington Post* said, "[t]here are no rules. Journalism today in the U.S. is just what you make of it," and a former radio and online journalist (2015) said, "I think objectivity is overrated—the voice from nowhere, two-sides. [The news organization] said we will not have two sides if one side is to be patently false. Trying to be 'fair and balanced' can be more damaging to the public interest." The former radio and online journalist said that some very thoughtful journalism was taking place, but being drowned out by the chaos.

Some of that chaos can be attributed to punditry in news. In a June 2016 feature in *The Washington Post*, Paul Farhi announced we had reached the "peak of punditry":

> These days, the people of Punditstan are a critical part of the cable news-industrial complex. The leading news networks—CNN, Fox, MSNBC—don't report the news as much as they talk and speculate endlessly about it. For at least the past year, as well as for the next six months, the only thing they're talking about is the presidential campaign, a story perfectly tailored for 24-hour cable with its built-in conflict, historic importance and, yes, ever-changing "narratives" (plus, who in America doesn't have

something to say about Trump and Clinton?). That means just one thing: Right now, we're at peak punditry.

In tracking the recent evolution of news, it is helpful to remember the different models of journalism that have come before.

Journalistic Models*

America's founders valued the ideal of press as a check on government and power and guaranteed press rights and freedoms in the Constitution to preserve media as the fourth estate. However, they did not specify in what form that media would operate. Prior to the Commission on Freedom of the Press[1] in 1947 (Vaughn, 2008) and the advent of the social responsibility movement in American journalism that led to the ideal of objectivity in news coverage (Pickard, 2010), the press in the United States operated under the libertarian model as a predominantly partisan press system. Under this partisan model of journalism, ideally citizens would inform themselves through consuming news. It did not matter which version of news they consumed as long as multiple and divergent voices were expressed through media.

It would be in the clash of ideas, through discussion and debate, as envisioned in conceptualizations of the public sphere by Tarde (1989) and Habermas (Calhoun, 1993), that individuals would arrive at considered opinions. Then, in conjunction with myriad factors, including technological and political ones (such as the invention of the telegraph, formation of the Associated Press, fears of communism and socialism, doubt that average citizens would be motivated, and able to discern the truth from multiple versions of news), the American press system shifted to embrace the objective model. The Watergate scandal ushered in an era of investigative and more strongly critical journalism, at some points verging on what some say was adversarial journalism. And interspersed in the 1960s and 1970s was the rise and fall of the advocacy and new journalism—also known as literary journalism—movements (Pauly, 1990). Advocacy journalists gave a voice to marginalized groups who previously had little to no presence in professional media (Janowitz, 1975). In the 1990s, the public (also known as civic) journalism movement rose, calling on journalists to take on the role of convener and moderator of community discussions about public issues, with the goal of reengaging citizens (Merritt, 1999). This run through U.S. journalism's evolution shows that rather than the objective model being a constant and long-held norm as

---

*Passage included with permission from Sage Publications/*Electronic News*.

is often misremembered, it is but one of many journalistic models that have flourished. Recently, Zelizer (2012) and Nerone (2012) have made a similar point that objectivity and democracy have both played too great a role in scholarship about journalism. Nerone (2012) has tracked the normative history of journalism and how it was in vogue for a time in the West. Williams and Delli Carpini (2011) identify the different prevailing journalistic models throughout history as "media regimes." While the objective model was internalized by many journalists, their organizations and culture, other journalists may have felt limited or like pretenders during that era.

Many observers see a move back toward the partisan model and a hybrid news environment today. As this book's findings will reveal, journalists and others have given reasons for the increase in opinion and commentary: the rise of online news, citizen journalism, news through social media, competition, and polarization of the electorate. Arceneaux and Johnson (2015) "contend that the emergence of partisan news media is more a symptom of a polarized political system than a source."

In transitioning from the discussion of what journalists have said post-2016 election to these chapters covering 2004 through 2016, it is interesting to compare what journalists say now about opinion, commentary, and news versus the before-2016 period. Some now say stay the course; objectivity is still important. Others say that the danger of false equivalence and moral relativism of the administration and supporters means journalists must take a stand and hold power accountable; that is more important than being "objective." Accuracy and transparency on one hand are being advocated for in journalism (Hellmueller, Vos & Poepsel, 2013), but the use of anonymous sources is prevalent.

The analysis in this chapter centers around several key case studies of this movement toward "talk," also known as opinion and commentary in news, including on TV with the increase in opinionated talking heads and the ushering in of a new era of talk and entertainment programs, the strategy by CNN to broaden its definition of news by adding non-news programs, and online and mobile news with the bevy of star journalists starting their own self-branded sites.

The purity of television news, in particular, has always been in question. In 2010, Ben-Porath (2010: 340) wrote:

> At this point, it is relevant to consider whether TV personalities who specialize in political interviews are journalists at all. A vast majority of journalists believes that the cable-news presenters are not (Jamieson et al., 2007). However, the same study finds that the general public is not as decisive in distinguishing between

personalities such as Bill O'Reilly and Chris Matthews and the journalistic profession. In other words, what this study finds is that the on-air actions of personalities who are perhaps merely quasi-journalists can affect viewers' attitudes toward journalists as a whole.

Ben-Porath, and Jamieson, Hardy, and Romer, were calling out partisan or opinionated TV hosts, as opposed to the related but distinct pundits. As previously mentioned, the rise of talking heads, or pundits, on cable news in particular, has been the source of much discourse. A relatively new luxury for some of these more-sought-after talking heads who are not full-time anchors or hosts but have recurring guest roles, is to have a camera and uplink installed in their homes so that they don't have to travel to a studio for their television appearances (Martel, 2012). James Carville, Mary Matalin, Sarah Palin, and Ari Fleisher were among those said to have these home setups. They can just mic themselves up, apply their own makeup at home, and go on the air. Sometimes the network pays for it, and sometimes, the individual covers the expense of installing the equipment.

Farhi (2016) provided a taxonomy of pundits:

> The secret pundit decoder works like this: A "contributor" (such as Meghan McCain) is an exclusive network hireling who gets paid for his or her sound bites. He or she earns a fee for each appearance or a flat amount for being on call, like a firefighter, whenever his or her services are required. The amounts can range from around $150 per "hit" to the mid-six figures for a marquee name such as Karl Rove or David Axelrod, both former campaign savants and presidential advisers. An "analyst" (such as CNN's David Gergen or David Gregory, the former host of "Meet the Press") is a salaried or contract employee who is expected to analyze the day's Narrative rather than opine about it like a contributor. A "strategist" is usually a part-timer and a partisan hired for his or her political experience and insight. . . .
>
> Then there are "guests," Punditstan's temporary-worker class. Guests typically aren't paid, and often aren't even identified as guests. Guests are free to peddle their thoughts to whichever network will have them (full disclosure: I've been an occasional guest on cable, like just everyone in Washington who has ever had a byline). The ever-itinerant nature of this class of talking heads explains why you're likely to see vaguely familiar faces such as

political scientist Larry Sabato or think-tank wise man Norman J. Ornstein on MSNBC one day and on CNN the next.

CNN has pioneered another variation on the theme during this election season: the "supporter." Last year, it hired two commentators to defend Trump, Jeffrey Lord and Kayleigh McEnany (Scottie Hughes, another Trump supporter, is a frequent CNN guest). It has also had a Bernie Sanders booster (Jonathan Tasini), one for Ted Cruz (Amanda Carpenter), one for Jeb Bush (Ana Navarro) and multiple ones for Hillary Clinton. Poor John Kasich; no one on CNN was paid to spin for him.

"The revelation that Donna Brazile, while a CNN commentator, shared CNN debate questions in advance to Hillary Clinton's campaign demonstrates how deeply the cable TV paid pundit model is broken," said NPR's David Folkenflik (2016).

Ironically, Brazile (2010) had previously written an opinion piece in *The Washington Post* in which she advocated for the end of punditry:

> It's time to abolish punditry. If a single move could restore civility to politics, that is it. Get rid of the left-vs.-right commentators who are just out scoring points for their team. This sort of opinion-mongering is not only boring and predictable, it is destructive of the truth.

Brazile suggested replacing pundits

> with people who have genuine expertise—whether from their academic work, professional life or personal experience—on the key issues of the day. Instead of partisan talking heads or mad hatters from the "tea party" preaching their views on, say, health care and taxes, let's hear from doctors and insurance professionals, or the number-crunchers from the Congressional Budget Office. They're much better equipped to help viewers, listeners and readers wade through the facts, arguments and data.

In January 2017, Margaret Sullivan reported statistics from a Gallup poll that public trust in media is down, but in a Pew report, "Three of four Americans give the media credit for keeping public officials from wrongdoing." "The watchdog role has stayed consistently high," said Amy Mitchell, director of journalism research at the Pew Research Center (Sullivan, 2017c). And "more than three in four Americans want the media to 'emphasize inaccurate statements,' Pew reports" (Sullivan, 2017c). "[T]here is this conundrum: As high as the numbers are for watchdog work, there are also high numbers of those who see bias. That hurts trust," said Mitchell (in Sullivan, 2017c).

Has Opinion in News Increased?

In addition to Pew data (2013), which has shown an increase in opinionated news content, scholarly research also shows that the increase in opinionated and interpretive news is not limited to television. Scholarly work by Jacobs and Townsley (2011) supports the increase in commentary and opinion in newspapers and television, and work by Esser and Umbricht (2014) also supports the use of more opinionated and interpretive news in U.S. newspapers. They found an increase in information mixed with interpretation, opinion, and commentary in U.S. papers between 1960/61 and 2006/07. Studies by Ben-Porath (2007) and Cushion (2015) refer to this as "dialogical," "mediatized," and "interpretive."

In all of my interviews with journalists, I asked them if they agreed with the assumption underlying our conversation—that there has been an increase in opinion and commentary in news. Several interviewees asked me to clarify in which mediums, and so I asked about television, and also print and online news, over the past ten years.

Most of the journalists interviewed gave their unqualified agreement that opinion and commentary have increased. Michael Calderone (7/2/14) agreed, "especially on cable news and on the internet."

Josh Altman (7/6/14), formerly a reporter with *The Hill*, also agreed that there has been an increase in opinion and commentary by professionals and laypeople–participants:

> There is, I would say on both sides. I think there's been an increase over the last 5 years, over the last 10, and over the last 50. If you put that out over any period of time, there's always been opinion and commentary, you could take that back 100 years back, 2000 years back. And it has increased in any perceivable amount of time since then on both ends. You see it more by professional pundits. And you see it more by anyone with an internet connection. You don't even need a connection necessarily; you can share an internet connection.

Dave Mastio (8/7/14) said:

If you look at the innovations in media since the birth of the Internet, since 1995, every big movement, like comments, the rise of the blogosphere, the rise of the new cable news channels, Fox and MSNBC. And the big success stories within that. Things like Huffington Post and Drudge, it's not just overwhelmingly opinionated media, it's all opinionated media.

According to Richard Benedetto (3/26/14), 2007 marked the edge of the era of increased opinion and commentary:

> [T]he last presidential campaign I covered full time was 2004. And in 2004 I could see . . . you'd be out on the road with the campaign. And you'd be out there to cover how are they, what are they saying, how are people reacting, what is the situation in the place, why are they there in that particular locale. reporting the story. And you'd get phone calls from editors back in Washington, saying to you 'So and so said something on TV,' you know, 'Some talking head said something. Follow that!' Here you are, out there, and you gotta chase back to somebody who's sitting back in Washington, hasn't been out on the campaign trail probably at all, and you're not doing what you're supposed to be doing, which is reporting. And it becomes, 'interpret this story based upon what somebody back in Washington said on TV.' And it was this convoluted. I found that jarring. And I found it difficult to reconcile with my instincts. My instincts were to be a reporter. I always called myself a reporter. Because, I define reporting very simply. I say, reporting is going some place other people don't go, and coming back and telling them what you saw and heard. But today, they don't want you to do that. They want you to go other places that people don't go, but they don't want you come back and tell them what you saw. They want you to tell them what you should've seen and should've heard, or what you didn't see and didn't hear. And it becomes an entirely different thing. And so I think what people are missing, the public. They're missing information. Good information. And, I always remember my first day in graduate school [at Syracuse University]. The dean is standing there, welcoming all the graduate students. And he's standing there and he says, 'Just remember one thing. You're in the information business. Give people good information. They can figure out what to do with it.' . . . Just give them the information . . . I took that to heart. Maybe too much to heart. It became difficult to be that

interpretive. I can do interpretation, I can do analysis. But, I liked the part . . . going out and reporting what you saw and heard. Less and less did they want that.

Rem Rieder (1/20/15) agreed that there is more opinion and commentary today:

Absolutely. I don't think there is any question about that. But it is at least important in these conversations such as these to make . . . distinctions. Certainly, with the rise of Internet, there are so many venues for . . . blogs or different sites where there is heavy use of opinion(s). You've got cable news that is so guided by a point of view. Ah, in newspapers and in traditional journalism . . . newspapers online, whatever, has been to me a really interesting change in that maybe not, it has not gone from news to opinion.

A former news producer (6/16/14) said,

I definitely think there's a lot more opinion in news in general. When you see a channel trying to get its bearings, like CNN per se, trying to get their bearings, and MSNBC is like, doing really well when there's a lot of politics going on. When they're not doing well, no one's like, no one blames their low rating on producers not being smart enough, or reporters not being smart enough. They're like, "Oh, they don't have a voice," or, "their anchors don't have charisma or a personality for you to tune in for." I think the success of certain shows is often in that. Sometimes it's pinned on production quality. A lot of the shows have the same type of set behind it. It's like, intelligent people who know what they're doing, maybe some people are doing something more innovative, but a lot of people are doing the same. The way that people are trying to differentiate themselves now is with stronger voices. Certain things are doing better. I think there are some long-form programs that are really interesting. Like, CNN has The 60s, which I have on my DVR. I haven't seen it to know if it's good or not. But it sounds like a different thing to watch. In general, when the shows are or aren't doing well, everyone blames it on them being boring or not having a good voice. So I think that that—I don't know. Channels are trying to tap into a voice or personality or an opinion. And the voice and personality—It doesn't have to be opinion, but often in this area, you're not going to voice an opinion and not say what the network is looking for, and not what the people are blaming it on if they have failure.

Liza Mundy (7/30/14) of the New America Foundation, formerly of *The Washington Post* and a contributor to *The Atlantic* and other publications, was also in agreement about the increase in opinion and commentary over the past ten years. She said,

> I do feel like there's, certainly the proportion of opinion journalism to reported journalism, it definitely, I think, at least anecdotally I think to me, trending in the direction of opinion.

Frank Sesno (10/9/14) said:

> Oh yeah, there's no question about it. And in many ways, this tracks from the revolution that I was part of, which was the CNN revolution . . . CNN started bringing 24/7 news to the public. What news executives started finding was that, especially in the traditional printed press, by the time people got to their articles, they'd already seen a lot of pieces and facts of their articles on television. CNN had carried the president's speech live, CNN had taken the press conference live, CNN had chewed over the story for 24 hours live or whatever. And so it started leading, and we started seeing, that really in the '90s to what the papers referred to at the time was a more interpretive style of reporting. That obviously went into high gear—high, high gear—as traditional news organizations went online, because it wasn't just a cable channel anymore, it was a cable channel plus New York Times dot com and CNN dot com, and everything else that was preceding this. Then it went into a high, high, high nuclear drive when social media took off, because now my friend Chris tweets me or texts me, "Hey, you've got to check this out." And there's a link and I'm going into the side door to Huff Post or somewhere else that's telling me that the Supreme Court just declined to rule on the same-sex marriage 9th circuit case. So what has happened is that we've now gone from interpretive to opinionated. This is driven by the same cycle because of what then was the world of cable started getting siphoned off to this online world, and that's when we started seeing the cable ratings decline. And we know that what works on cable is opinion. So then we had the rise of Fox and when MSNBC first launched in '96, they were trying to

be a hipper, cooler CNN, not the counterweight to Fox, it was not opinion. They got no ratings, they got no numbers. Brian Williams arguably had the best newscast on television when he had a prime time hour long newscast on MSNBC, drawing from all the traditional news talent that would be on the NBC network. No one was watching and they cancelled that show. It was his warm up gig, it was his farm team . . . there is absolutely without question opinion and outspoken opinion, the coin of the realm is now the observational, experiential, opinionated sound bite. It is not the straight observation of event or fact.

When I was bureau chief at CNN, I actually wrote a memo to the staff, or to the correspondents, urging them to avoid two words in their live shots. And the two words were "I think." Not that I didn't think they thought, but that what I was saying to them was that the audience isn't here and doesn't especially care what you think, they care what you see and feel. And now, it's really much more, even with the straight correspondents, a matter of what they think and they call it this idea of experiential reporting. You see the reporter walking through the hallway with the senator. It's not just the senator talking on camera doing a sound bite. In every way, the personality is more injected into the news and it expresses itself most notably in the high end opinion shows and opinion leaders who dominate on the air.

Paul Farhi (6/4/14) of *The Washington Post* cited two ways in which opinion in news has increased. The first is that ideological organizations are starting "news" sites online, and the second is journalists appearing in other venues and either being asked to comment on what they've reported on, "or what their opinion is of some other news story."

On the second way, Farhi talked about being prescreened by news program bookers and not selected for some cable news segments because he wouldn't provide conflict:

> [W]hat they do want is conflict. They want one opinion—another opinion; they want clashing views, because clashing views make really good television. So, it's kind of a dangerous game. But you know, these two things actually come together in the sense of— since there's so much opinion out there masquerading as journalism or, frankly, not masquerading at all, going on television and giving opinions would have been shocking a generation ago. It's not terribly shocking now. But, I think, where my opinion comes

in, it degrades the whole process of news reporting and the whole image of news reporting as somehow separate from opinion and objective. Because we're throwing opinions around all the damn time, it's hard for, perhaps a reader to take seriously anything as a straight up news story. They are right to be skeptical about what opinions are being embedded . . . So, I think these two things [ideological organization starting "news" sites, and journalists appearing in news in other venues] are sort of gravitational pulls on the objective nature of news reporting. Look, let's not be naïve: reporters always—as I said—have had opinions, and those opinions, one way or another, found their way into news. But, now we live in a world in which it's becoming much more transparently opinionated. And I think there's something lost. I think, as an old editor at *The Washington Post* used to say, readers, viewers are entitled to one clean shot at the facts, and it's getting harder and harder to find one clean shot at the facts.

Farhi's observation that "clashing views make really good television" is consistent with Mutz's (2015) research on hostile and in-your-face television discourse.

In other journalists' views, one cannot simply say that opinion in news has increased; once opinion is contextualized historically, it is less of a recent change, or they describe it another way.

For example, Erik Wemple (6/12/14) said:

I think inevitably there's more opinion now than there was 10 years ago, but there's more of everything than there was 10 years ago. So I would be hesitant to say that there's more opinion as a ratio, or as—the proportion of opinion to news has gone up. I would guess, probably, depending on how you qualify things—I mean, there's lots of news sources out there, and it seems as though any news source that comes out that does a fair amount of opining. But I would be hesitant to say that it has proliferated more than other forms of journalism. Look how many fact-checking outlets have proliferated in the past 5 years. That's certainly a trend, too. So, you can't call that opinion—of course, you could call that opinion. A lot of people say fact-checking is opinion journalism under a false representation, so that's fair. But, I don't know.

Wemple made a useful point about the sheer volume of content that exists today, and with that increase in volume has come an increase in opinionated content. I and others have located data which serve as evidence that the proportion of opinion versus news that calls itself objective or still aspires to be objective, has in fact increased in several sectors of news (Wemple, 2013; Pew Research Center, 2013).

Jack Shafer (2/11/15) and a TV journalist in Washington (6/18/14) made points similar to Wemple's. Shafer (2/11/15) said,

> I wouldn't make too big a thing because there is more of everything. There is a proliferation of comedy. There is a proliferation of situation comedy. There is a proliferation of drama. There is a proliferation of documentaries. It's an increase in all kinds of media across the board. Hard news to soft news to celebrity news to opinion. It is a true statement, but I think it is a richer statement if you acknowledged that everything is ballooning. Therefore, they are fighting, everybody is fighting, for an audience. They are mostly returning with slivers.

Shafer (2/11/15) went on to say:

> there is a huge explosion of accessibility to hard news that rivals anything we've ever seen before. I would factor that into anybody's calculations when they are trying to talk about the explosion of one kind of news over the other. The whole business of political commentary that is comedic in its nature, historically, you can find that in the earliest newspapers. Right now, I'm writing a Williams and Stewart column and there is this great old, what year is it, there is an academic paper about The Needlers,[2] journalistic satirists throughout the ages. And that has been a parcel of journalism since from the earliest days, the cartoonists and essayists . . . the more people want to say that things have changed . . . I always want to dip back into history and say, no no, things are pretty much the same they've always been. It's just now they are dressed up in glitter and tights.

A TV journalist in Washington (6/18/14) said,

> Well I think first of all that assumes that the amount of TV news will stay the same, right? There's a whole lot more news and a whole lot more information out there. I haven't done a study of it, but it's possible that the same amount of news is out there or even more news is out there, but there are also all these opinion things.

The same correspondent also wanted to distinguish between a news outlet airing someone else's opinion from the outlet's own reporter or anchor giving his or her own opinion:

> [D]o you mean they're airing more opinion or showing more opinion? Because you could have an hour long show where all you do is have the speaker of the house talking for an hour. Airing an hour long opinion. That's not Fox airing it. Or it could be the anchor saying it for an hour. Is it one and the same? Or is it different?

David Mastio of *USA Today* (8/7/14) also agreed that opinion has increased:

> I think it is accurate. I think if anyone would argue with you it would be about, you know, what's the line between opinion and analysis that's traditionally been part of news but is not really opinion.
>
> The way that news editors talk about it is, you know, they want people to write with more voice or more edge, or, you know they use kind of euphemisms for opinion in order to make themselves feel a little, in order to feel a little bit better, but you know, it's really, it's a big gray area between what's absolutely opinion and what's analysis. Like, for instance, we recently added this thing called "Voices" on page 2A there where every day, someone who reports for us or is a news editor, writes a column, and they are, they try to be more reported and more perspective they've gotten from covering an issue for a long time, but you know, it strays pretty far into opinion, into opinion often. Sometimes they're clearly analysis but sometimes not. And, you know, we've done other things online that kind of amp up the opinion like you know, CNN's iReport kind of stuff, you know that's putting reader . . . We have a similar thing to it.

Jon Allen (6/9/14), head of community and content for *Sidewire* (formerly *Bloomberg News* Washington Bureau Chief; Vox senior political correspondent), generally agreed with the assumption about the increase in opinion and commentary in news:

> I think we've seen an increase in subjective analysis in news reporting, some of which is what you might typically consider opinion, some of which is simply more colorful observation than sort of your dry, just-the-facts news.

But like Wemple and Shafer, Allen (6/9/14) qualified his agreement when I asked him if he thought the increase in subjective analysis he described is happening in one type of medium more than others (i.e., more on TV? Or just as much in print and across media?) He drew interesting contrasts between different kinds of outlets, and said that the increase in subjectivity by some outlets might make things easier for those who are still in hard news:

> It depends on the outlet. So, the 24-hour cable news cycle has necessitated an injection of color. Some of that is opinion. Some of it's simply a little bit more subjectivity . . . But I do think the 24-hour cable TV news has to talk about something, and they have to—in order to attract eyeballs—keep the people interested even though there's a dearth of actual breaking news for many parts of that day. And as a result of that, you end up getting more analysis, more opinion. The people that are on television talking, often for long periods of time, are a Democratic strategist, or a Republican strategist; they might be on for 10, 15, 20 minutes, an hour, at a chunk. Just in and of itself, forget the basic cast of the cable news outlet, in addition to that obviously. You've got Fox which caters to the right, MSNBC which caters to the left; that is their business model. That said, I don't see the same thing happening with NBC News, ABC News, CBS News. I don't see the same thing happening with the *New York Times* or [*T*]*he Washington Post*, or *Bloomberg News*, or the *Wall Street Journal*. So you go through your various media outlets, I think there's a proliferation of media choices for the consumer. There's a broader array of things that you go to, and as a result of that, also more partisan choices, more subjective or opinionated choices as a reader. I don't necessarily think that's a bad thing. For one thing, it makes those of us who are sort of in the hard news business stand out even more for continuing to operate in a straight-up fashion, as compared to others.

Opinion Journalism Is Increasing through Journalists' Social Media Use

According to journalists, another way in which opinion by journalists is increasing is through journalists' own social media use. Paul Farhi (6/4/14) said:

Twitter was adopted early by journalists, because, of course, journalists like any new communication technology. Twitter got adopted early by journalists, and then by the rest of world. And Twitter is just an opinion machine; Twitter is a way for journalists to throw opinions around about every damn thing in the world. Sometimes it goes overboard. We've seen—here—instances in which reporters were kind of overstepping their boundaries as news reporters, and, on Twitter, going into being opinion columnists. It's inappropriate, and they had to be, essentially, disciplined, although that's probably too strong of a word. What they had to be told was, "you know what, tone it down, cool it, that's not appropriate," and they have. But it goes on all day long. Twitter is a seductive kind of thing because at any given point, you are your own publisher and you can throw anything around that you want. Facebook is the same way. These are personal medium(s). You think you're talking to your friends, but in fact you're talking to the world. And it's just unseemly for us to be doing some of that stuff. I know I have to stop myself from doing it. I'll have opinions, but about things I don't cover, so somehow that makes it ok.

I asked Farhi about the Post's policies on its journalists' social media use. He said,

The rule is that you should not tweet anything that you wouldn't want to see in print under your byline, which I think is a very good rule. You wouldn't write that in a day's story, or an enterprise story, or whatever kind of story, so why are you tweeting that? You're tweeting that because, mainly, you can, and that's really the point of what goes on.

Rem Rieder (1/20/15) implied that most journalists at *USA Today* are unfamiliar with the company's social media policies, even though journalists are strongly encouraged to use social media:

Yeah, but they [policies] are not widely known . . . There is a great premium placed here on social media. There is a social Tuesday or something like that. And there is, very much, being very active on social media is very much encouraged. . . . They [the policies] are not a part of the conversation. Maybe they should be more . . . I think it is kind of common sense. That basically you don't . . . It's like the pornography thing, you should know it when you see it. There are certain things you don't do and you don't say.

I enjoy Facebook a lot more than Twitter. But, to me, Facebook and I, obviously, I circulate all of my columns on both, but I enjoy Facebook and do it more as a personal thing. It is both personal and professional, I guess, but I enjoy it for the silly conversations, the favorite movies, the back and forth stuff. Twitter is obviously an extremely valuable tool both distributing material and for monitoring the zeitgeist . . . But I should like it more than I do. But I do have a real weakness for Facebook. I like it a lot.

[I have] [j]ust one profile and kind of in my life, I've thought this for a long time, it's hard to know, I think journalism is all encompassing field, such an intense thing. It becomes a part of you. It's hard to know, there is a blurry line between the personal and professional. There is that whole part of who you are, some of your friends are journalists, and so, yeah, so I've always had one account and it will always kind of be a mix. On Facebook, I find really good journalism that other people de-flag. So I like it for that, but it is more the personal and the fun that I really like about it.

Rieder said that while he doesn't feel pressured to use social media, "you do and you need to." However, a television news correspondent (2/9/17) said she quit Twitter and Facebook and doesn't find very much use for them. She said she thinks if all journalists stopped using it [social media], it would go away.

A TV journalist in Washington (6/18/14) said that items he reports can end up on any medium first:

> It depends. It's situational. It could end up on Twitter, anywhere. Twitter, it depends. It's situational. Twitter, TV, for the web . . . Probably like . . . at the same time, you know we'll do it on TV, Twitter, and all at the same time. If it's sort of, let's say it's new, something, I just got to . . . if it's new, you know, you don't have a show again until 6:30 at night, the morning show is over, we'll [T]weet it and put it on the internet. If it's of less importance but I think it's sort of funny, a good little tidbit to have, but it's not worth a whole story online, I'll tweet it.

This correspondent enjoys having more outlets for the work:

[I]t's a great chance, for me it's fun. I love it when five of us get to have a byline together and we're all sort of swapping ideas. And don't forget to put that in, and change this line to that. It's a little bit more of a creative process. You get to be part a little bit more of the creative process.

These journalists' sentiments about social media are consistent overall with those found by Holton and Molyneux (2015), as summarized by Ordway (2016):

- There still is uncertainty among reporters and editors about acceptable practices on social media, especially as they relate to personal branding and company branding.

- Reporters are being asked to read and respond to social media posts at all times, which they view as an added burden among a long list of job responsibilities.

- Editors said that they are sympathetic to the branding-related demands being placed on reporters but feel "hamstrung" by the policies and expectations of their news organizations. Few said they monitor their reporters' social media activities but acknowledged that their news agencies "made examples out of individuals who were not falling in line."

Another study (Lee, 2015) examined how journalists' social media activities affected audience perceptions of them and their news organizations. The study found that journalists' social media activities (specifically self-disclosure and interaction with other users) negatively influenced audience perceptions of the professional dimension of journalists and their news products, even though it positively influenced audience's perceptions of them personally. So while news organizations encourage their employees to be active on social media, it may not improve audience perceptions. Still, there are other reasons organizations pursue social media, such as increasing viewership of their stories and promoting their brand.

It's interesting that Farhi (6/4/14) said that journalists like any new communication technology and that Twitter was adopted early by journalists. Whereas I and others have asserted that in the past, journalists and their news organization in general have been slow to adapt to change—chiefly technological—and did so late and only when facing obsolescence, there have always been some journalists who were on the forefront, embracing new technology and figuring out how to utilize it for their work. This time around (over the past ten years), some of these trailblazing journalists are the journalist-hackers, data journalists, and social media gurus for their organizations.

Increase in Opinion and Commentary in Radio News

Although I only interviewed one radio journalist for this research—Rick Massimo, web writer and editor at Washington, DC's WTOP—Massimo (6/10/14) was able to provide his perspective on how the increase in opinion and commentary has affected local news:

> One of the things that I'm sure people have told you is that it's cheaper to produce commentary than news. It's much easier to have somebody sitting in the studio talking about what's happening in the Middle East than it is to send somebody out to find out about it. And what I have been finding in the local TV news is the micro version of that. Which is that every story is padded by asking somebody in the neighborhood what they think about it . . . And what I'm realizing is, whether it's on purpose or not, and I can't say, but I bet I know. You're padding. And that's fewer stories you have to send people out on. So, to me that's sort of like the micro example of the same principle.

However, Massimo said that radio news has not been affected in the same ways as print and television:

> The idea that it [radio] was always free. Right, and that the Internet presence would only sort of complement or help . . . Maybe that's why, I mean, there are pure talk radio stations, but maybe that's why, but this is news radio station, maybe that's why, in the case of the trend you're talking about, there hasn't been this huge shift to commentary . . . And that's the other thing. Radio is local. . . . It just occurred to me now that by getting rid of the reporters and replacing them with a bunch of commentators, wouldn't actually save us any money. Because we're not sending people to Vietnam anyway. We're sending people to Frederick.

Massimo said public radio is in a different situation:

> I mean the thing about public radio is that they are, there's government funding, and maybe the thing more volatile than the advertising dollar is the government funding and foundation funding.

Massimo acknowledged that WTOP is owned by Minneapolis-based Hubbard Broadcasting, but said it doesn't have the same issues with chain ownership of homogenized centrally created content that some other chain-owned stations have:

> That's not happening here. I mean, you know, to an extent, we're a CBS affiliate so, in that sense we're broadcasting some of the same stuff that stations all over the country are.

Why Has Opinion in News Increased?

Journalists tend to provide several reasons for the increase in opinion and commentary. They relate back to some of the causes that I have speculated about; One, financial—the low cost of creating opinionated content; two, competition and being able to differentiate your product. Dave Mastio (8/7/14) provided a third reason. He said,

> Well, I think there's a huge demand to be heard. And while it's true that you know like Fox and MSNBC were launched as businesses to, as businesses to make a profit and that cheapness might have played a role there, in their opinion route there. I mean just look at the amount of unpaid work that's poured into social media, into blogs and all of that. That's not about making a buck. It's about people wanting to be heard. And I think that drives opinion into the news just as much. Because people don't want, don't just want to be heard, they also want to see, they want to read things that reflect back at them what they think. And so, giving readers what they want is another big element.

Cable News Was a Factor in the Increase of Opinion in News

Richard Benedetto (3/26/14) and Jon Allen (6/9/14) both said they thought the 24-hour cable news cycle was a reason for the increase in opinionated news. Benedetto said,

But CNN came along and then followed by the Fox Network, followed by MSNBC, which changed how you present news in a 24 hour format. What do you do to fill a 24 hour format? The networks only had to fill 30 minutes at night. And a few minutes up on the morning shows like "Today" and "Good Morning America" when they filled them with fluff as well as news, which they still do.

Benedetto traces the talk and commentary format on cable news back to "Meet the Press":

Now the eighties was not a period where we had a lot of war so that that was not a big part of their agenda at that time, but so they found ways to fill in the time with these talk shows. Because they had this long period of time to fill. 24 hours a day. So these talk shows where you bring people on. And some of them were like, just adversarial where they'd bring one Republican or one liberal or one conservative and they would go at it for a while. Or they would have panels. So that more and more opinion was coming into the daily presentation of the news. And Roger Ailes came along and figured out a way he could make money with it, by attracting a liberal, conservative audience. So that had a lot to do with changing the dynamic of reporting the news. The only thing you saw on regular news programs was Meet the Press. And Meet the Press in those days was different. Meet the Press used to be a guest, a moderator, and some journalists asking questions. Meet the Press had been on from the fifties.

The newspapers found it very popular because it was on Sunday, and Sunday is a dead news day so therefore they would monitor. The newspapers would all cover Meet the Press so that they would have stories for Monday's paper about what was said in that particular venue.

Allen (6/9/14) also indicated he thinks that competition and narrowcasting to niche audiences are behind the shift in opinion:

So, there are a couple of ways I would look at this: one is—and I think you see this to a large extent in print, online, on television as well—I think in what had been a shrinking news environment, in what had been a shrinking industry, there is an understanding that there is a lot of demand for good storytelling, and good storytelling isn't necessarily dry news, but it's often the opposite.

So, I think part of that is an injection of writers trying to find a way to grab their audiences, and sometimes that can come off as opinion or not objective enough. So I think that part of what drives sort of a change in the news atmosphere. I also think consumers are increasingly isolated, in a way, and able to sort of live—in a media sense—in an echo chamber. They can go to the sources that give them the news that they want to hear and provide it to them in a way that has a partisan bias if they want it. In the old days, media outlets were broadcasting—and not in the sense of broadcasting like television or radio, but broadcasting in the sense of trying to attract the most readers, the most viewers, the most listeners—and as part of that, they had to work hard not to offend anyone with particular viewpoints on politics and partisan viewpoints. That's not necessarily what we're seeing anymore in the media market; what we're seeing is increasingly narrow casting, where you're just trying to pick off a particular percentage of the market and you want to get a smaller set that's very loyal, or get people who advertisers want paying attention to your media. So I think there's been that change as well. I think it makes it harder for the smaller share of media outlets remaining that are objective and balanced and seeking simply to get news out there to people who would read it.

Benedetto also believes the changes are generational:

Well you know, there, when we think about changes in the media, we think of changes in the delivery of media. The technology part, and that's certainly a big factor. But there's also another part of the media that have changed and that is the people. There's generations of change too so that people who went into journalism in my day, let's say, which would be in the sixties. Coming out of college in the sixties, and going into journalism at that time, were a lot different than people who went into journalism, say post-Watergate. We, if I think about what people like me wanted to do when we wanted to be reporters, basically we liked to write, we liked politics, we liked politicians, we liked to be in the middle of the action, we were nosy, we wanted to be in the middle of the action. We liked it. We saw it exciting. We didn't hate politicians. We didn't hate government, we didn't hate politics. We kinda liked all of those things and we wanted to be in the middle. We weren't necessarily, didn't want to be politicians, but we liked being around politicians.

Benedetto continued:

> Younger people today who have . . . I say people who have come into business after Watergate, let's say. Because that is kind of a watershed. They came in with this kind of a get the politicians attitude that the role of the journalist is not just to provide information but is to dig out all of it. Now we do have a watchdog function. I mean, we are supposed to in fact, if there's anything that's wrong. . . .

Benedetto reflected on his thoughts that on the one hand, journalists seem to be more watchdog since the seventies, but that today we are seeing this taken to the extreme:

> But as a watchdog, with the watchdog function, I tell the students, we don't go in there and try to point out wrongs to bring the government down. We point out wrongs so they can be fixed and the government can work better. . . . If somebody does something right, it's as much a story as if somebody does something wrong . . . If you go up to an editor and say, 'I want to do a profile of a politician who I think is a nice guy' they'll say 'you must be crazy. What are you, going soft?'

Benedetto (3/26/14) believes the rise of cable and the lifting of the Fairness Doctrine in the 1980s contributed to the rise of Rush Limbaugh and more opinionated media:

> Well it's technology and it's also legislation, or regulation. Up until the early 1980s, we basically had the three major TV networks and we had the newspapers and radio networks. And that was it. Two things happened. Cable TV came in. Cable TV came in in the eighties. And the Fairness Doctrine was lifted in the eighties. When the Fairness Doctrine was lifted it made it possible to have shows that took political ideology and promoted that particular political ideology. It contributed to the rise of a guy like Rush Limbaugh, for example. Very, very much so. The other thing is cable news, with all these new channels available, people decided that there would be ways that we could provide more news, more sports, everything.

Talk Is Cheap. Financial Incentives to Moving to a Talk Format

Rick Massimo (6/10/14) traced the change back to the financial models for news, and said that fortunately radio has not been affected in the same way as newspapers:

> And don't forget the process, the underlying what's behind all of this is the idea that news organization have to make money on their own, as opposed to they were just thinking everyone knew they didn't make money but they knew they ran soap operas and sitcoms to pay for the news. Once that stopped happening, then the floodgates opened to a whole lot of change.
>
> And as soon as you have, as soon as you talk about making money, then you've got businessmen, and as soon as you've got businessmen, um, then you've got problems. But one of the reasons you've got problems is because businessmen say cut costs, because we still think that when a businessman comes in and says cut costs, he's saying something intelligent, but you know if he came in and said, uhh, if he came in and said, let's be better, everyone would say, well that's a stupid thing to say, and you know, well this is my agenda here, but for them to come in and say cut costs . . . [i]s no more intelligent than saying, be better, and yet we treat it like it is. And the thing I kept saying at the paper every time there was a cutback, every time there was a buyout, every time there was a lay off, every time there was a cutback in coverage, every time they closed a bureau, I, every time I would say, well, evidently the philosophy is that if we keep making it worse, sooner or later more people will buy it. And you know, one of the things I can say about WTOP is that it's successful . . . they do actually think, let's make it better. We'll make more money if we make it better. They are actually expanding. And this is such a refreshing change. . . . [N]ewspapers are bleeding because of the Internet because people are getting all the content free. Radio, radio is already free. We don't care. He said, radio, we love the Internet because now we get to give more free stuff for more people.

Mundy (7/30/14), also citing the proliferation of outlets, and highlighting the low cost of opinionated content, said, you can either blog yourself or there are so many publications now that people can write for. It's, I think much easier to publish. It's probably gotten harder to get paid for your publishing. But there's just a literally an endless amount of space to fill now, so it's much easier for people to write or express their opinions, and I think too on television . . . the proliferation of cable and 24 hour news channels just means there's so much air space to fill and shrinking news budgets that of course you're gonna have people opining . . . It's the cheapest form of journalism. Literally the cheapest form.

David Mastio (8/7/14) also cited the low cost of opinionated talking heads:

I think it's fairly cheap. There's lots of people who want to do it. For nothing or very little, because they wanna have a voice in the debate, so I mean it's just a really good business move all around.

I don't know the economics of how people are paid and stuff, beside Fox and CNN. I only know very little, but you know, there are some people who get paid really well for their opinions, and there's some people who don't get paid at all. The ones who don't get paid at all far outnumber the ones who can make a living at it. And I think that's the same as, same at newspapers. It goes right back to the readers. Just like there's gradations between news and analysis and opinion, there's that big gray area where it's a matter also of opinion. In, there's a huge gradation in who the people are who contribute to the opinion. You've got, you know, you start with the readers and then you slowly move your way up into more and more expert people, and then the most prominent experts, and then the people who make their living doing that and there's you know, everybody's got an opinion.

At his own organization, *USA Today*, Mastio said,

Most of the people who write for us for print, just because there's such a premium on the highest profile people, the vast majority are paid. And for online the majority are unpaid, but even, you know, there's people who bring followings with them who you know, you just know you're going to get a certain amount of traffic with, and that, you know that creates more demand for them and so even if they're writing for online, where we have infinite space and infinite number of people who want to write for us, we pay for that too.

Michael Calderone (7/2/14) also cited the low cost:

> I mean in some ways opinion is cheap. Reporting is very expensive business, and you know in parts of the news business, you know, that have been strapped for cash, you know, opinion is much easier. And like I was saying, opinion can do much better at times online than a reported article that may take weeks or months to report out. So, I think there is a tendency to kind of increasingly do opinionated pieces or riffs on the news than creating news. And part of it is an economic factor in that it costs a lot more money to have reporters on the ground doing these stories, whereas you could have somebody at their desk knocking out five or six posts of opinion on the news throughout the day.

Calderone went on to say:

> And those stories may do very well traffic-wise. And they may get shared, and they create controversy. Controversy that spills out onto Twitter and other platforms where people will engage in these ideas, so I mean, there's still very much a need for reporting, in the news business, obviously, but you know, I think in a lot of ways it's cheaper and easier at times to do opinionated posts. On cable television, we've seen you know, Fox News has been the leader now for 50 consecutive quarters by doing news with a conservative bent. Both their news coverage as well as their nightly opinion shows are, their nightly opinion shows like The O'Reilly Factor has been the top rated cable news show for years and years. They've had a lot of success with this model, and it's a model that's then been emulated by MSNBC and at others, trying to do the liberal side of news. Liberal talk shows throughout the day. You know a liberal or conservative talk show is very cheap. You just have a host, or a couple hosts who can bat around the news all day, versus actually a news show that's focused around doing well-produced segments by reporters in the field. So it's, on cable news these shows are very cheap to produce . . . The sets are pretty much interchangeable, it's just requiring a different host, and you've got a whole new show.

Josh Altman (7/6/14) cited the low costs associated with expressing opinion today, as well as the protection of anonymity that emboldens some people to express their opinions:

> I think we are also louder. We are certainly more vocal in it. And I think part of that just comes with the ability to comment more when commenting had a transaction cost when, I mean let's go back a little bit, anything more than 150 years, paper was expensive. I don't mean paper down here at the paper source; it is all going to be very nice paper that you would use for like an invitation. And I don't just mean 8.5 × 11 paper, that was expensive. Ink was expensive. These were commodities that not everyone had a means that you could use just to dispose of to write an angry tweet. Not even ease, the actual cost. I mean, it's no harder to write a tweet than it is to scribble it out on a piece of paper. That paper and that ink cost money. Then you have to fold it up and actually put a stamp on it that has value. Not just transaction costs—actual costs.

Competition as a Reason for the Increase in Opinion and Commentary

In addition to the low cost of some forms of opinion journalism, Mastio (8/7/14) also agreed that the need to distinguish one's news content plays a role:

> It's differentiation. You have a little more edge in your piece, maybe it's going to be more likely to get linked and drive traffic. And there's also an element of, you know, going back to the readers and . . . experts and stuff and all the people who add to our content for free or for very little. There's an element of, the technology has made it so easy for them to do that stuff anywhere and have a good audience for it. It'd be, you know, folly for us to just say, 'Oh no, you can't do stuff for us for free.' You know, 'Go to the *Huffington Post*' or whatever.

Perlmutter said opinion has increased as of five or even ten years ago, also due to the need to differentiate content from competitors:

> Well the reason is, is because, again, it goes back to technology and social media. On the technology side there are just so many options now for people to get their news anywhere, any time on

demand, up to the second. But what probably is the most important factor is social media, Facebook feeds, Twitter, Snapchat, you can get your news on demand. And the reason why the opinion pieces started to happen more and more on news channels and television is because when you go to watch news, what happened today, what happened five, six hours ago, people, the audience already knows that. They've seen it, they've heard it and they're aware of it. So there's no point in continuing to deliver them, here's the news of the day, here's what happened. Even 24/7 cable, they are even late because people are not watching that, they're getting it from their handheld device, they're getting it on their computer. So, you have to, somebody had to think about what it is we can give them that's different, that they'll want to engage in if they already know the news. And the answer is, opinion. So people are not going to cable news anymore for straight news. People are not going to the nightly news shows to find out what happened, because at 6:30 at night, they already know all that, which is why the evening news shows, it might be less opinion, because they're a little bit harder news, but that's why the evening news shows on the traditional networks are doing more features. They have to do it. They've gotta provide something different.

A TV journalist in Washington (6/18/14) made an interesting observation, however, about the morning shows:

> The one thing that the morning shows have, that no other shows during the day have, is that people have been asleep before they tuned into that show, so there is eight hours of people not checking their phones and not on the Internet. So the morning shows have a little, I don't know if it's a benefit or an edge. They apparently offer something that other shows don't.

Rem Rieder (1/20/15) also cited competition as a reason for the rise of opinion and commentary:

> Well, I think that the Internet, in general . . . has a more freewheeling form. You've got, in the old model, you had a finite number of news organizations and they were all pretty traditional and you've the gatekeeper approach. So, if a handful of news organizations decided something wasn't a story, it wasn't a story. You don't have that now because you don't have gatekeepers. You

have so many players and so much, and this is kind of related, you have so much competition. So many people clamoring for attention, it puts a premium on doing something to stand out. You know, at the best of it, that is unearthing great investigative stories that no one else has or doing something like 'Snowfall' like the *New York Times* did. But, but what it does on the other hand is putting a premium on sexy headlines that are misleading or sexy stories that are empty calorie, click bait, that don't really add anything. But, like everything, it's like a multi-edged sword. But, I think the end of the gatekeeper era, the emergence of so many players, immense competition, you have to do something to get noticed, some of what you do can be really good and some of it can be pretty sleazy.

Amber Phillips (7/23/14), reporter for "The Fix" at *The Washington Post*, who at the time of our 2014 interview was a Washington correspondent for the *Las Vegas Sun*, also described the immediacy of information and competition among news providers as a reason for the move toward opinionated news content:

> . . . as a regional Washington correspondent, the challenge is: how do you write what no one else is writing. What the wires are writing, what the DC inside publications are writing. And I'm proud to be part of a publication, the *Las Vegas Sun*, that wants to find a way to kind of cut through all that noise of what people are writing. You know, "So and so lawmaker said this," and that's the story; ten inches, done—not even—six inches, done. And, I think there's value in terms of journalism of record, but it's not the way that correspondents need to be going, because anyone in Las Vegas can get their news anywhere online at this point. What I need to do is find a way to tell the broader story—cut through the noise and tell the why and the how something is happening. And to do that, I think you have to kind of walk a new line in journalism, and that is a very thin line between opinion and commentary and objective journalism.

Phillips went on to explain:

> Like, I feel like I can't just say, "lawmakers are pushing this bill; here's what the bill would do," and at the very bottom, after my readers have invested their time and their clicks to read my story, say, "but this bill will never happen." That is kind of the old model

that's great for the wires, that's great for a lot of other DC publications, but to help my readers and cut through the noise, I need to kind of get to the point really quickly. For example, I wrote a story that said, "Senate Democrats proposed this bill and it isn't going anywhere, and here's why." Some people might classify that as opinion or commentary, because I'm taking a hypothesis and making a point, even though it's a reported point. But I think more and more of that is kind of necessary in journalism, especially as a regional Washington correspondent, to help people who aren't in DC understand what's going on and make it worth their time to read the story.

The former news producer (6/16/14) also agreed that technology, which has enabled increased competition among news providers, has been the driver of many of these changes in news:

people can get news everywhere, so however you're presenting your news has to be some sort of new and interesting way. Otherwise, what are you offering people? I think that has a lot to do with opinion, because I think everyone can get the story, everyone can read it online . . .—and everyone's read that article on their own news aggregator sites, but people kind of want this because they are tuning into opinion news. People want to hear pros and cons. Even though a news article does have a quote from someone for it and a quote from someone against it, I feel like, when people are hearing impassioned arguments for either way, I think it either helps solidify people's opinion—I think it probably helps solidify people's opinion; I don't think that they're completely turned in the other direction . . . it's helpful for them to hear the other side if it's a boxing match sort of debate, cable news thing. It's helpful for them to hear the other side, . . . Devil's Advocate argument for their own side, and possibly to see the other side and say "oh, I hadn't thought about that concept." So yes, digital has something to do with it because the opportunity for people to learn about straight news . . . that has forced TV to rethink how they're presenting things. What are they doing that [gets] someone to tune in if they already saw the story on their iPhone . . . You have to advance the story or no one is going to watch.

Jim Henderson (12/10/14) also cited technology as a driving factor of changes in journalism:

Technology, as in the internet, has hurt advertising for newspapers, and the whole business model has changed. So, technology has created the business need for—so, what more and more has happened is, I think publications both print and online are trying to give readers what they want. And so if you're in an area where much more of your readers are liberal, you're going to feed them—unconsciously or consciously—more of a liberal bent. Likewise, if they're conservative, you might be doing it that way. If your readers are more prone to stock-picking, you might be focusing more on that. So, that's created some of it: giving the readers what they want. The old days, when you had monopoly newspapers somewhere, and you could give them what you feel they need because they can't go anywhere else, that's long gone. So that's sort of splintered things a lot. And I think some of it also comes from so many different news outlets, that you have a lot of people coming into journalism—they probably didn't think they were even going to be in journalism—but they're landing jobs on websites and things like that. And, actually, on major publications, too, is that you don't have the bench strength. So in the old days of newspapers where reporters just didn't write headlines, the editors didn't write the headlines, the copy desk wrote the headlines—the editors might look over them—you've got reporters now banging stories out quickly because that's their job. And they're also putting the heads on—the headlines. And they go right in online. And then, maybe somebody will be looking over their shoulder at some point and changing it, but it's up there. And so, that could—and not just the headlines, but the leads of the stories. So that's happened, a lot, in a sense. But that's a millennial generation coming on very quickly. But they're also learning very quickly, and they're smart, and they're being trained as journalists on the job. And it's—that is taking place, which is good.

Political and Social Changes Are also Factors in the Increase in Opinion and Commentary

In addition to technology being a driver of journalistic changes, Henderson (12/10/14) also discussed the political and social changes that have been a factor:

I mean, there's certainly growing polarization politically in the country that's been going on for a while now. So that's lent it. And there's also growing polarization socioeconomically, too. We've got that 1%—is out there, and . . . there's polarization between generations, too. I mean, the baby boom generation, they started life just flat broke. The Millennial generation is starting life deep in a hole—they'd love to be just flat broke. And so, there's polarization there. That's some of it. But also, historically, I think if you look back, the fact that there was not so much polarization in the past—'70s or '80s—that was probably more of an anomaly, historically speaking, in this country. You know, before WWII, politics was extremely polarized, and certainly in the 1800s—it was just—that's what the country's built on . . . but there's something recently on how WWII may have done a lot, because there was such a shared experience by a huge generation, and that sort of brought things politically together, and the media as well. And that generation has kind of faded out; we're back to good old USA.

Maria Bartiromo (6/19/14) also cited divisiveness in the country as a reason for increased opinion. She said,

> I think there's a lot of finger-pointing going on about whose fault it is for a weak economy, and whose fault it is after the 2008 financial crisis, and as a result, the public has become more divisive than ever before. And, you know, the president has in some ways divided us; in other ways, people who have opinions and do not agree with him have divided us. But, I think people are divided, and it has taken the press with them. I am stopping short of blaming any one administration, but I think going into Iraq under President Bush was not popular. So that was one issue. President Obama is also very divisive and blames the Republicans a lot for everything, and that sort of fuels the fire. And so, as a result of that, I think people have made their own opinion about where the country should go, how it should be governed, and they speak out about it. And the bias has clearly gotten into the media.

This belief that media reflect the polarized political environment, rather than contributing to, or being responsible for it, is consistent with the comments made by other journalists, such as Brian Stelter.

Rieder (1/20/15) also sees the demand for opinionated content: "But, I think there is a market for it, too. I mean you see—the emergence of Fox is really significant. Fox came into the market place when television tradition was trying to, pretty much, be straight down the middle to draw the broadest audience possible, you don't take sides." Rieder said,

> Fox came in here and clearly there was huge pent up demand for it. I guess it was being fulfilled to some extent by talk radio, but Fox came in and has been an enormous success. There are a lot of people who really want to hear their news filtered through their beliefs. They want to hear what they want to hear and to a lesser extent (I guess) that's true of the left, but MSNBC never emerged as a force to the extent that Fox did. But, for a time, I think it subsided now. But it has a substantial audience as well. And you have a world now, where you can kind of just listen to your own news, you can listen to talk radio, and Fox, and conservative, and right wing conservative; if you are liberal, you can watch MSNBC and go to the *Huffington Post*. So, ah, there is, so to some extent, it is a response to the market place . . . the people they, the side I'm not crazy about, want to hear what they want to hear. But also they are seeking the thirst for sharper edge stuff, and part of this was because traditional journalism was dull. High minded, maybe, but dull and unsatisfying.

Frank Sesno (10/9/14) offered a different thought about the reasons behind the increase in opinion and commentary:

> When I joined CNN in 1984, I was told we do not have stars, the news is the star. When I started my program, "Late Edition," in 1991 I think it was, it was just "Late Edition." It became "Late Edition with Frank Sesno" and that was a—it was married to a really hard campaign to get in a little box that lifted our guests in the Sunday shows and [T]*he Washington Post*, I was considered a big deal so the name was part of that. No show 20 years ago on CNN carried the name of the host. They all do now. People watch people. And one of the first things that we were told after one of our—after the AOL merge for example—was that the AOL people and the Hollywood people had come in to help run it, where we had started to see the serious ratings decline and defections to Fox, was that CNN was too bland, too generic, and that the news did not sell. People watch people. And so the entire business, same with print. Go to a columnist now, an online columnist and there's a picture of them. That never existed before.

Sesno (10/9/14) elaborated on the elevation of individual journalists and the segmentation of the audience:

> It's all gotten much more personality driven. And . . . one is the competition, the other is the disaggregation of audience. The audience is disaggregated, the audience is collapsed, certainty eroded for almost all news organizations. And so, it's not just competition, that's always existed. The dramatic erosion of audience and the need to have a Tom Friedman, a Maureen Dowd, a Bill O'Reilly, and an Anderson Cooper, someone who is sort of the brand of the brand.

CNN's (Jeff Zucker's) Strategy to "Diversify" Programming

CNN's new emphasis on "broadening" the definition of news was the brainchild of its new president, Jeff Zucker, who not so coincidentally, came to his role at CNN after leaving as the Executive Producer of Katie Couric's talk show. Zucker said his strategy was to "broaden" the idea of news by putting different kinds of content on CNN's programs (Wallenstein, 2012). In winter 2014, he announced it was the year of "shake up" (Steinberg, 2014).

CNN has long, and arguably always, done more than just the news (Meltzer, 2003). In January, 2011, Piers Morgan had been the replacement for Larry King's talk show with newsmakers, an example of hybridity. Morgan's show was cancelled in February 2014 amidst poor ratings (Yahr, 2014; Carr, 2014). Don Lemon's show on CNN has been more successful. Lemon's profile on CNN rose during the coverage of the 2009 Obama inauguration (Flaherty, 2009). He and others also filled in as CNN experimented with Erin Burnett's time slot while she was on maternity leave (Steinberg, 2013; 2014). One Wemple article (2015) mentions CNN's strategy:

> CNN strives for a tricky balance in its news programming. It wants spicy, watchable coverage enlivened by perspectives and opinions—but no partisan biases from its corps of reporters and anchors. Take controversial anchor Don Lemon, who is licensed to express opinions on air on the condition that they're not "predictably partisan."

When Zucker came to CNN in 2012, he announced a new strategy to create other kinds of programs that clearly aren't news, such as Anthony Bourdain's show "Parts Unknown," and some documentary-type long form programs such as "The Sixties," and "Blackfish" about the killer whale at Sea World who killed its trainer. Bourdain's show on CNN has achieved great ratings for the channel and even featured President Obama in one episode in Hanoi, Vietnam (Yahr, 2016). Bourdain died in June 2018; CNN has not yet announced plans to replace the program. While not airing on CNN, Anderson Cooper, a CNN host and news anchor, was permitted to produce an HBO special about his mother Gloria Vanderbilt (Lawson, 2016).

Journalists had different thoughts about Zucker's strategy for CNN. A CNN employee who worked on digital content (4/14/15) referred to CNN's "identity crisis," and a "culture shift in the organization" as fewer people are buying cable, shifting more and more to digital platforms. The employee said, "The impression I get is that he's [Zucker] very into trying stuff, sort of throwing everything at the wall, seeing what sticks . . . Which is a good atmosphere for sort of innovation, but he also has definitely brought a sort of like a morning show mentality to the whole network, from what I can tell." The CNN employee went on to say:

> It seems like a common refrain from folks, that they don't really—I wouldn't say they don't agree with the way that we spend our 24 hours of television time, but there can be some frustration from producers who feel like there might not be enough news. Because the other sort of—on top of it aside from coming up with these perky experimental shows, is—he will sort of pluck out three news stories of the day and we'll just focus on them. I'm sure you've read that—what CNN does—has to at least be in keeping—is breaking news . . . He's got a real mix of viewers so who am I to sort of criticize? I guess I come from like a little bit of an old school point of view about what news should be.

This idea of trying many things at once to see what works was echoed by a former news producer (6/16/14):

> Speaking of opinion, I don't even know if their longer form pieces, whether you consider it opinion. I actually think that there's so many channels and voices trying to fight for initially the same user base. Some people are actually, ok Fox News, they're not even going for the same audience. I'm going for the older person, or Republicans or Democrats. . . . It's like a mix . . . They're all trying to fight for the same viewers, they're just trying to come up with different unusual things that might attract people's atten-

tion. You know, the ads for "The Sixties" are like, you know what, kind of interesting to talk about the '60s because of Mad Men, and every once in a while, something comes to remind younger people of what an important generation it was. Not just the people who lived through it. . . . They probably have a huge white board or electronic spreadsheet of different ideas, and they're thinking which ones are we going to try first? And see if we give it a little try for a while, if the ratings are going to do better with this. It's not opinion, but following the missing flight for weeks and weeks on end, it's kind of obsessive news coverage. So I think trying different things and seeing what sticks, really.

The former news producer (6/16/14) also thinks it's possible that in the future, CNN and other outlets could outsource, or acquire programs, from other content producers:

[S]ome places have the manpower within their own network to create really unique content, but other times they just don't have—I don't know if it's the money, or the capability, or the infrastructure they already have is based on daily or weekly programming. They don't have the manpower for specials. Some of them do; it depends on how in depth and polished you're going to make it. I don't know that a lot of networks have man power.

Sometimes, doing a special is—if they can re-run it, it's cheaper and easier. You can re-run a special four times, than one long news program—maybe you can re-run it once that night, but you can't re-run the same program over the whole weekend. Some networks, if they're doing it themselves, it's cost cutting. And other places, I think they're doing it either because they think viewers will tune in for it, or they think—this is something, we've already been covering this, maybe it would be helpful for our viewers to go more in depth on this topic that we've been covering . . . election cycle time, focusing on hot primary areas, or new up-and-coming people. At the end of the day, everyone is always chasing the ratings. I think if long-form programming continues to work, which just depends what age they're going for—so, if older people are watching the long-form programming, but they're really still going for the demo, then we'll see less long-form. And if the demo's [18–49] starting to tune in for long-form programming, like Anthony Bourdain: Parts Unknown and The '60s and things like that, then there will be more of that. It's similar to the increase in opinion. There's so much of the same on TV that everyone's trying to stake their claim into a new area. And that's a lot of what the opinion programming is all about, I think.

Others defend or justify Zucker's strategy at CNN. Bruce Perlmutter (8/7/14) said,

> What Jeff is doing at CNN can be equivocated with the opinion networks are doing. You know, he's just not doing opinion. He's finding other ways to deliver news in a different way. CNN has an entire films division that deals in acquisitions, they're doing themes around decades, and more. And that's all he's doing . . . back in the day when I was at CNN, it was the same quandary that CNN had back when you and I were working there. The question was, what can we as a network do that is just not the daily news because people weren't watching that, unless there's a huge big breaking story, but for the most part they're not. And that's when we came up with magazine shows. It's the same notion. And now . . . Jeff has got his strategy and Fox News has their strategy.

A confidential source who works in TV news also noted that CNN thrives during breaking news but there's not always breaking news. So it makes sense to have other programming that holds viewers during those lulls. This source still considers CNN's brand to be hard news as opposed to other networks.

According to a CNN employee who works on web content (4/14/15), CNN has become "very personality-driven."

> They [CNN] have started with . . . it's clearly a different strategy to create franchises around their quarters. And that includes sort of to venture further—they've just hired up a bunch of big names to throw around town. So, they hired . . . you know, guys like Chris Moody. So, relatively well-known names in the political sphere and so they've branded sort of web videos around them. I think they're taking lessons from what's worked on TV with, you know, all of these personalities that become friends of CNN—wider brand—and trying to transform that into sort of like viral web videos which I don't know if it's working. I don't really know how they're gauging whether it's working; it seems like a very new thing. But, it's an interesting form of journalism.

The employee further suggests that personality and point of view make sense in the current media environment:

I just think, like, where I hope that Fox is going is that the efficiency of getting your news on like the television or via video, I think is going to become less efficient as we come up with better ways to sort of deliver news online textually. Because I don't have time to watch an entire hour.

The CNN employee has also been told to be "voicier" in her work:

[It's] being a little more fun than not delivering the straight news, just that I was learning to develop from my previous network. So they like us to do these Q&A's, [. . .] explain the news of the day but there's no conversation on it; it's supposed to sound like you're talking to your friend or if I get to write perky news . . . If I get to like christen news about—when it comes to politics or something, they encourage me to be funny about it or—and that doesn't come naturally to me but I don't think that it's necessarily a bad thing, I think that's sort of where a lot of online news generally is going. And then even with the hard news, when I'm writing an analysis piece, they want your writing to be a little bit more interesting then, you know, I might have written it like my old outlet. And I think that it's currently because they're trying to write towards a more national audience than it's not just, you know, political press to Washington. So that makes sense to me, I think; a wider audience.

According to Brian Stelter, CNN's strategy to diversify programs is ". . . entirely logical, and I think we are. The evidence is that it's working. It is a response to the same forces that MSNBC and Fox are responding to. If people think they already know the news at night, then what can CNN do that's different? And Anthony Bourdain is an answer to that question that seems to be working. Anthony Bourdain is also a point of view."

Stelter distinguished between program content with a political point of view versus other types of viewpoints:

You might not call it point-of-view journalism, . . . but there is news and information embedded within the hour. But it is definitely a point of view, right? He's the character and it's about him and his travels. So it's actually another way to go toward opinion or point of view . . . you're seeing his point of view as he travels. It's definitely not political, but it is point of view. Mike Rowe's show will be the same way. John Walsh's show obviously has a point of view, which is, we need to find these bad guys and lock them up. They at least come from somewhere.

But other journalists, like one veteran TV reporter (7/3/14), find CNN's strategy undesirable:

> They got rid of everybody, and nobody is watching. Nobody is watching CNN . . . I try to watch it and it's unwatchable. I mean how much Anthony Bourdain can you watch, and look at Candy Crowley, one of the top. I mean, she's been sidelined . . . one of the best political reporters of all time . . . Oh, it's just absolutely criminal.

Rem Rieder (1/20/15) tended to agree:

> CNN seems kind of lost in there as a cable pioneer. What is the answer there? They seem to have gotten into this mix of let's go crazy about one big story at the moment and then have like programming and MSNBC, I think, is totally, it needs, George W. Bush. It needs another Iraq War.

But Rieder lumped CNN in more broadly with cable news, saying "Cable news is certainly a business in transition."

Maria Bartiromo (6/19/14), who previously worked for CNN, also views CNN's shift in strategy negatively:

> Well, I think audiences are not sure who to trust, and some audiences are believing what they're reading and what they're seeing. So they're taking everything that they read and they see as fact. And other audiences are feeling like—other parts of the audience are feeling like, "well, I don't agree with that." So, I just think that it's dividing us even more. CNN is a good example. CNN was the leader in news ever since it came on the scene and really started doing things in a different way than the rest of the broadcast networks. I started my career at CNN. I was a writer and a producer during the first Gulf War, and we had Bernard Shaw . . . in Iraq telling about the bombs that were going off. It was an amazing moment to actually watch real-time stories playing out in real-time, as it was happening. It was just extraordinary. And I think people like that very much because they were able to see really what was happening raw and straight from the [scene].

Bartiromo also said:

But today, you heard Jeff Zucker just recently say, "you're not going to shame us into covering Benghazi." That's what he said. That tells you that he doesn't believe the Benghazi story, and he's not going to cover it. So, I mean, ok. That's his opinion. But I don't think we should be hearing that from the head of a news network.

Bartiromo continued:

I mean, it's the same thing with MSNBC. You know, and Fox. I recognize that people see Fox as the conservative network, but they're not saying that they're not. So I'm less bothered by it. I'm bothered by it when someone tells me they're a journalist and a news person when in fact there's an agenda. That's what bothers me. And so, if you're all the way to the left and you tell me you're all the way to the left, then I know. If you're all the way to the right and you tell me that, then that's ok. But when you tell me you're something and you're not, and you creep in agendas, that's a problem. And I think—I'm a journalist, so I'm keen to it. But I think someone who's not aware of this can get sucked up in thinking there are the real stories when it may or may not be.

MSNBC's 2015 Strategy Change to Return to Hard News

While CNN was broadening its content, beginning in early 2015 under new news Chairman Andrew Lack,[3] MSNBC began to change its programming line-up and strategy to focus more on hard news and less on opinion. Former programs hosted by Ronan Farrow, Ed Schultz, Al Sharpton, Joy Reid, and others were canceled (Steinberg, 2015a, 2015b). MSNBC also severed ties with host Melissa Harris-Perry amid its strategy to move back toward hard news (Farhi, 2016). Harris-Perry had "complained about preemptions of her weekend program and implied that there was a racial aspect to the cable-news network's treatment, insiders at MSNBC said" (Farhi, 2016b). According to Farhi (2016b), this followed:

. . . a strategic transformation of MSNBC that has swept up several of its minority program hosts. Specifically, the network—which typically finishes far behind Fox News and CNN in cable-news ratings—has been trying to emphasize breaking-news coverage during daytime hours while maintaining a slate of liberal hosts

> during prime-time hours at night. Like its competitors, it has emphasized breaking campaign coverage, which lately has bumped Harris-Perry from her regular spot. The network earlier faced some outcry on social media over its irregular preemptions of Jose Diaz-Balart. . . .

According to Steinberg (2015a),

> MSNBC's ratings have dropped significantly over the past two years as it veered away from coverage of breaking news. The network's viewership losses have outpaced those of the collective cable-news juggernaut: While the total median viewership for Fox News Channel, CNN and MSNBC over a 24-hour period fell 7% in 2014, according to Pew Research Center analysis of Nielsen data, MSNBC's tumbled 14%.

Some reports also linked the new strategy to a motivation to continue to repair the network's news image after it was tarnished by Brian Williams. Lack returned to NBC amidst the Brian Williams scandal in 2015.

According to Byers (2015), "The changes are part of MSNBC's effort to shed its reputation as a liberal platform and rebrand as a nonpartisan news channel—at least in daytime." But some were skeptical that the new strategy to turn away from more progressive programs toward hard news would be successful (Chariton, 2015a, 2015b). As has been the case in the past, all of the news channels see rises in ratings during election coverage, including the 2016 cycle. In January 2017, NBC, with Lack still at the helm, hired Megyn Kelly from Fox News (Ellison, 2017).

Journalists Starting Their Own Self-Branded Sites

Many journalists have gone out and started their own blogs—or entire news websites—because they've cultivated a relationship with their readers, and they've created such a strong brand for themselves. These include Andrew Sullivan's now-folded *The Dish*, the launching of *Vox* by Ezra Klein in April 2014, and Nate Silver's *FiveThirtyEight* blog (Massing, 2015). Sullivan was formerly the editor of *The New Republic*. Klein had started Wonkblog at *The Washington Post*, and Silver previously wrote for the *New York Times*. Entire news organizations are also capitalizing on this trend. *The Washington Post* has initiated or acquired a number of blogs, an accumulation over the past few years, many of which are very clearly opinionated. Interviewees talked about the fine line between objective journalism and opinion. Not all of these new blogs and news sites toe that line. Some of them are clearly over the line, and very opinionated, and not just offering news analysis based on the facts.

I asked interviewees about this increase in the personal branding of journalists in general and the link between self-branding and content with a point-of-view. I also asked for their thoughts about more and more journalists who are going out on their own and starting their own sites. Their views were generally consistent with those found by Holton and Molyneux (2015) in their study of journalistic perceptions of self-branding.

Amber Phillips, who by December 2015 was writing for *The Washington Post*'s "The Fix," thinks that Chris Cilizza pioneered "brand journalism" with "The Fix" ("The Future of Journalism and Politics," 2015).

Michael Calderone (7/2/14) said,

> I think there's a positive, probably a positive and negative for the overarching news organization. I mean, I think it's better that a news organization allows journalists to kind of have their own voice, and be able to engage with readers, you know, on social media. I think it's sort of essential and you know, it's something that I always recommend to young journalists or students you know, to definitely have their own Twitter feeds, and to use it in a way that their, you know, alongside with doing journalism or studying journalism, not just you know, their personal stuff all day. But yeah, the downside then is that you can kind of take your following with you [if you leave the organization].

Erik Wemple (6/12/14), of the "Erik Wemple Blog," said,

> I think that is definitely—while I am circumspect about how much opinion journalism has exploded because of the other forms—I think it's safe to say that journalistic self-branding is on the rise, given that there's so many more platforms for doing that stuff. There's Twitter, there's Facebook, there's Instagram, there's all these new places where you can, sort of, sell yourself. You can get appearances galore in ways that probably were not—there weren't as many opportunities before as there are now. So this whole notion of branding yourself, or of becoming—sort of transcending your own media outlet is definitely, I think, something that is—it strikes me as having picked up—I'm not saying it was never happening before, obviously people outgrew *The Washington Post* or wherever and went on to radio and television careers to become

their own brand, but I think there's probably a little more of it now. Given, as I said, the social media opportunities and other avenues of exposure, I think that it's definitely a thing. There's lots of debate out there about is branding a good thing or is branding a bad thing. I don't know.

I asked if, aside from there being more places and ways to do this, so journalists have a greater ability or it's easier to do this for oneself, there are other reasons for it. I asked if people are just not as interested in working for traditional, mainstream news outlets anymore.

Wemple said,

> . . . I think primarily it's technology-assisted. And a fun one too. I don't know that it's—is it demand driven? Do people want their journalistic brands? It's possible, it's possible. Look, as long as newspapers have been around, there have been people who flock to their favorite columnist who have the little woodcut, the little picture of themselves on the page. That's an early form of branding. Certainly I have always had my favorite columnist that way, so I suppose you could just say that it's the full flowering of something that has its roots deep in journalism. That could well be, it's just the way people have their trusted news sources, their trusted news reporters and personalities. So, you know, it could be demand-driven. And maybe it's just the fact that the internet, aside from giving these platforms for journalists to put their stuff out, has resulted in more news consumption. And so, given that there's more news consumption, there's more opportunities for branded journalists to crop up. I don't know. I think it's a fun thing to watch.

Commenting about the individual branding of journalists and journalists who have decided to go out on their own and start their own site, or become part of a new site or news endeavor, Jon Allen (6/9/14) seemed to support the trend, saying that branding, and reaching out through social media are "absolutely helpful to consumers to know who it is who's delivering information to them. I'm totally for that kind of accessibility." Allen said:

> I think there's an accountability factor in it, which is nice for the reader; that you can actually seek out the journalist. A lot of news organizations, including my own, list the reporter's email

address at the bottom of the story. I'm on Twitter; you can reach me that way. I get phone calls from people who are irate, and very occasionally people who are happy. I think the familiarity the audience has with the person who is reporting is important. I think it's too easy for journalists to become detached from their audience—at least in the past I think it was. I think it's one of the reasons there are trust issues between the public and the news media, and I hope that some of the accessibility that's offered by modern technology—some of the branding, so that your reader is familiar with the person that's writing the story, or talking about it on television—helps build that trust back up over time.

I'm aware of a lot of journalists who are branded, so to speak. Some of them are people who have started their own ventures, Ezra Klein being one of the more recent. Even my former bosses at *Politico*—John Harrison, Jim VandeHei, Mike Allen, also *Politico*, and a number of people at the *New York Times*. There are a number of ways to create those brands. What I find is most effective, usually, is a personal brand for a reporter that is both good for them and the organization that they work for. I think a lot of the times when journalists leave their publications and try to start their own thing it's a hard road to hoe, so to speak, and what can be really powerful is an organization that has a big brand alongside a reporter who has a big brand. It's nothing new; opinion columnists were the branded journalists of long ago. So now you may find that it's Jay Mart[4] at the *New York Times*, or Peter Baker at the *Times*, or any number of people who aren't really opinion journalists, who have become really well known through their work. And the important thing is that they write. Woodward and Bernstein through their book and through their reporting on Watergate, and through the movie that was made about them; John Heilemann and Mark Halperin who wrote *Game Changer* now work at *Bloomberg*, are people who are extraordinarily well known for their political coverage—their independent, objective political coverage. We see a lot of our industry now.

I do think about it. I think it's silly not to think about it, as a modern journalist: how do you brand yourself, how do you elevate above the pack. But at the same time, if it becomes all-consuming to do that, you can lose focus on the work itself. Which is counter-productive, because if you're selling a bad brand, people figure it out. You can dress Alpo up in a nice package, but at the end of the day it's still dog food.

When I asked Liza Mundy (7/30/14) about journalistic self-branding, she said,

> Sure, yeah. David Pogue. Sure. To create their own vertical. I mean, I think this is fine, I don't think, again, it would take Jack Shafer or a more sophisticated media analyst to tell me whether I should be worried about it. But I don't feel worried about it, I feel like, actually I feel like we're in a, it's funny . . . we were talking about opinion journalism, but these verticals that we're talking about are really explanatory journalism, they're really, very, usually very statistics heavy, deep dive into a topic like technology or various other subjects, you know, electoral data. I mean, I think they're great. I think that we're, at the same time that we may be in a sort of peak period in opinion journalism, a lot of these verticals that you're describing are actually very data heavy. They may not be the kind of reporting that involves leaving your office and going out among people, but they do involve a lot of statistics and a lot of expert knowledge. They're often very wonky, very deep dives, and I think that's great. I mean I love explanatory journalism. I have no problem with these brand verticals.

When I asked about Mundy's characterization of these "verticals" as explanatory journalism, Mundy also said,

> Well Andrew Sullivan would be different. I mean his is more of a sort of a bloggy, opinionated, Andrew Sullivan's take, but I think that's great too actually. I found the argument made recently that readers are moving away from, like a blog-like, not necessarily Andrew Sullivan's, but a blog like that, that's kind of one person's opinion on any number of topics and that they're trending towards these explanatory deep dive channels or verticals on a single topic. I don't know whether that's true or not.

David Mastio (8/7/14) said of journalists starting their own self-branded sites:

> I think we're absolutely going to see more of that because, you know, newspapers and other traditional publications are shedding great talent all the time. It's not, when there's layoffs or whatever, it's not always the dead wood that goes out, that goes out the door. And I also think there's, along with the layoffs at various times, there's rounds of voluntary buyouts, and people who feel most comfortable going out on their own are going to

go out on their own. And there's all kinds of local stuff going on around . . . I think it's only gonna get bigger and more competitive and then you also have this phenomenon. I know people at all the big newspapers, and there's a frustration inside when you want to do something new and interesting, you know, there's a certain amount of resources inside the organization to do new and interesting things, and so the wait to do something new and interesting can be really long, and sometimes you can never get to the front of the line, so I think people are gonna be leaving, leaving for that. You know the web company that I started was an idea that I had previously, you know, I could never get anybody to understand what I was talking about or to pay any attention to it, so I just did it myself. And that wasn't with a personal brand or anything. I was trying to build a whole separate brand. But if you have ambitious, passionate people who want to do new things in journalism, they're gonna, they're gonna do them. And those are, it's those kind of people that the *New York Times* and *USA Today* and [*The*]*Washington Post*, those are the people that they want in their newsroom. But when they get them in their newsroom, they're not free necessarily to do what they just passionately want to do, and so you know, of course they're gonna get frustrated and some of them are gonna, go be their passionate selves somewhere else.

I asked Paul Farhi (6/4/14) about watching some of his colleagues starting their own news sites and about the focus on the individual persona of the journalist. In contrast to other journalists I interviewed, he said:

I would say two things about this from a personal perspective: one, I'm uncomfortable with it, and two, I'm not good at it. And those things go hand in hand. If I were better at it, I'd be good at it. I mean, if I were better at it, I would have a better personal brand. I've always thought—and this is such old-school thinking, because I'm old—is that if I do good work, people will discover it, and maybe they'll read it, so I don't have to self-promote. I hate self-promotion. But there is something to the self-branding thing, and self-promotion. I hate it, and again I'm not good at it because I hate it, but I guess on some level it's necessary. I wish I were better at it. I wish I could stand doing it. On the other hand, I generally tweet out something I've written. I don't know how many followers I've got—1,500? Not many. So maybe those people will discover something I've written. I don't even go on Facebook anymore, I don't care . . . but you need to go beyond that. You need to all day long keep up this dialogue with people. A) I don't have time for it, or at least I think I don't have time for it, and B) I think in some ways it's a waste of time, too. Because you spend a lot of time doing it, or some time doing it, that you could be spending in some other fashion. I'm not entirely sure that by doing it I bring myself any other attention or readers. Again, maybe I'm underestimating this, because again, I'm lousy at it, but I'm just uncomfortable with it. It feels so egotistical, and I can't get over that.

The lobby of the old Washington Post headquarters had several huge monitors hanging on a wall. One had the day's events, and one had information on the reader metrics of their stories. This ties into comments Paul made in our interview about caring about what the audience wants versus needs. I asked Farhi if, even though he doesn't enjoy promoting his brand and presence through social media, he recognizes that it's something he, and all journalists, have to do to some extent. He said:

Sure. So we're told. I don't know what to tell you other than ok. I guess you're right. A lot of our readers come from Facebook—I mean lots. Our homepage is useless—well, not useless, but it's less useful than ever. A lot of our readers come from Facebook and Twitter, and that's undeniable. So it would help if you could push your stories that way. But, I'll tell you something: the stories that I've done that have gotten the most attention, or, generally speaking, tend to get the most attention by getting links on Yahoo, on Drudge, on other big websites like that. And I can't control that. Again, I figure there's a self-fulfilling prophecy here—which is the wrong way to think about this—which is, if the story is interesting enough, people will find it, they'll like it, they'll tell their friends about it. It's the ripples on the pond. It will go out unto the world and come back, in terms of interest. Somehow, I'm not sure I control that. And my brand, what the hell is that? . . . Yes, [T]he Washington Post is still—It's not my brand. It's [T]he Washington Post's brand. And the fact that I'm associated with that brand is what helps me the most. If I were writing the absolute same things on my own website, who would ever see it? I mean, it happens, but it would be much harder.

In summary, most journalists interviewed believe that opinion and commentary in news—or talk—has increased. They attribute the increase to several factors. These are: (1) cable news; (2) competition from new sources of information, many enabled by changes in technology; (3) the low cost of producing opinionated content; and (4) social and political changes. Journalists also shared their views about CNN's strategy to broaden its programming. Some journalists thought CNN's move logical, and others see it as a confused or panicked mistake. Most journalists interviewed view the branding or self-branding of individual journalists as a necessity or advantage in the competitive news environment, even while it does not come naturally to all of them. In addition to their thoughts about the increase in talk in news, other programming strategies to retool or diversify news programming, and the branding of individual journalists, journalists have also offered their perspectives about opinion, commentary, and incivility in all types of news as well. The next two chapters will explore their sentiments.

3

Journalists' Perspectives on Incivility and Opinion in Digital News Media*

> News and analysis go together, and they're only a heartbeat away from opinion.
>
> —Erik Wemple (6/12/14)

Through the personal interviews with journalists and analysis of their published and broadcast discourse, the views of journalists with regard to opinion, commentary and civility in all types of news media are discernible. This chapter will illuminate journalistic perspectives about opinion and incivility in digital news media. This provides the longer-term, more historical viewpoints of journalists since the 1990s. This sets up the following chapter 4, which will provide the contemporary perspectives of journalists shared through interviews about opinion and incivility in news.

Research confirms that unpackaged, unproduced "talk" in news and opinionated journalism are growing (Pew Research Center's Project for Excellence in Journalism, 2013). Some of that talk has been called uncivil. In a recent nationally representative survey (Weber Shandwick and KRC Research, 2013), the government was considered the most uncivil aspect of American life (69 percent) followed by the American public (63 percent) and the media (63 percent).[1] Fifty-nine percent of respondents said online news article comments are uncivil, and 47 percent said blogs are uncivil. Fifty-nine percent of respondents cited the Internet and social media as one of the leading causes of incivility.

---

*Passages included with permission from SAGE Journals. doi: 10.1177/1940161214558748.

Veteran newsman Ted Koppel wrote an op-ed in *The Washington Post* deriding opinion news (Koppel, 2010), and former Federal Communications Commission Commissioner Michael Copps "sharply criticized U.S. television (TV) news for failing to produce 'the body of news and information that democracy needs to conduct its civic dialogue'" (Irwin, 2010a). In October 2010, Comedy Central TV program hosts Jon Stewart and Stephen Colbert held their Rally to Restore Sanity in Washington, DC, in support of restoring the civility of public discourse and giving a voice to political moderates who felt that their views were absent in a media landscape where only extremely polarized views are represented. Tom Brokaw fronted a documentary for the USA Network in December 2010 in which he denounced divisive dialogue in the media (Irwin, 2010b). But not everyone agreed. Keith Olbermann, one of the objects of criticism for his brand of opinionated news, rebutted Koppel and others, citing the history of opinion in news (Poniewozik, 2010). In January 2011, in the wake of the shooting of Congresswoman Gabrielle Giffords and 14 other people in Tucson, Arizona, the *Financial Times*, along with many other media outlets, published articles blaming their media peers for perpetuating a "viciously partisan tone" of political coverage that some argue set the stage for such violence (Edgecliffe-Johnson & Gelles, 2011).

Then, in March 2012, *The Washington Post* published an article about the potential chilling effects for talk radio, or the "Limbaugh Effect," from the backlash Rush Limbaugh received for his name-calling attack on Georgetown law student Sandra Fluke for her congressional testimony about access to contraception (Farhi, 2012). In November 2013, Martin Bashir resigned from MSNBC after making "coarse" and "graphic" remarks about Sarah Palin (Bauder, 2013; Collins, 2013). This latest reincarnation of the concern about civility in news and politics has particular characteristics and is shaped by several key events. These events also include the gridlock in federal government amid an economic recession, which led to a government shutdown in October 2013 due to an inability to pass a new budget (Associated Press, 2013); and finally, incivility in online reader comments on news sites and elsewhere. The 2011 shootings in Arizona prompted the founding of civility initiatives across the country,[2] President Obama called for civility (Cooper & Zeleny, 2011), and there were attempts to revive the Congressional Civility Caucus (Cohn, 2012).

Scholars have identified reasons for what they see as the devolution toward incivility in American public discourse. According to Dalton and Kramer (2012), a marketplace in which whatever kind of communication that achieves our strategic goals—whether those goals are to draw the largest audience or change policy in our favor—is considered "good" leads us to communicate whatever and however we want. For Gutmann and Thompson

(2012), structural features of our political system, particularly the never-ending campaign, accompanied by habits of media coverage, contribute to political gridlock. And for Rountree (2013: xix), "current problems in American political discourse have relatively recent origins stemming from cultural and technological changes in political news coverage, the reshuffling of political parties, the campaign finance revolution, and a new culture of fear . . . These sources have contributed to venomous and problematic discourse from both sides of the political spectrum."

Although some believe that a lost civility of discourse is problematic in a democratic nation, the concern about civility in public discourse, including media discourse, is not new (Herbst, 2010; Tannen, 1998; Wyatt, 2012). However, "more than 8 in 10 adult Americans view the lack of civil or respectful discourse in our political system" as a "somewhat serious" or "very serious" problem (Public Religion Research Institute, 2010, as cited in Kenski, Coe, & Rains, 2012). Often, they point the finger at opinion or partisan news as the culprit. It is difficult to disentangle uncivil media and uncivil politics and figure out which came first. They appear to go hand in hand.

Some would argue that incivility in public discourse, and the concern about it, has always been around (Herbst, 2010; Papacharissi, 2004). They trace incivility in politics and media back to the founding of the country and the first presses (Daniel, in Boylan, 2009). But uncivil speech today has more outlets, can be highly public, and travels and spreads faster; its impact can be greater, and strategies for dealing with it are still being tested.

This section analyzes what journalists think about the increase in opinionated, sometimes uncivil, political commentary in digital news media. It analyzes what a group of journalists—primarily those who participate in professional and trade venues—have written about uncivil commentary online, what their perceptions are of the effects of this shift on audiences and political culture, and how journalists think uncivil political talk affects journalists' roles and authority in society.

Definitions of Civility

"Civility, or incivility for that matter, has no one commonly shared definition" (Ben-Porath, 2007: 4). From French Jesuits in 1595 to George Washington to Tocqueville, characteristics of civility have been laid out over centuries (Herbst, 2010).

Some of the most striking ones include "a willingness to listen to others and a fair-mindedness in deciding when accommodations to their views should reasonably be made" (Rawls, 1993: 217 in Ben-Porath, 2007) and "an agreement on how to disagree and the exercise of self-control" (Peck, 1996, in Ben-Porath, 2007). The list of uncivil characteristics is long: name-calling; lack of respect (Brooks & Geer, 2007); "aspersion, hyperbole pejorative words, vulgarity and non-cooperation" (Jamieson & Falk, 1998, in Ben-Porath, 2007); "character attacks, competence attacks, insults, maledictions, teasing and ridicule" (Infante & Wigley, 1986, in Ben-Porath, 2007), and violations of tenets of Grice's (1975/1989: 29, as cited in Ben-Porath, 2007) cooperative principles, such as the "maxim of quality" that commands, "do not say that which you lack evidence for," as well as standards of politeness. Evident in these works is a spectrum of aggressiveness measures, ranging from probing to confrontational, adversarial, attacking, and uncivil.

Sobieraj and Berry (2011) differentiate between "incivility" and "outrage," writing that "outrage is incivility writ large." Whereas incivility involves "gratuitous asides that show a lack of respect and/or frustration with the opposition" (Mutz & Reeves, 2005, in Sobieraj & Berry, 2011: 20), outrage is the term they give to "more dramatic types of political incivility." Outrage discourse involves "efforts to provoke a visceral response from the audience, usually in the form of anger, fear, or moral righteousness through the use of overgeneralizations, sensationalism, misleading or patently inaccurate information, ad hominem attacks, and partial truths about opponents" (Mutz & Reeves, 2005, as cited in Sobieraj & Berry, 2011: 20). Their analysis of media content demonstrates that outrage discourse is extensive, takes many different forms, and spans media formats.

But Papacharissi (2004) asserted that it is important to differentiate between mere rudeness and incivility. Heated discussions, she argues, may be central to democratic discourse. According to Papacharissi (2004: 267), incivility "can then be operationalized as the set of behaviors that threaten democracy," and only when a behavior affects the common good, rather than isolated individuals, such as when a social group is attacked, should it be termed uncivil.

Recent work by Stryker et al. (2014) and Muddiman (2014a, 2014b) has made progress in identifying specific dimensions of speech and behavior that lead people to characterize political discussion as uncivil. These include "insulting utterances, deception, and behaviors tending to shut down or detract from inclusive ongoing deliberation" (Stryker et al., 2014). They also found that different groups of people have different levels of tolerance for political incivility. Muddiman (2014a: 1) found that younger people are more accepting of incivility than others, and partisans are more accepting of uncivil behaviors when they originate from their own party.

What these definitions of civility and incivility make clear is that there is a fine line between opinion, disagreement, and incivility. Although they are often related concepts, there is an important distinction between opinion and civility (Meltzer & Hoover, 2014). Throughout the history of American journalism, expressions of opinion have been accepted by the journalistic community when they are designated as such. Prior to the late 1940s, the American press operated as a partisan press system (Pickard, 2010). Even during the objective age of journalism, editorials, opinion columns, and the new or literary journalism and advocacy journalism movements (Pauly, 1990) all involved the journalists' opinions and perspectives in stories. What's at issue is not the mere expression of opinion, but journalists' thoughts about when the expression becomes uncivil.

Research about Civility, Politics, and Journalism

Many scholars of deliberative democracy "presume either explicitly or implicitly that civility is required for genuine, successful deliberation" (Stryker et al., 2014). Research finds that the civil delivery of opposing political views is more likely to lead audience members to consider the rationale for the opposing views legitimate (Mutz, 2007), and the civility of online discussants affected readers' perceptions of source credibility and dominance (Ng & Detenber, 2005). Uncivil political discourse adversely affects people's trust in government (Mutz & Reeves, 2005). While Papacharissi (2004) found that most messages posted on political newsgroups were civil, Coe et al. (2014) found that incivility in newspaper website comments occurs frequently and that frequent commenters are more civil than infrequent ones. Vraga et al. (2012: 5) found that journalists acting as neutral moderators of political discussion, versus as "comic" hosts or "combatant" hosts, increase perceptions of informational value, enhance host and program credibility, and reduce erosion of media trust. Feldman (2011), however, found that people can learn as much from opinionated news as from traditional, objective news. Anderson et al. (2014) found that exposure to uncivil blog comments can polarize user perceptions of the issue covered in the news article, and Santana (2014) found that anonymous comments are more likely to be uncivil than non-anonymous comments.

Journalists and audiences have been found to have different ideas of what constitutes being uncivil (Ben-Porath, 2007). Journalists' use of confrontational interviewing, a style founded on attacking the interviewee, is registered by audience members as uncivil discourse (Ben-Porath, 2007: 3). Wyatt (2012) prescribes that journalists should not cast blame without ensuring that they meet certain ethical standards (i.e., blameworthiness). To do so without meeting these conditions would be acting in an uncivil manner. Journalists should avoid rancor and seek constructive engagement for themselves and their guests (Wyatt, 2012: 190). Reader (2012) found that "journalists and audiences" have very different conceptualizations about "civility and the role of anonymity in civil discourse" in online comment forums.

Other researchers have investigated journalists' views about online comment forums in particular. Meyer and Carey (2014) found that journalists' views of their papers' community comment forums were at odds with those of participants in those forums. While participants were more likely to post if they noticed moderation by journalists, the journalists were more likely to view their audience negatively when more comments were posted. Nielsen (2014) found that "journalistic norms and conceptions of expertise prevent journalists from engaging with readers" in using online reader comments to shape their news content. Loke (2012, as cited in Stroud, 2013, also see specific report on "Journalist Involvement in Comment Sections") and Diakopoulos and Naaman (2011, as cited in Stroud, 2013) found that journalists expressed concern that uncivil online reader comments could harm their brand, reputation, and ability to get information from sources in the future. This seems particularly salient in light of data which show a further decline in credibility ratings for most news organizations (Pew Research Center for the People & the Press, 2012). McElroy (2013) bridges the divide between newer online comment forums and letters to the editor in her examination of the process by which newspaper editors selected online comments from readers for publication in the printed version of the paper. McElroy found that editors allowed for anonymity of commenters and a "wider rhetorical range" than traditional letters to the editor, but editors altered online comments that were selected for publication in the printed newspaper to meet the more traditional standards and style of letters to the editor. Older research found that editors were reluctant to reject letters that contributed to public debate even if they violated the principle of civility (Wahl-Jorgensen, 2004: 102).

Most of these findings lead to an argument for more civil discourse in news commentary. There are, however, scholars and others who justify incivility and argue its merits. Bennett (2011) explains that incivility may be necessary at times: "When the other side declares those differences to be irreconcilable, civility becomes a losing strategy. Indeed, when facing stark absolutism, civility seems to entirely miss the point" (p. 1) . . . "Incivility is a winning strategy for an underdog determined to defend fundamental principles and win the political game at any cost" (p. 3) . . . "A public that is largely turned off to politics is hard to reach with logic and reason . . . it is not news to observe that the media feed on spectacle" (p. 5). Herbst (2010) suggests that incivility may be viewed as but one rhetorical strategy among many that a speaker or author may choose to advance his cause, rather than a state of society (p. 133). Other observers have also noticed that the discussion of civility in political discourse has been robust in recent years. Roy Peter Clark (2007), Senior Scholar and Vice President at the Poynter Institute, observed that people who discuss civility do so in particular ways. Clark cataloged the five "frames of incivility" that are employed by those who talk about it: (1) The Freedom Frame: valuing freedom of expression, adherents to this frame assert that civility can be, and has been, used to oppress by censoring speech and ideas; (2) The Responsibility Frame: values responsibility over unfettered free speech; (3) The Business Frame: values profitability for news sites above all else. Legal and financial reasons limit the ability of news organizations to police comments, although some controls are needed; (4) The Journalism Frame: concerned with values in the practice of journalism and their survival in the digital age, civil discourse should be "encouraged and enforced" online; (5) The Self-Policing Frame: believes in the power of self-policing online communities to shape the valuable practices of journalism online and democratize the process. I found that Clark's categorization of civility frames is consistent with several of the themes we also detected. Although we did not perform our analysis through this particular lens, we do map our findings onto Clark's frames when appropriate. While a growing body of research focuses on the effects of incivility on audiences and their participation, and another burgeoning body of research looks at journalists' views and actions specifically in regard to audience feedback, this research aimed to provide a broader picture of what a group of journalists—namely those who have written about civility in media discourse in professional journalism venues—have expressed about the increase in opinion and incivility in news media.

Method

This study examined intramedia discussion—the discussion among and between journalists, in keeping with the interpretive communities (Zelizer, 1993) and communities of practice frameworks. A graduate assistant, Layan Jawdat, and I performed qualitative textual analysis on the materials in which journalists discussed their thoughts about civility and opinion in media discourse. This analysis employed a grounded theory approach to identify themes present in the articles and blog entries written by journalists across these sites (Lindlof & Taylor, 2011: 250–52; Glaser & Strauss, 1967, as discussed in Holton, 2008). We searched the websites of journalism organizations, journalism blogs, and online news websites to see what journalists have said about civility and incivility and how they're dealing with it. The websites searched were those of the *American Journalism Review* (*AJR*), *Columbia Journalism Review* (*CJR*), Nieman Journalism Lab, Poynter.org (The Poynter Institute's website), Google Blog searches, Google News searches, and regular Google searches for the following search terms: "civility," "civility in news," "civility in news discourse," "civility AND news," "civility AND media," "media news AND opinionated journalism," "media news AND opinion news." EBSCO was also searched to retrieve results from *AJR* and *CJR*, but those searches returned very few results. The search dates for Google News spanned a ten-year period between February 2004 and March 2014. The searches of the organizational websites set no date limits and considered all articles that were returned.[3]

The two researchers met periodically to discuss the criteria for selecting and saving returned items to the database that was created. Items had to involve a journalist expressing a view about opinion, civility, or news commentary to be saved for analysis. Approximately 230 items were analyzed. Both researchers engaged in open coding (Strauss, 1987, in Lindlof and Taylor, 2011: 250) in which they read the saved articles and took notes on themes present related to the research questions. The constant comparative method (Lindlof & Taylor, 2011: 250) was then used to further develop and refine the themes. When it was agreed that theoretical saturation (Glaser & Strauss, 1967, in Lindlof & Taylor, 2011: 252) had been reached, four key themes were identified in the articles. These key themes were then connected to examples from individual articles that illustrated them, which are presented in the analysis.

As the study examined mostly professional/trade venues where journalists and academics are the audience, and where the authors and readers are particularly interested in these sorts of issues, our findings may not be representative of the perspectives of all journalists. In addition, the analysis was of what has been published, and those journalists and media observers mentioned here may hold different views today and into the future.

Analysis

Our analysis identified four main themes in journalists' writing about civility, opinion, and commentary in digital news media.

These themes are:

1. Concern, or lack thereof, about uncivil mediated discourse through digital news media.

2. The causes of an increase in opinion and incivility.

3. Awareness of academic research about opinion and civility in news and reader comments.

4. How journalists are dealing with the increase in opinion and incivility in online political news discourse.

We will describe each of these themes in detail and provide examples.

Theme 1. Concern, or Lack Thereof, about Uncivil Mediated Discourse through Digital News Media

Of the articles analyzed in which journalists wrote about civility or incivility, the vast majority indicated a concern with civility and belief that journalists should act to improve the state of things. Several of these articles date back to as early as 1993. In one such article in *AJR*, the author described and reported on the *AJR* conference and report, "Public Perspectives on the Press" (Cleghorn, 1993; Pagano, 1993). What is striking about this conference report is that the issues being raised in 1993 were some of the same ones being raised today—participants complaining about incivility of the press. Another 1993 article, "The Right Stuff" (Kaufman, 1993), was about the *Wall Street Journal* editorial page and its lack of civility, and again in 2004, journalists were calling politics uncivil (Stranahan, 2004). There are also recent examples. In one article, Bob Steele, the Nelson Poynter Scholar for Journalism Values at the Poynter Institute and a former journalist-turned academic, was quoted as saying:

> As media professionals and journalists we certainly have a responsibility for the quality of the content we produce. It is about civics and it's about the civility of the discourse. I believe respect is a linchpin value in a healthy society. When respect diminishes or disappears, the society corrodes from within. This is also about ethics, of course. We have a responsibility to use wisely the tools we have at our disposal. (Ward, 2007)

The Association of Opinion Journalists (Formerly the National Conference of Editorial Writers) launched a Civility Project in 2011, which was then renamed Civilitas, and PBS aired the documentary, "Out of Order: Civility in Politics" in February 2013, which interviewed Bob Schieffer among other journalists, academics, and elected officials (*KPBS*, 2013). These examples illustrate the "responsibility frame" in discussions of civility that has been identified by Clark (2007).

Theme 2: The Causes of an Increase in Opinion and Incivility

Journalists whose writing expressed a concern with civility attributed a decline in civility to many different causes. Frank Partsch, the Project Director for the Association of Opinion Journalists' Civility Project, wrote, "The incivility of the era cannot be realistically discussed without considering the culture of irresponsible anonymity that the Internet not only facilitates but, in some instances, encourages" (Partsch, 2011).

Others cited online user comments as a source of incivility (Kennedy, 2012). In addition to anonymity enabled by the Internet, Partsch also identified campaign rhetoric and the audience's lack of ability as causes of incivility (Partsch, 2011):

> NCEW recognizes that more than one factor have conditioned society for the occurrence of incivility in public discourse. One is the simplistic rhetoric of modern campaigning, in which ideological assertion is substituted for appeals based on fact and logic. The adversary is presented as not merely philosophically opposite but morally flawed, its representatives regarded with contempt and its ideas distorted so as to present them in the worst possible light. This situation is abetted by a lamentable lack of analytical ability on the part of some audiences. Politicians sling mud, as has been said, because mud-slinging works . . . The audience must develop the skills to avoid being bamboozled.

Thomas Kunkel, former dean of the Philip Merrill College of Journalism at the University of Maryland and former president of *AJR*, also blamed "media partisans of every stripe" for having been "enablers in the current plague of public gridlock and incivility" (Kunkel, 2004). Others also attributed incivility to journalists and the media:

> The anger and the hatred and the sniping, that is, the loss of civility in public discourse all began with James Kilpatrick and Shana Alexander on "60 Minutes." Jim and Shana no doubt were just trying to introduce a bit of a spark to involve people in the important subjects of the day. Who knew it would descend to "Spark this, you treasonous loser." (Bluhm, 2004)

Another *AJR* article connected civility and incivility to patriotic coverage after 9/11 in that although there was shift toward civility right after 9/11, the sensitivity wasn't lasting, and humor and political criticism soon went back to their usual levels (Tugend, 2002). In a *CJR* interview by James Marcus (2009) with *New Yorker* film critic David Denby, who wrote a book in 2009 about "snark" (a close cousin of incivility), Denby attributes snark to journalists' insecurity about their own future:

> **Marcus**: You write that one of the optimum cultural conditions for snark occurs when "a dying class of the powerful, or would-be powerful, struggles to keep the barbarians from entering the hallowed halls." Are traditional journalists such an embattled class?
>
> **Denby**: I think so. I just feel this tremendous collective anxiety among established journalists that somehow they'll be left out. There will be a game of musical chairs and they're not going to get a chair. So one way of seeming to embrace new media, one way of staying in the game, is to get snippy and sarcastic and snarky. They're certainly not encouraged to be more analytic, more intelligent.

Theme 1. Concern, or Lack Thereof, about Uncivil Mediated Discourse through Digital News Media

Returning to Theme 1, although the majority of the items analyzed for this theme indicated a concern with, and interest in, improving civility, there were some articles (ten) that instead questioned the outcry for and focus on civility. In the *CJR* article "Giffords Analysis Machine in Overdrive," the author questioned the connection between the Arizona shootings and political rhetoric that others were so quick to make (Meares, 2011). In a Time.com article, another author wrote that civility has been "fetishized" (Liu, 2012):[4]

> Focusing on civility makes us pay disproportionate attention to the part of politics that's rational. Which is tiny . . . It's right to want to convert that combative instinct into nonviolent expressions like legislative action. But it's wrong to imagine that the instinct itself can be legislated out of existence. The Constitution our framers gave us did not ask that we be mild or moderate; it anticipated and channeled our immoderation . . . The danger with pushing for more civility is that it can make politics seem denatured, cut off from why we even have politics . . . a virtue isn't to have more polite arguments but to have less superficial ones.

Some of these concerns expressed over the rallying around the cause of civility are similar to those put forth by Bennett (2011) and Herbst (2010), and others reflect Clark's (2007) "freedom frame." In contrast to a previous *AJR* article discussed here about returning to lower levels of civility after 9/11, in a 2004 *CJR* article on George Bush titled "A Summer of Lies," the author wrote that journalists won't question the government because of a "misplaced notion of civility" stemming from patriotism after 9/11. More broadly, some journalists wrote that the movement toward opinionated commentary in the place of news is a logical and perhaps necessary reaction to threats and impingements on more traditional social responsibility journalism from newer technologies and news venues.

While they were not explicitly defending uncivil journalism, several journalists pointed to what they saw as a natural evolution toward opinion news as a strategy for maintaining audiences and the careers of individual journalists. As NPR's Ira Glass said, "Opinion in all its forms is kicking the ass of journalism" (Glass, 2010). Glass explained that "commentary is trouncing fact-based reporting" because of its "casual, approachable style." "One way the opinion guys kick our ass and appeal to an audience is that they talk like normal people, not like news robots speaking their stentorian news-speak" (Glass, in Myers, 2011). This assertion is supported by findings from a 2010 Pew study, "Fewer Journalists Stand Out in Fragmented News Universe" (Pew Research Center for the People & the Press, 2010).

The Concern about Civility in Media Discourse is not Limited to Online

Most cases described thus far demonstrate that journalists have expressed concern about regular people (non-journalists) posting uncivil comments to news articles online. But other cases show concern about public figures and other professional journalists/pundits saying uncivil things on TV, radio, newspapers, and through social media. All the way back in 1994, Reese Cleghorn, former *AJR* president and former Dean of the Philip Merrill College of Journalism at the University of Maryland, wrote about Paul Duke leaving PBS "Washington Week in Review," about his civility, and the lack of civility by others on TV (Cleghorn, 1994). He was lamenting the state of civility in media twenty years ago:

> Amid the strident opinionatedness that often now characterizes journalists' analysis of public issues, he [Duke] had been a moderator in the best sense of the word: not moderate as in milquetoast, because he sometimes was visibly restraining some

private passion . . . but reasoned and mannered. Moderation and restraint are not now hallmarks of journalists' analysis on television. Opinions tend to be torrid rather than tempered.

There are also recent cases of journalists expressing concern about civility in television in particular. A 2012 Poynter article (Moos, 2012) summarizes two segments on "Rock Center," where Ted Koppel spoke with Bill O'Reilly, Ann Coulter, and David Carr about the business of broadcasting hate. In the segments, as reported by Moos (2012), Koppel said, "[t]he bar for civility on cable television and talk radio has fallen so low . . . that by comparison [Bill] O'Reilly seems almost reasonable." O'Reilly agreed:

> You can make money by assassinating people that differ from you. There's a success that wants everybody to come into the tent and watch. That's me. And then there's the success where you make money speaking to the choir, the haters. So if you're a liberal, they hate George W. Bush. They hate him, so you smash him every single day. Same thing on the other side. They hate President Obama . . . You look for ways to smash him. You don't really care what the truth is, you just want to smash him. You can make a lot of money doing that, especially if you do it loud enough and vicious enough. And that's what happened once cable news went up. You had some of those people come in. Some of them have washed up, but some of them haven't. And it's nasty.

This excerpt of the conversation reveals that some television journalists themselves—even those who are involved in the so-called uncivil discourse—find it problematic, while acknowledging that in the commercial marketplace, it can be a successful strategy in terms of ratings and revenue.

Commenting on this exchange, and the difference between broadcast television news and its cable counterpart, which has been much more criticized, Greta Van Susteren pointed out the difference between performance style and opinionated content. She wrote,

> Broadcast news people may have deluded themselves into thinking that they are pure because they often show no passion in their voices or volume in the talk. A modulated voice and soft volume does not mean no bias. It only means modulated voice and soft volume. They THINK their bias is not shown (or even that they have none) and therein lies their self delusion. (*Gretawire*, 2012)

There are also examples from radio, such as the canceling of Tavis Smiley's show by four stations who felt that his advocacy journalism was too political for public radio (Powell, 2012). He was even compared to Bill O'Reilly (Powell, 2012). Examples from online and print news include the suspension of Joe Williams, White House correspondent at *Politico*, for remarks he made on Martin Bashir's MSNBC show about Mitt Romney and comments he posted on Twitter about Ann Romney (Beaujon, 2012). The coverage of Williams's Twitter comments (Wemple 2012) shows that journalists are also concerned about their fellow journalists' posts through social media. Williams's comments through social media were made on his "protected" Twitter account, "which means that only 'confirmed followers' have a view of what he's tweeting" (Wemple, 2012), but according to a memo by *Politico*'s top editors, they compromised Williams' journalistic responsibility and failed to meet *Politico*'s "standards for fairness and judgment."

Theme 3: Awareness of Academic Research about Opinion and Civility in News and Reader Comments

Several articles provide evidence that some news organizations have actually made changes and decisions based on academic research, specifically about anonymous posts and moderating comments. Based on research from the Engaging News Project (Stroud, 2013) about the use of a "respect" button on news websites versus a "like" button, the *Tampa Bay Times* and *Huffington Post* now feature other buttons on their sites (such as important, inspiring, sad, amazing). The project found that having a journalist moderate reader discussion leads to more civil comments, and the "Respect" button leads to more consideration than "Like" or "Recommend" buttons. Another such case was when the publication *Popular Science* decided to get rid of comments on its site completely, citing, among other things, the study in the *Journal of Computer-Mediated Communication*, "The 'Nasty Effect:' Online Incivility and Risk Perceptions of Emerging Technologies" (Anderson et al., 2014), which suggested that uncivil comments skewed people's understanding of an article (H.G., 2014). These are not the first cases where journalists made decisions based on academic work. In the 1990s, journalists took up the public journalism charge outlined by academics, and Tenenboim-Weinblatt (2009) found that the journalistic community's eventual acceptance of Jon Stewart as a quasi-journalist or new kind of journalist was aided by political communication scholarship that legitimated him as an educating source of political and news information.

It is important to note that the journalists who have written about opinion and civility for the professional journalism organizations (*CJR*, *AJR*,

Nieman, and Poynter), where discussion of academic research about journalism is part of the standard fare, likely pay closer attention to academic research than other journalists who do not participate on these sites. These journalists are also more likely to make use of services such as Journalist's Resource (JR) featured on Nieman Lab's site, which provides ongoing updates about the top academic articles published on social media research and other topics of interest to journalists (Wihbey, 2013, 2014). JR is a project of the Shorenstein Center on Media, Politics, and Public Policy at the Harvard Kennedy School. A Brookings Institution report suggests that "[m]edia organizations should consider partnerships with universities and nonprofit organizations and leverage their expertise" (West & Stone, 2014). In addition, two *CJR* articles focused on the relationship between journalists and academics. The first, "Embrace the Wonk" (Marx, 2010), mentioned The Monkey Cage, the blog by several political science professors that is now part of *The Washington Post*. A more recent article, "Political Science and Journalism: BFFs?" (Nyhan, 2014) mentioned several academics who have been hired as columnists or contributors to news sites.[5] The latter article also discussed how journalists are increasingly more open to and interested in academic research and that academics are getting better at connecting their work and making it known to the real world. This finding is in contrast to Zelizer's (1998: 118) assertion that "journalists remain closed to and largely unaffected by external opinions, particularly academic ones."

I also found evidence from the interviews I personally conducted with journalists about how journalists are influenced by academic research. For example, in my interview with Rick Massimo (6/10/14), he said he had gone to a talk at the Nieman Foundation at Harvard and "the guy who founded MinnPost was there" and talked about financial aspects for newspapers and why newspapers were failing. Andy Carvin ("The Future of Journalism and Politics," 2015) mentioned the work of Nick Diakopulous at the University of Maryland, a former Columbia Tow fellow, who identifies algorithmic bias in news and social media software. Other journalists I spoke with, such as Richard Benedetto, Michael Calderone, and Bruce Perlmutter, also have adjunct professor roles at universities.

Theme 4: How Journalists Are Dealing with the Increase in Opinion and Incivility in Online Political News Discourse

Articles turned up in this study's searches discussed many of the ways in which journalists are dealing with incivility online. These include requiring identification of commenters or requiring that commenters link to their own Facebook, LinkedIn, Google+, or other profiles to verify identification. For example, *USA Today*/Gannett switched to Facebook for reader comments to require identity of posters (Ebner, 2011), and *The Portland Press Herald* uses Facebook Connect, Twitter, and WordPress logins (Ellis, 2010). Some news sites, such as the *New York Times*, use a two-tiered approach of verified and unverified comments (verified may be those with a history of high quality contributions, motivating those labeled "verified" to remain high quality so that their comments are posted directly and without moderation); crowdsourcing the review of comments and using ratings systems for comments, which some research has shown to be effective (Lampe et al., 2014) and placing reader comments directly next to the content on which they are commenting, thus encouraging commenters to read before sharing an opinion (H.G., 2014). Other sites, such as the *LA Times*, use automated filters (Edgar, 2011).

Other approaches include providing etiquette guidelines for comments, such as the political discussion website Politix, which has its own "Engagement Etiquette," forbidding "the use of profanity, personal attacks or off-topic commentary" and spam (Bond, 2012). Yet another approach is having journalists and non-journalists police comments. AOL and Yahoo! have hired journalists to create original content and to police the comment sections on their articles to maintain civility (Shiver, 2010). Gawker Media has created a separate commenting platform, Kinja, that users control. Kinja "gives readers the ability to initiate discussions surrounding a particular Gawker article through their Kinja account and then manage them with tools like reply, dismiss, share, follow, or even 'heart'" (H.G., 2014).

However, news sites still face challenges in choosing and executing these strategies. As a 2008 *AJR* article describes, there are different thresholds for crude language at different news organizations (Macy, 2008). Furthermore, newspapers have grappled with where to draw the line vis-à-vis coarse language "in the digital world, where almost anything goes" (Macy, 2008). Questions also remain about not allowing anonymity. While some argue that anonymity creates an environment for bad behavior, others say "anonymity has value because it encourages honesty and empowers creativity" (Ingram, 2014). In addition, "[a]lthough news organizations can employ moderators to remove uncivil comments from these online forums, the practice can be both time-consuming and expensive," so the Engaging News Project (Stroud, 2013) promotes preemptively moderating comments and posing questions to readers to increase civility on the front end.[6]

While these examples illustrate the many different ways news sites have dealt with reader comments, there has been some blowback in the recent cases, with news sites deleting and controlling comments in ways that turn readers off. For example, one Nieman Lab article (Phelps, 2011) told the story of WHYY Philadelphia, whose commenting system was so good at keeping out trolls and flamers that hardly anyone commented. They overcorrected for the problem (Phelps, 2011). As a result, WHYY's "The Speak Easy blog will bring a new comments system with no registration wall, and blog host Eric Walter will serve as sergeant-at-arms until the community (hopefully) becomes too big to manage." When that happens, they will recruit volunteers from community users.

Another example of negative results from dealing with user comments in heavy handed ways is an incident at the *St. Louis Post-Dispatch*, where an editor observed that extremely vulgar comments originated from a local school's IP address and informed the school, which eventually resulted in the resignation of the employee who made the posts (Peters, 2010). When the editor posted the account on the paper's website, he received hundreds of comments from upset readers who felt he had overstepped his role.

Still other examples, such as the "NewsTrust Baltimore" experiment, which let readers critique its stories in civil ways, raised the question of whether civility is sustainable (Wallace, 2011).

> Unable to get continued foundation support, and not close to being commercially viable, the project finished without hinting at a workable business model. And the relatively small number of articles that sparked robust discussion suggests that there are limits to how deep news consumers want to get in the news-critiquing business. (Wallace, 2011)

The project localized the online social networking/media watchdogging tools developed by the national nonprofit NewsTrust. Other news organizations, such as *The New Haven Independent*, a nonprofit site launched in 2005, have decided to suspend all user comments (see Kennedy, 2012).

In discussing how journalists are dealing with incivility and opinion, it should be noted that many, although not all, of these examples come from what may be considered "elite" media, which tend to have more resources available for handling large volumes of feedback than other news outlets. Smaller media outlets may receive more manageable volumes of online comments that can be handled more like traditional letters to the editor with regard to prescreening and rejection.

Research continues to explore how journalists' management of online comments affects their organizations. Recent studies have found that online incivility in reader comments can negatively affect users' perceptions of the news product and organization (Prochazka, Weber, & Schweiger, 2016; Anderson, Yeo, Brossard, Scheufele & Xenos, 2016), and news organizations' commenting policies have an effect on the quality of user comments (Ksiazek, 2015; 2016).

Discussion

In revealing four main themes and several subthemes in journalists' writing about civility and opinion in digital news media, this research found that most, but not all, of the journalistic writing examined here about civility and incivility expressed concern for the state of things as uncivil. Most, but not all, articles indicated it needs to be improved. And most journalists' writing indicated that they or their organizations are responsible for keeping things civil on their own sites. The journalists' writing indicated that they think incivility affects society, the public, political culture, and their own organizations. Analysis of journalists' articles also revealed interest in academic research about civility, and some of the many ways journalists are dealing with incivility online are based on academic research. Those who did not express a concern for civility wrote that it has been "fetishized," cite the first amendment, and equate calls for civility with attempts to censor certain viewpoints.

The indication that journalists and their organizations may be motivated to, at least outwardly, advocate for, and take actions to improve, civility out of a fear of losing favor and credibility with audiences, and consequently audience share and revenue, led me to consider whether it might be appropriate to invoke theoretical concepts about journalism such as paradigm repair, critical incidents, or boundary maintenance (Meltzer, 2011). Unlike in paradigm repair (Bennett et al., 1985; Berkowitz, 2000; Hindman, 2005; Reese, 1990), there hasn't been a specific breach of good and normal practice per se surrounding civility that needs to be restored. And unlike a critical incident (Zelizer, 1992, in Tumber, 1999: 340–54), there also has not been a singular event or evolution pertaining to civility that has led to the reexamination of journalistic practices. Boundary maintenance (Gieryn, 1983; Lewis, 2012) may be the best analytical framework available for understanding journalistic discourse and action related to civility, but it, too, is an imperfect explanation.

Because the threat to journalism from incivility is happening on all fronts, from both users and journalists, across all types of media, and it is attributed to many causes outside of journalism, none of the above frameworks seem to adequately capture the journalistic quandary and response. Rather journalists are engaging in not just image restoration (Benoit, 1995), but in image defense, protection, and maintenance. It is possible that journalists have simply been following the lead of academics, politicians, and policy workers in their calls for efforts to improve the state of civility, but it is difficult to prove with certainty the root source of this latest round of concern and calls for action about civility in public discourse. In addition, as we and others have demonstrated, the roles inhabited by academics, politicians, advocates, and journalists are increasingly blurred. In addition, it is difficult to know whether all of the above-named groups are merely paying lip service to the cause of civility or whether their rhetoric and efforts are sincere. Tandoc, Hellmueller, and Vos (2013) found a gap between journalistic role conceptions and enactments. Two examples of apparent hypocrisy about civility by journalists and their organizations have raised doubt about the sincerity of these individuals' and groups' concerns. One is the 2012 case of Froma Harrop,[7] the former President of the National Conference of Editorial Writers (now AOP), the same journalism organization that launched a Civility Project in 2011. Harrop was called out in a *Daily Show* interview parody for having used uncivil language in describing members of the Tea Party in one of her syndicated columns (*The Daily Show*, 2012).

In another case, *CJR*, one of the sites of journalistic discourse about civility that was examined for this study, received letters from readers criticizing the magazine for printing the "F" word on its September/October 2013 "Journalism Is" cover (Romenesko, 2013). But whether sincere or feigned, journalistic discourse reflecting a concern for civility meshes with Bishop's (2001) and Zelizer's (1997: 17) contention that journalistic self-reflection is also designed to deflect potential external criticism and distrust. The concern expressed in the journalistic writing analyzed in this chapter about lack of civility in audience feedback, however, is having real effects on journalism practice, as described.

4

Journalists' Perspectives on Opinion, Commentary, and Incivility in All Types of News

While the research discussed in the previous chapter found that most, but not all, published journalistic discourse analyzed from the 1990s on expressed concern about opinion and incivility in mediated political discourse, Diana Mutz's 2015 book, *In-Your-Face Politics*, provides evidence for the negative *and* positive effects of televised incivility in particular. " 'In-your-face' politics refers to both the level of incivility and the up-close and personal way that we experience political conflict on television."

> Incivility is particularly detrimental to facilitating respect for oppositional political viewpoints and to citizens' levels of trust in politicians and the political process. On the positive side, incivility and close-up camera perspectives contribute to making politics more physiologically arousing and entertaining to viewers. This encourages more attention to political programs, stimulates recall of the content, and encourages people to relay content to others. (Mutz, 2015)

Research by Muddiman and Pond-Cobb (2015) contradicts some of Mutz's conclusions, finding that civility in online news increased engagement, and news articles that included incivility discouraged people from engaging, but the difference between text-based incivility and audio-visual incivility could be a factor in the discrepancy of findings. Similar to Mutz, Taylor's (2017) research found educative effects of "extreme television," but also negative effects. According to Taylor (2017), "extreme media produce higher levels of political knowledge and that they also produce higher levels of negative affect among viewers compared with control groups." The study also finds that "extreme media are at least as informative as traditional news."

In addition to research that examines the effects of opinion and incivility on audiences or users, other work focuses on the implications for journalism. Ben-Porath (2007) suggests a different term and conceptualization of the increase in opinion and commentary in news:

> Unlike the edited news package, which dominates network and local news in America, the cable news channels recount the day's news predominantly through conversation, a format dubbed here dialogical news. At the center of this article is the concept of internal fragmentation, a consequence of the turn to conversation-based reporting, and its central implications: (1) the authority of the news reporter diminishes; (2) question-asking replaces fact-checking; (3) news organizations relinquish their accountability for news content; and (4) the news audience assumes the role of witness or participant rather than receiver. . . . In the short-run, journalists are losing their battle to control their sources and maintain their gatekeeping function. In the long run, journalism might lose its significance as society's reflexive storyteller, reverting instead to its former role as a partisan instrument, a source of entertainment or a bit of both.

Cushion (2015) views the increase in mediated and interpretive journalism as potentially positive:

> the rise of live two-ways can potentially enhance viewers' understanding of public affairs—moving reporters beyond their visual backdrops and reliance on political soundbites—by asking journalists to scrutinize the actions of political elites, interpret competing source claims and to explain the broader context to everyday stories.

Now that I have established what journalists who wrote about opinion and civility in professional and trade journalism venues said, this chapter will explore the contemporary perspectives of journalists from the personal interviews about the reasons for the increase in opinion and incivility in political media discourse, their evaluation of these forms of discourse, their concern for the audience, and what they see as the most problematic aspects. This includes a section focusing on what journalists who are engaged in opinion and commentary themselves, have said.

Reasons for the Increase in Incivility, Uncivil Tone of Political Discourse in Media

Does It Reflect What's Happened in Government and Politics? Or Is It the Other Way Around? Do Media Contribute to the Tone of Discourse?

Jim Henderson (12/10/14), former Money editor at *USA Today*, thinks there are lower levels of civility in culture and society, and that impacts media civility, not the other way around:

> [C]ivility in general in this society, or at least language civility, the bar has fallen a lot. There's so many movies you go to, you listen to them and you just sort of think, "gee, if they cut all the swear words out of there, that would have taken 20 minutes off that movie."

Dave Mastio (8/7/14) also believes media reflect politics and not the other way around:

> So much of the commentary that is made up particularly on television of former government officials, people who want to be in government in the future, or you know, committed partisans . . . who see themselves as on a team, and so with that critical mass they have brought what was the behavior of politicians into the behavior of, you know, because that staying on message having the specific points you want to make, you know. Even fifty years ago you didn't go into a press conference without talking points and knowing what you wanted to say, what questions you wanted to get asked. So I mean, I think it's politics that's corrupted our debate, not the other way around.

Brian Stelter of CNN's "Reliable Sources" tends to agree:

> Yeah, I don't think I have a good, smart answer to it. I think it's probably a vicious cycle and I don't know where we would assign the beginning of the cycle. I don't know where we'd assign

blame to initially. I would like to think that the press responds to the country, and not the other way around, in this particular case. And certainly I think Fox gets the bad rap and in general, I think point-of-view media probably gets a bad rap because the most divisive, most outrageous comments are highlighted. And you know, made out to be more than what they are. I mean, the thing about cable news is, something is said and then ten seconds later, it's over, unless it's picked up by the blogs and repeated and replayed and regurgitated. So, I try to be sensitive about that on my show. I mean, I did it yesterday, talking about Dr. Keith Ablow on Fox saying Michelle Obama needs to drop a few pounds. You know, I did play that clip. But where we took it was, what responsibilities do doctors on TV have? As opposed to, 'God, Keith Ablow is a jerk.' Which is a useless conversation. You know, so, I think there's sort of something to be said for not overreacting to some of the vitriol and foolishness that happens on live television sometimes. However, I know, it can add up to something that's disturbing to people. I realize that.

Amber Phillips (7/23/14) also agreed:

[A]re voters and viewers more partisan than ever before? And politicians and media are a reflection of that. That's my theory. What gave rise to these commentary cable news shows, that's, perhaps, a very good reason. Producers saw—executive producers saw a niche there . . . I think it was the Pew Research[1] . . . that recently said they've noticed that voters tend to live in communities that jive with their political views.

In contrast to these other journalists, Michael Calderone (7/2/14) said the media have had a role in the increase in incivility:

I think that the case can be made that the media certainly has played a role in the, in the coarsening of civil discourse. Because, I mean just going back to what we were saying about commentary and opinion. You know a lot of opinion and commentary is cheap, and often the more harsh opinion, or the stronger, you know the harsher opinioned stuff may jump to the front of Twitter and get a lot of attention online. Because, you know, the stronger a statement a politician makes, on Fox News, that becomes a clip, which then becomes, gets passed around and gets them a lot of attention. You know, and it may be negative attention among people who don't subscribe to the same politics.

But it may be very positive attention for core Republican viewers and potential voters. So I mean, I think you will see politicians you know, often, just as we were talking about how there's a conservative bubble, you know, I think politicians will go on conservative outlets and make claims and make statements that you know, are very harsh, but that readership and that viewership, you know, will love it. And that viewership and that readership potentially are voters, as well. So, you know, I think the bifurcation media can play a part in politicians just catering to one, to their potential audience. And not looking to make inroads with the other side. . . .

Is Opinion a Successful Business Strategy?

Several journalists, particularly TV journalists, suggested that opinion is a successful business strategy and that's at least partly why it has increased:

> Some people like it [uncivil shouting] because they're still putting it on TV. I mean, I don't know, it's hard to separate myself from a viewer versus a producer. I don't find it enjoyable to watch people scream at each other. It's unpleasant. But then again, I wouldn't necessarily rather have two people with a black screen behind them sit there with hushed radio voices talking about the same thing. That's totally boring. And so, yeah, that's a valid argument that it is more interesting to watch. And listen, everybody likes a good fight; the time where someone argues and they take off their mic and they storm off, that makes for viral videos. So, are we supposed to stop that people encourage boxing matches? No, because you're hoping to get a viral moment. . . . (Former news producer, 6/16/14)

From the point of view of journalists at *USA Today* who had to adapt to a strategy to produce "first takes," more opinionated shorter content for the paper, Jim Henderson (12/10/14) said that the "first take" strategy

> was uncomfortable at first, but you do . . . quickly realize that these reporters who are not fresh, new reporters to the beat at

all—covering their beat for years and years, if not decades—they really do know their stuff, and you suddenly were quite impressed with their first take opinions. It did add—at least in business journalism—add some value for the reader. What would creep me out more is when you would see them in print. So sometimes you would take that first take opinion piece and put it in print right next to the reporter who's done the same story on the straight news story. And, now the opinion piece, you make sure it's labeled properly, maybe even have the reporter's picture there so it's kind of clear, but that took some getting used to. But, you know, I think these days, readers are so accustomed to different things coming at them, they can tell the difference between the two.

Asked if there was an initial period of adjustment for the journalists writing the first takes, Henderson (12/10/14) said:

Yeah, they got used to it. But the hard part of getting used to it wasn't so much—at first it was, "oh my God, what are we doing? This opinion stuff." But quickly it also became, "holy cow, this announcement came out, I have to do three stories in an hour and a half." But that's important because, as you know, a story can break quickly, and somebody puts up two or three sentences, or a two-paragraph, and that story will get five times as much traffic as the good, in-depth story that goes up three hours later because it's old news by then.

Henderson said that rather than spending much time lamenting the fact that they were being asked to do opinion, they realized that traffic was increasing, which helps the bottom line:

We were business reporters, so you kind of do know that things are—the reality of things. And you need to do it. *USA Today*, there was also more advertising inventory than we had stories to put it on. So, the more stories we created, the ads were just sitting there on the shelf waiting to be put on them. I mean, they're not high revenue ads, but it's money sitting there on the floor waiting for you to pick it up, if you have a story to pick it up with. So, that also was impetus to create more headlines.

Frank Sesno (10/9/14) said that this more diverse news environment "provides an opportunity for news organizations to further define themselves."

Just as Mercedes Benz says, "yes, you're going to pay extra for us, and we're not going to sell as many cars as Toyota, but they're doing just fine as a company because they've got a particular brand and they've got a particular level of quality." Just like the *New York Times*, the *Wall Street Journal*, and Fox for that matter. But I think a good example used to be that CNN would not report on bomb scares on the northwest gate of the White House, that went out the window in the early 2000s after Fox—or maybe even the late '90s because I was there when this happened—when we had did not have our cameras on a little robot trying to check out a suspicious package and we looked up at the monitors, and MSNBC and Fox did. And the decision was made that we could not sit this one out anymore or we would look irrelevant. So the standards changed, and the pressures are intense on all news organizations to have a very dynamic conversation internally about how they're going to respond to this world. Where everyone has a competing stream of information.

Amber Phillips (7/23/14) believes providing analysis, or a point of view, beyond just giving the facts, is not only successful, it's necessary for journalists today:

I run into a lot of these people that I'm talking about. And one thing that worries me from my other regional reporting colleagues is—you know, I ask them what news they're covering for the day—and this is just unscientific observation, it's just my friends—and they'll be covering the Bowe Bergdahl army hearing because they'll have one senator from their home state in the hearing and they're just going to write up a straight news story: "this hearing happened, our senator said this." I talked to my competitor, another Las Vegas correspondent here, who does that. He's very much the paper record. But at the same time, his stuff isn't that different from what the wires are writing. And, you know, it's not really justifying their salaries. I get—I don't want to say concerned—but I don't think they're going down the right path of journalism. And it's so easy, I almost wish that I had that job; it's so easy to write a 20-inch story about nothing—it really is. It's a lot harder to do the analysis—it's a lot more fun, but it takes more work.

According to Brian Stelter (8/18/14),

Not only is it [opinion] a successful business strategy, I would also say it does fill a market void. I mean, it, I don't subscribe to the theory that all other networks lean to the left. I think that NBC, ABC, CBS, CNN try really hard to be fair. But Fox provides a conservative point of view of the world and that does fill a void. That's why I think it's so important that MSNBC does what it does, and provides a truly progressive point of view to the world . . . I don't, I try to say on the air all the time, I love Fox. I try to, because, I really do. They help me understand, you know, conservative politics. I mean, they really serve, they really do good work. You just gotta know what you're seeing, what you're watching. And I, and God I hope [other] people, turn the channel and try other sources too.

Differences in Success with Opinion between Conservative and Liberal Outlets

Erik Wemple (6/12/14) commented on a Brookings survey (PRRI/Brookings, 2014) in which MSNBC barely registered for people's trust in media. When asked what he thought were the reasons for the PRRI/Brookings survey outcome, Wemple said:

That's a really good question. Here we go. I think that one of the reasons is that . . . during the course of the day, MSNBC just does all these panels where these people just spout off about stuff. And they'll throw some news in if big news breaks, but it's basically a ton of talk. Now, Fox News is a lot of talk, too, but I do believe that they get onto news stories a little more. I think that—I'm talking primarily about the big time—they're all blab pretty much at night. So I think that, in terms that, that was a story about—you know, what your most trusted outlet is—and MSNBC was way down, even among liberals. It wasn't a go-to place even among liberals . . . But, that is really bad news for MSNBC because you've got to corral the audience at least that you're pitching to. There was another study today that I just wrote about, which was the Pew Center has found that almost 80 percent of conservatives have an opinion about Fox, of course, mostly favorable—predominantly favorable, like 74–75 percent. Whereas only about half of liberals have *any* opinion or are aware of MSNBC. So, either the problem is that liberals don't care about TV and don't care about cable news, or MSNBC isn't really doing much for them. Who knows which it is; I really don't.

When I asked Wemple if that forecasts anything for the future of cable news, or at least liberal cable news outlets, and MSNBC, he said:

> Yeah, it means there's trouble. I think it means, maybe there's a big TV cultural difference between liberals and conservatives. Maybe conservatives like TV more than liberals, but I'm not exactly sure. In some ways, it might be the opposite of what we think. Maybe what Fox News has done, is that Fox News is just a stroke of genius. I mean, they found that there was so much disillusionment with the mainstream media—*so* much disillusionment with mainstream media among conservatives that ties all conservatives together, and has since Spiro Agnew made that speech about the mainstream media back in the late '60s. And so Ailes and Murdoch harnessed all that conservative disaffection with the mainstream media and created a phenomenally successful cable network, with 900 million in annual profits and almost 2 billion in revenues, and amazing, amazing ratings. And so perhaps what Fox has done is created these outside expectations for what cable news can do, and perhaps MSNBC and CNN are more like the natural water level of what a cable news outlet should be. I mean, they're both profitable, but they just don't do it with [an] audience the way Fox News does. Maybe they should be happy registering where they are.

Differences in Opinion and Commentary According to Medium

Journalists had different views about which medium was seeing the largest increases in opinion. Stelter focused on opinion in TV, whereas Henderson pointed to online news.

> The point of view journalism, point of view television, you know, I think there's a rise in point of view journalism, which I guess I would describe as reporters who come from a certain place who have a certain set of beliefs, who may even advocate for those beliefs, but you know, but engage in reporting, conduct interviews, write articles, etc. I guess I think of point-of-view television as being more about Rachel Maddow's op-eds, her essays, or about

> Sean Hannity's guests, you know? I guess, what I mean is the building blocks of television point of view are different than the building blocks of an op-ed column I guess. (Brian Stelter, 8/18/14)

Jim Henderson (12/10/14), formerly the Money editor at USA Today for three decades, agreed that "there's definitely been an increase" in opinion and commentary in news, but that it's occurred "more online, of course, than in print." By online, Henderson was referring to the change in nature of the content created by journalists that he witnessed firsthand:

> For example, at *USA Today*, for online, one of the things to help draw traffic is this volume of stories. Lots of entry points, lots of headlines. And so, if you have a breaking news story, you'll not try to do one story, you'll try to have maybe three different angles on it. And maybe smaller stories. And what we were encouraging reporters to do—expert reporters—would be something called a first take. And that's what you'd see on the headline: first take. And it would be the reporter's sort of opinion of what this event might mean; what it could portend . . . But there is that first take that gets that opinion out there quickly. Then you have four headlines there. People just, you know, click on it to get the different points. So that's almost like a formal way that it's happening.

Henderson (12/10/14) said that the editor of *USA Today*, Dave Calloway, devised the first-take strategy when he was fairly new at the paper, and brought the strategy with him from MarketWatch.com: "I mean, Calloway is by far an expert on online journalism and how to create traffic and what draws readers. And so he taught us that. It was effective. It works. It's compelling."

David Mastio (8/7/14) also made a distinction among types of media when it come to an increase in opinion, citing increases in opinion in cable news, fact-checking sites, and what he calls "explainer sites."

> I mean it's true on the cable networks, which now seem like half or more opinion. I think it's much less in newspapers but you've also got these fact checker sites, those are not reporting. I'd say, you know, like maybe two thirds of them are like, you know, you can give a clear answer, but if you really know the policy areas that they're talking about, there's so much more nuance and it's, you know, more a matter of when you stop reporting, you know, you choose to stop when you've gotten to a certain conclusion, but if you went, you know, a couple of other layers

deeper, you might find the opposite conclusion, and if you went a couple layers deeper than that, you might get back to where you started. . . . And the same thing with these explainer sites, you know, both the one that was born from the *New York Times* and Ezra Klein's that was born from, I mean, those all have a tendency to come down in one direction.

Increases in Opinion and Commentary Are Positive or Neutral

A number of journalists I spoke with viewed opinion and commentary in news as beneficial or at least not detrimental. According to Bruce Perlmutter,

> It's a free marketplace you can go to watch and listen to and read straight journalism without any name-calling or any issues with civility, or there are places where you could go and you can hear varying opinions and there may be some stronger than others. I mean it's just, it's a free marketplace. I don't believe that that's an issue, because it's not like those are the only places where you can get your content. So choose what you want. Go to Fox if you want one type of commentary, go to MSNBC for another brand of commentary, and that's just on cable. There are so many opinions now coming from influencers on social media. That's what it's about. Or go to, you know, read the AP wires if you want to have it played straight, or to some degree, the evening news shows still continue to exercise I would guess more straight journalism and less opinion so that's, they're all there. It's what you want, and don't be offended or put off if there's one outlet that does something that bothers you, don't watch it.

Tim Carney of the *Washington Examiner* (3/16/15) agreed and said that he thinks reporters having opinions is the way things are going.

A confidential source who works in TV news said that news reflects the society and culture we live in, implying that if the audiences want and watch certain things, that's what the TV network and journalists will provide. So whether it's continuing coverage of a story, such as the Malaysia Airlines missing plane, or expanding into commentary and long-form or documentary-style programs, the network's offerings reflect society, and if ratings are good, they'll keep doing it. This is basically the chicken-egg argument about supply versus demand, or giving the audience what it already has a taste for versus feeding it what you know or think is good for it and hoping it can learn to acquire that healthy new taste. However, this same confidential TV news source said he wouldn't "sell out" and go work for another channel or outlet that only does opinion.

Brian Stelter (8/18/14) views the current news environment positively:

> Right now we're talking about the independent autopsy of Michael Brown. Well, you could read about that on your phone via the *New York Times* last night. But the *New York Times* story is never gonna be a point-of-view story. It's always gonna strive for objectivity. You're gonna get those raw facts, and then CNN will help you digest them, with point of view and commentary and reporting. To me that feels like a pretty comfortable news environment.

Paul Farhi (6/4/14) said,

> There's this whole debate among journalists as to whether we're in the best of times or the worst of times, and the answer is yes. It's both things simultaneously. There's a lot of junk, and crap, and false stuff. My wife always says that everybody needs a media education class to understand where people are coming from, how the news is made, and to become more discerning consumers of news to figure out what's left, right, and center, and she's right. It would really be good for people to have a bullshit detector, to be able to say, "come on, we know this is not—we know this is implausible," and to be able to figure out what's credible. Look, I think everybody today is a media critic. Everybody has an opinion about the news media and how badly it does its job. And the fact of the matter is the media doesn't do badly; the media actually does quite well. It's when somebody sees something that they don't like that all of a sudden, this notion that there's something called "the media" doing badly, they're aware of it. Now what's "the media?" People think the media is anything they see; and they're right, it is anything you see. But, "Entertainment Tonight" is the media every bit as much as Twitter is the media, as the *New York Times* is the media, as *The Washington Post* is the media.

Farhi also used the healthy versus junk food metaphor in discussing people's media diet, but didn't come down on a side:

> And again, back to media education, what kind of journalism is it? ... So in other words, to make people more discerning

consumers of the news would be a very good thing, because we know that these things, while fact-based, aren't always coming from the same place as a reporter trying to cover some hard news story objectively. CNN's coverage of the Malaysia Airlines jet is a very interesting living media example for people. Why did they cover that story? I mean, there really wasn't any new development about it. The reason they covered that story is because—great insight here—it moved the needle on the ratings, and people were interested in it. And it told you, are we here to cover the news in some way that we as the priests of the news determine? Or are we here to serve the audience's demand and needs? And the answer that CNN gave is, it was the latter. We could go for weeks on this story whether or not there was anything new to report because people were interested in it. So maybe that's one definition of news: facts that people are interested in at any given point. Not spinach that they need to eat because it's good for them.

Farhi (6/4/14) said that because of the tremendous diversity of media, we shouldn't put too much stock in the surveys that show a decline in trust in news media over time:

. . . surveys, about the news media, about public opinion. Of course, it goes down year by year. We are held in lower and lower esteem all the time. And I would also say that one of the things that those surveys never quite ask is, what exactly are you taking about when you talk about the media? When you drill down into these things and you see what people say—"this is the most credible news source, and this is the least credible news source"—the news source that people choose themselves tends to be very credible to them. It's sort of like your congressman—"I hate all those other congressmen, but I like my guy." It's because you know something about it, you've experienced it. It's the perception that the news media that I don't consume is biased and incredible. But the news media that I do consume has integrity and is honest and is straight-forward. . . . You're opining on the things you know nothing about, is my point. So I can't hold a lot of stock in those surveys.

Rem Rieder (1/20/15) thinks there is an upside to opinion and commentary, but cautions against those at the expense of solid reporting:

I think a weakness of the traditional journalism was it was almost in a straightjacket, the old kind of objectivity was carried too far. So somebody says this and somebody says that period. And what I think has really been helping and is, it is not quite opinion, but it is in the ballpark of what you are talking about, is that more analytic writing and less fear of reaching conclusions, in other words, it is not opinion it doesn't really have to do with what your point of view is, but if your research shows that whatever candidate you are talking about that their assertion is nonsense, I think there are more places you can see it labeled nonsense now. And I think, overall, that has been a healthy trend because I think there was a lot of kind of weak-tea writing . . . with an excess of caution.

One thing I would underscore is all the smart commentary and analysis in the world is no substitute for reporting. There is a danger, I think, in getting away from hard edge reporting and unearthing the facts and I don't think that has happened. But, it has sort of come under challenge in this area as traditional news outlets have been so challenged financially and so they backed off: their staffs are smaller, there are fewer people doing things. There is this kind of tension in the digital world of getting clicks, getting audience, which sometimes puts more of a premium on the empty calorie story and that's, then, that's a tension in every newsroom now. I value commentary. So, I think, there's an upside to more livelier writing, more analysis, to sharper edged stuff; there is no substitute for the bedrock, nuts-and-bolts reporting, uncovering things, finding out things people know and need to know. And investigative reporting, for example, was really a casualty in many traditional news outlets and so you've seen a different landscape with the rise, where you've had something I never thought I'd see, and that's nonprofit journalism, sometimes funded by funders with (with) a point of view, something like ProPublica, which has done some really good work. So we've set new forms coming into the market. Some place like BuzzFeed doing investigative reporting . . . but I think it would be a really sad place if you didn't have the bedrock reporting that all this needs to be based on.

Like Rieder (1/20/15), Liza Mundy (7/30/14) was concerned about the increase in opinion journalism because of the simultaneous loss of reported journalism, in her view:

I sometimes thought it must be a good time to be getting started in journalism or writing because you can certainly get published, but it's I'm sure harder to get paid, and maybe it's harder to get noticed. I don't know. I think it's a mixed thing. Certainly people are able to write and express their opinion who maybe couldn't have found a format back in the days when space was limited. I do think that the proportion of opinionating to actual reported pieces has gone up. . . . And so, you're gonna have, I think, less scene-based journalism, less immersive journalism, maybe, less, you know, less journalism that takes you to a place that you haven't been, or don't have the opportunity to go to. Because that's expensive journalism and, I mean reporting outside your office or your home, offline is time-consuming, you don't know if it's gonna work out. You have to often travel somewhere and immerse yourself in some place for eight hours and maybe you get a scene and maybe you don't, and I just think that's, that, whether people consider it a loss I don't know. I consider it a loss because I like doing that kind of reporting.

Opinion and Commentary from Regular People/Bloggers/Citizen Journalists through Social Media Are More Important than What's Coming From, or Through the Filter of, Legacy/Big Media

Some journalists think the content posted by non-professional journalists online is more important and, at times, problematic, than professional journalists. Richard Benedetto (3/26/14) said,

> Blogging, the Internet has a lot to do with the decrease in civility. Not only people who blog, just feel free to be critical as hell, and it [may] be personal, and make wild accusations, because they're not trained journalists, most of them. First of all, they're not trained journalists, but they are practicing journalism per se. They are communicating, let's say. I think I agree, it is the language. But it's again, it's generational. Younger people feel free, much freer, to do this kind of thing than older people do. We have different sensitivities, we have different . . . , we've been brought up different ways. And so that we, even if you had something tough to say, as my grandmother would say, "If you haven't got anything good to say about somebody, just don't say anything."

According to a confidential source who formerly worked in TV news:

> About the people out there who aren't journalists, but are providing just as much information to the public as journalists do, but they're not really regulated. They're just posting stuff and people are taking this stuff very seriously, as though they've got some authority and knowledge as well. That to me is really interesting of what's happening these days. . . . there's a freedom of speech and people can post anything they want. And to be honest with you, bloggers and people that are out there posting on Twitter and on Instagram, they have sometimes more knowledge than actual journalists, because they're right there. So the information speedway is just it's crazy with all these types of content coming in.

The same confidential source who formerly worked in TV news said:

> But here's the thing. CNN can do iReport, that is a traditional news organization trying to tap into people reporting. That's not what I mean. I don't mean how CNN is dealing with it. I mean how real people are just posting stuff as they see it. I think CNN smartly tried to get into that game to see if we can get real people to do it for us. But that's not what people want. I spend a lot of time right now in the world of digital and social media. And the word is authentic. People want authentic information from people. If you filter it through CNN's iReport, that's not what I'm talking about. I'm [not] talking about Andrew Sullivan and I'm not talking about CNN, I'm talking about real people finding the ability and the, shall we say the form of self-expression to put it out there. . . . That's people commenting and responding and posting things on Twitter. That's the direct, there's no filter, there's no middleman.

Not Concerned for the Audience because of Opinion in News

Among the journalists I interviewed, there was a split in concern for the audience because of opinionated news content, and even uncivil content. Some of these concerns reflected scholarly theories and research about selective exposure, attention, and retention, and confirmation bias. Some journalists, however, expressed concern over incivility, but not over mere opinion.

Among those not concerned about opinion because they believe consumers are capable of discerning among outlets, Amber Phillips (7/23/14) said,

> It is tough for a reader to, who doesn't know "so-and-so columnist is definitely conservative, and I'm reading her column right now," as opposed to reading "The Fix," which is a blog on *The Washington Post*, but it's more objective. So, it's tough for readers to navigate that, but I think that—and I give readers the benefit of the doubt. They know when they're reading something that is objective but still kind of cutting through the crap and the noise versus something that's trying to drive a point home, even if it's not labeled. I think most of the journalism world does a good job labeling it, but even if the reader doesn't recognize that they're reading—I'm trying to think of her name, Jennifer [Rubin]. She's a conservative *Washington Post* columnist—versus, you know, "The Fix." Cause it does take a certain amount of educating yourself to know right off the bat that's what you're reading, but I give the readers the benefit of the doubt that they . . . say, "oh, ok, this is a column; this is clearly a blog with a slant and a tilt."

Phillips (7/23/14) believes viewers are capable of distinguishing what they're watching on TV as well:

> I think stereotypes of TV programs, of cable news programs, play a lot more into a viewer's perception of the program—so, I think for the most part, viewers can kind of listen to Erin Burnett ["Out Front" on CNN], which I think is pretty objective, and say "ok, you know what, she's not trying to spin me one way or the other." And then . . . turn on a liberal program from MSNBC and be like, "ok, I'm being spun; I can tell by the way the host is asking questions.

Jim Henderson (12/10/14) said,

> I think viewers are also pretty savvy. They know when they're tuned into a program on Fox that's meant to be like that, versus maybe a program on Fox that's a bit meant to be more of the straight news. Same with CNN. Because they do have—you know, it's not 24 hours of the same show. It's 24 hours of different types of shows. I think they're becoming a little bit more civil there.

In our interview, Henderson mentioned a study[2] he'd recently read about on media "catering to a niche audience, and reaffirming what they believe."

> But there's a study—I was reading in the paper the other day—about, some guys at the University of Chicago, they did a study. They found that a lot of liberals will go to the conservative sites, and conservatives go to the liberal sites, just to check them out. So it's not like the traffic on those sites is entirely one or the other.

Henderson, however, also said,

> I mean, the overarching concern is that because people aren't reading newspaper as much, or there isn't just the one newspaper where you get your information from, or that the only news is not on at 6:00, is that there becomes, sort of, two groups: one, people who are actively engaged in the news, looking at everything we're talking about, and there's this other huge group that's just tuned out. They've become indifferent to the whole thing, and it's a less informed populace than it was when people would sort of watch the 6:00 news 'cause that's all there was. Or get the local newspaper because, even though they might not be interested that much in the news, they needed to know what time the movies were going to start, or what's on TV. And they'd stumble across the headlines.

Like Henderson, Dave Mastio (8/7/14) also mentioned audience segments, but as a reason not to be concerned, saying that opinionated TV content in particular is not that influential:

> That's the other thing. It's that, the audience is not that big, and if you look at the demographics of the Fox audience and you look at the audience of the MSNBC audience, I don't know whether this applies to CNN, but you know they're committed partisans too. It's a really small echo chamber and I think if you combine the peak audiences of all three of the big cable news networks it's like, you know, less than 6 or 7% of the U.S. public.
>
> You know, that they're not persuading each other isn't much of a threat because they weren't open to persuasion to begin with. And so, it's one of the reasons that I really like my work at *USA Today* and even though I have a strong point of view, I'm really committed to the way we approach things in the opinion section here is because we really want it to be a conversation. We really

want the facts to be straight, we want, you know every sentence in the liberal thing to not be misleading, and every sentence in the conservative thing to not be misleading, and try to avoid talking points and, I mean there's counter forces, but I just don't think the cable shoutfest is culturally influential enough to matter. I think people in Washington confuse themselves by watching it and thinking that's what's going on out in the country.

Bruce Perlmutter (8/7/14) also thought consumers are capable of discerning and making a choice among news providers. He said,

No, I mean the reason why cable news started to exercise their option to do opinion journalism is because it's the same as an op-ed page in the *New York Times*. I mean, you know, so last, OK so if they have lack of civility, I mean, that's what happens when you get into a little political, or a large political debate around the dinner table.... Everybody's got an opinion, and that's what cable news is putting on the air. They're putting on those varying opinions. I mean, if you as a network decide that you are going to exercise your option to do opinion journalism, as opposed to straight down the line journalism, which by the way, also has two sides, it's just there's no question, you need to balance it either way, that's what you're gonna get. And I honestly think people just need to understand, you don't have to watch it. You don't have to read it. Get your news somewhere else. I mean, that's what you're getting when you have opinions.

People are smart enough to know. If you watch any prime time show on Fox News or MSNBC, you're not hiding the fact that it's an opinion show. No one, I mean I think people are much smarter to know when it's opinion. I mean, a dead give-away is when there's a talking head that's got an opinion, as opposed to watching. I mean I think people are really, Americans are smart, they get it. No one's camouflaging the fact that there's an opinion piece but they're passing it off as news.

Of the audience, Richard Benedetto (3/26/14) said:

You respect people. They don't know all the issues. They don't. But they vote sometimes on their gut, sometimes on just one issue, sometimes on . . . but you know, I respect the voters. I think that's where the action is. And they're smarter than you think. You

> know, this idea that somehow or another voters are dumb, well certainly they don't follow every dotted "I" and exclamation point in the campaign. They don't. It's not what they do. But they have gut feelings. That's why the debates become so important, because people will tune into those, because they get gut feelings. Not so much that they, the performance itself. But they get a sense of who this person is and whether they can trust them as president. It's an important thing. It's become a very important thing. But the public is smarter than we think they are. And it's because they're not political scientists. And to think that they should be is really crazy.

Benedetto, however, thinks other journalists have little faith in the audience:

> I think that a lot of journalists think that the public is ignorant and they can be fooled easily. I just don't think that's true. When somebody wins or loses an election, there are reasons. Part of it has to do with being able to connect with the public.

While journalists interviewed here variously expressed concern or not for audiences amid the increase in opinionated news, and concern for the loss of reported journalism, the results of two surveys released in June 2018, one of journalists, and the other of U.S. adults, showed that the public thinks the most useful kind of news reporting mostly provides facts but also combines some background and analysis to give audiences context. However, many Americans think most of the news reporting they see is opinion and commentary posing as news reporting, and others say coverage includes too much analysis (The Media Insight Project, 2018).

Opinion in Filter Bubbles and Echo Chambers Is Concerning

Other journalists, like Brian Stelter (8/18/14), said they believe point-of-view (opinion) news is serving the interest of audiences.

Stelter (8/18/14) and others, however, express concern for the echo chamber/filter bubble:

> I think the audience thinks it's beneficial or else the ratings wouldn't be where they are. I definitely worry about the effect of viewers living in a bubble, and not hearing things outside the bubble. No doubt about it. You could say that about MSNBC or about Fox or about the *Weekly Standard* . . . I don't have any brilliant solutions to the problem though.

Stelter went on to say,

> And I think the viewers, as a cable news, as a subscriber to cable, I like having a conservative point-of-view channel, and a liberal point-of-view channel. I like it. What I don't like is knowing that some people only watch one and not the other. Because I love watching both. And I don't say that to sound holier than thou. But I wish that people who watched Fox also watched MSNBC and vice versa. The research indicates that some do but most don't overlap. And that's where I think we should, there are reasons to worry about point-of-view television.

Rem Rieder (1/20/15) said,

> I guess I'm concerned by . . . people . . . living in their own world. I think it's healthy in a democracy to be exposed to a lot of points and views. . . . I think we have a lot of that now and whether it's kind of a who would come first kind of thing. But it kind of reinforces the polarization. It is a reflection of the polarization and a reinforcement of it. So, again, we have, the politics, the dysfunction of Washington doesn't come from nowhere, and we really have a body politic that is not really interested, a great many people are not interested in having a dialogue. And I think that's troubling.

Michael Calderone (7/2/14) also expressed some concern about the echo-chamber/segmentation impact of increase in opinionated content:

> Well, I think one of the concerns I have is that, there is this sort of choose your own adventure aspect to the news business now, where you can have, you know, there's less sort of shared experiences like there would have had a generation or two ago, where everyone watched nightly news, and may have read one or two weekly news magazines. There was, you know, there were stories that everyone kind of came in contact with, whether or not you thought the media was covering them fairly or not. We're at the point now, where a news consumers can read introductory part first thing in the morning to find out what stories they want to read. They'll read [inaudible] news during the day, have Fox News on in the background and basically have a completely different idea of what the biggest news stories of the day are than

somebody who's reading the *New York Times* and watching CNN, or moving further to the left, is primarily reading blogs on the left and just has MSNBC on.

Presciently, back in 2014, Calderone observed the echo-chamber effect on people in the 2012 election which proved even more significant in the 2016 Presidential election:

> So, you have . . . we saw this play out in the 2012 election, where a lot of conservatives thought that Barack Obama was going to lose reelection because they were in this conservative bubble of just seeing what was on Fox, just reading the Drudge Report and conservative blogs. So you had this sense that, there's no way Barack Obama could win, there's so many scandals surrounding his presidency, nobody likes him, he's been a terrible president. I mean this was the perception you would get 24/7 if these were the only outlets you were looking at. And of course, Barack Obama won reelection decisively, and a lot of pundits, including on Fox News, were completely wrong in telling viewers right up until election day that Romney was going to win the election. So I think that it's fine, if you're ideologically minded and you want to primarily read blogs on the left or right or news magazines on the left or right. I think that's fine. I think the concern that I would have is if you're only putting yourself in this one bubble, and you're discounting all other reporting, including nonpartisan, independent reporting in places like the *New York Times* or elsewhere. The caveat would be conservatives don't see the *New York Times* as nonpartisan.

Calderone continued:

> I think the problem is, you could be setting yourself up where you, you know, you have a different view of reality and what we saw with the 2012 election, the reality was that these scandals that were just huge on the right, like fast and furious, Benghazi, etc., these just did not have an impact on the way, they didn't' have a significant impact on the way people were actually voting. So, you know, that would be my concern with the way the news media has become so segmented in that, you're just, you're looking at a story in a completely different way . . . what I think is most problematic about the way the industry is being broken up

and where ideologically focused outlets are really just catering to this idea that they're the only ones that are gonna give you the truth. That reporting is suspect, that mainstream outlets that do original reporting should be discounted. So I think that that's a big problem.

Josh Altman (7/16/14) also expressed concern for the audience:

> I think from a viewer's perspective, you would like to think an educated viewer knows, but unfortunately most people watch one channel. Sitting in DC as someone who works in that industry, I'm thinking, "Well of course I know watching that, I know it's a slanted article and that it, you know, leans this way or that." Most people are not reading 3 newspapers a day and have a well-balanced Twitter feed with all these reporters and news feeds. That's just not the rest of the country. For some reason, the rest of the country doesn't have time for that. They have their jobs . . . this is my job.

Unlike Stelter, Calderone, Altman, and Rieder, Jon Allen (6/9/14) did not express concern over selective exposure and echo chambers:

> I think most people have some sense of what they're getting. I think those who want an objective news source certainly know how to find it. If they're having trouble with that, I can point some out [at you]; I think Bloomberg.com is a great place to go for objective news. But I do think most people have a good sense of what they're getting. I think most people are seeking out something that is objective, independent, or are seeking something that is partisan, or writes with a particular style or flair, or covers a certain set of issues that particularly speak to them. I think all of them are valid. My one [inaudible] view of all this is it doesn't matter what the political affiliation or lack of affiliation is of a news source, it just matters that they are reporting things that are true that no one knows.

Concerned for the Audience because of Incivility in News

Contrary to his lack of concern for the audience because of mere opinion in news, Allen (6/9/14) did express concern about incivility in political media discourse. He said:

> Like our entire public sphere needs a time out. Yeah, I think it's terrible. I think we don't treat each other with respect, with civility, with dignity. By and large, I think societal norms have broken down on television. People in Congress say terrible things about each other on the House and Senate floor, and I don't think it's the worst period we've ever had in American history in terms of political polarization, but I do think that we probably lost something in terms of our basic civility and the ability to have intelligent, and even divisive discourse without turning this personal and making our system a little uglier than it has to be.

Following up about it not being the worst that it's ever been throughout history, Allen replied,

> But that's a low bar to set. To say we're not slugging it out like cavemen is an endorsement of our behavior. I think it [incivility] makes our politics harder. I think with somebody attacking you on television, making it personal, I think it makes it harder to work with them. I do see a fraying, it's in our political system—and it's not just our political system, it's all of us who have some connection to public life, and I don't think of reporters as public life figures, but certainly the more we go on television, the more we talk openly about things, the more we're in that context, we're to blame, too. Look at reporters' Twitter feeds; they are injecting a lot of negativity and a lot of personalization of politics into the atmosphere. I think we would all do well to not tweet in anger, not go on television in anger, and try to bring a little more civility to our national discourse.

When asked about incivility on cable news in particular, Erik Wemple (6/12/14) said:

> Here's one of my sort of conclusions from watching thousands upon thousands of hours of cable news for the past three years. I do believe that cable news' "rap" as an uncivil medium is ok, but a little bit overblown. I think that mainly what cable news is, is boring and repetitive. Oftentimes, it's too civil. Oftentimes, it is softball interviews with people of the same ideological stripe. MSNBC will have some liberal on there, and they'll just sit there nodding their heads and say, "yeah, those conservatives are terrible." That's a lot of the programming, let's not forget that. I have a feeling that these networks—if they get strong opposing

opinions—their ratings go down. Fox has some liberals, MSNBC at least used to have some conservatives, but I don't know what their conservative count is right now—I have to check on that. They used to have—they would orchestrate—and FOX News does more of this, I believe, than MSNBC, but don't quote me on that—the fair and balanced debates, and stuff. But, I do believe that if you found that—if the conservative on MSNBC and the liberals on FOX started getting too good, then you might find viewers peeling off. That would be my guess.

Wemple, in the exchange above, did not seem overly concerned about incivility, which he viewed as a successful audience strategy. However, when directly asked about whether we should care or be worried about incivility on TV news, his response took a turn:

I would say that we—of course we should care about incivility. It doesn't set a very good footing for how conflict and disagreement should be resolved. It is quite clear that cable news shows are only too happy to see their guests become embroiled in a shouting match. That is what gets them—I have to say on my blog and it gets them on other peoples' blogs as well. In cable news, particularly, getting rotation, getting noticed on the Internet is an important element. Bill O'Reilly at one point, I believe, boasted about the fact that his stuff—cable news and O'Reilly's stuff—gets a lot of attention on the Internet in a way that the nightly news broadcasts, which are generally very formulaic and certainly not filled with shouting matches, do not. And so, that's a big sort of—there's a big incentive to create conflict . . . Of course, if you want to bash cable news for that, you probably should also bash Ted Koppel Nightline for that and Martin Agronsky and Company, and the McLaughlin Group, because they're all geared toward starting something—starting a fight, getting people to yell at each other. So this ain't new.

A former news producer (6/6/14) also has mixed feelings about incivility on TV news:

I don't necessarily mind or . . . think it's dangerous or bad for society to have these sorts of boxing match, pro-con debates. I think it's ugly sometimes when it's "I yell at you, you yell at me." I do think it's fair to—if a news network is going to put on three people in a row that are Republicans, and the host is not going to fight that person for each segment, I do think it's more fair to have a boxing match so that at least both sides are being heard. I don't think it's civil and I don't like it. You know I'm a producer; I'm just as annoyed hearing two people screaming at each other. That's not how I prefer to get my information either, but the actual content of each person's fighting for their side, I think that's so dangerous because—the other way is that one person who has their heels dug in on the right wing—or the left wing or whatever—if you have someone on the right wing doing four minutes of a talk segment, someone on the right wing doing another four minutes of a talk segment, another right wing Republican doing another four minutes of a talk segment. I mean, you're not really giving people many other viewpoints, so I think it is uncivil, I think it's too unpleasant; I think it makes people think that you're supposed to yell at people. . . . But I think there is value in presenting both sides of the argument. . . .

Although Amber Phillips was not concerned about mere opinion, she said incivility is problematic:

Well, yeah. I mean, I think it's pretty harmful, whether its politicians or the media themselves, having negative discourse. Because how many average voters do you hear who are like, "Oh, I just tune out. No one can agree on anything; they're all a-holes. I just totally tune out." And so I almost feel like it's—I don't know if I want to say this—but it's almost like a moral responsibility as a journalist to not focus on the, you know, Orrin Hatch—and this is a true story from yesterday—Orrin Hatch said the Senate is emasculated.[3] You know, one-time ally Harry Reid—they've been known to work together—and now he's bashing him in. It's just like, it doesn't help the average reader decide how to vote, unless they're from Utah. Or, what can be more news than politics, and I need my readers to care about politics, to keep me in a job. So, I would argue that it's pretty negative, and I think it's media and politicians. I would definitely agree there's more negative discourse [now] than there has been in 15 years, 20 years.

Rem Rieder (1/20/15), too, thinks there is much incivility and that is it problematic: "There is a much higher snark quotient then there used to be. There is a premium not just in politics, but there is a lot of snark out there. . . ."

> I think it is part of the same thing. When you don't hear other voices and see the legitimacy in the other point of view. It is easy to be really contemptuous and uncivil if you will, and snarky. I mean you see it (in) on the hill with the "You lie" comments, which is unthinkable. But you see it in a lot of more partisan journalism. And, again, I don't know that that's new, and some of this is cyclical . . . But, I do think that today's harshness is not healthy at all and it again feeds on what we just talked about before, the echo chamber and the denigration of your rival.

When I asked Rieder (1/20/15) what should be done about incivility, he mentioned that he had participated in an event held by the National Institute for Civil Discourse at the University of Arizona. Rieder said,

> something needs to be done and I think that's the next step, but how do you break that cycle. It's really difficult because you are not really talking, this is a point I made, you are not just talking about reforming journalism, you are, it's much bigger, you are talking about a certain kind of journalism. There is a lot of journalism that isn't tarred with this, at all, but the commentary part that is, is part of a much broader problem.

On the effects on audiences of the increase in opinion and toward emphasis on specific personalities, Frank Sesno (10/9/14) said:

> . . . the main effect on the audience has been to habituate the audience to more opinion and more personality. The flipside of that is that I also think it's helped to alienate a large part of the audience that don't want that personality or that opinion. So it's been then as a result to divide the audience more clearly and more ideologically.

When asked if he thinks audiences can be as well informed from opinionated news and news that focuses on the personality as from what we previously had more of, more objective-style type of news, Sesno (10/9/14) said the potential for being well-informed is there, perhaps even more than before, but it requires more responsibility and work on the audience's part:

> No, I don't think the audience can be as easily informed if they're doing a one-stop shop by the way. I think the audience can be more

easily informed now than it's ever been before if the people want to work at it. And I think that probably the big underestimated or underfocused—I don't know what the term is—aspect is the public's responsibility. . . . I know that I want to go to a number of different places [for news]. I also know the various agendas of the places I go. And that's where the public needs to become more news literate, more media literate.

Not Concerned about Incivility

Some journalists were not concerned about the impact of incivility on audiences. Jack Shafer (2/11/15) does not believe there has been an increase in incivility or opinion in news. Accordingly, he is also not concerned about the effect on the audience:

> It's not my job to worry about the effect on the audience. I mean the audience is so grand, we've got 315 million people in this country . . . I actually don't know what that means to say that you are concerned about the effect on the audience. Maybe the effect on the audience is to cause them to feel apathetic. Maybe another set of viewers become politically engaged. Maybe another set of viewers look at what Fox is doing and say that is just bullshit propaganda, they are not consistent, they are just a tool of Rupert Murdoch. And they go pick up a few books and (and) engage in some stimulating conversation. I don't worry about—I don't think that oppression is the nanny of his imagined audience, or the audience which constitutes the whole population.

Rick Massimo (6/10/14) also disagreed that incivility itself is always problematic, but said that he believes incivility is often linked to inaccuracy, which he does find problematic:

> Well, my feeling is, and this is only partially a journalistic feeling, and partially just a humanistic . . . I have no use for civility whatsoever. I have no concerns with the decline of civility. My concern is with the decline of accuracy. And I think the two go hand in hand. I think the reason people are uncivil is because they're wrong. . . . Now, if the last shred of freedom in this country were actually under attack, then it would be not so uncivil for people to be screaming in the streets and maybe shooting. It's the fact that they're this hyped up about health insurance. That's

the problem. And if you want to call that uncivil, OK, but I don't think it's that. I just think it's based on overheated rhetoric of something that is just, the problem is that it's just not true. It's not that it's uncivil, it's that it's based on something that's false . . . We should care less about how it's said. We should care more about what, the content.

Massimo (6/10/14) reiterated what my other research had found about journalists believing that they have a responsibility, but in his view, it's only to accuracy:

But it is a journalist's job, and you know, now it's considered taking sides to point out that something that somebody tells you isn't true. . . . Why is journalism the only private enterprise that's protected in the text of the constitution? Because that's where you go to find out what's happening. . . . And, you know, to say that it may or may not be our jobs to point out that this thing that somebody is telling us is not true. One of my favorite media criticisms is to ask, what do you even think your job is? Actually put it into words. What do you think your job is? What are you doing? I don't know. But yeah. I think that once there's more truth, there'll be more civility.

While Paul Farhi (6/4/14) had explained his concern for the blurring of news and opinion, especially on the part of journalists who give opinion in other news venues, and said that he thinks media [literacy] education would be beneficial, he expressed only mild concern for the televised presentation of extreme opinion:

I think it's performance art in the sense that that's what television wants in those forms. You don't want a civilized, calm discussion. You want fire, you want clashing ideologies, and it's kind of edited for that. Again, it's a stage production. . . . Remember the famous Jon Stewart calling-out of "Crossfire." I thought that was a little overstated on his part. It was, like 2004, so that was 10 years ago. They're not necessarily ruining the country, but I can see how you can construct an argument that says, "you are making people believe that extremes are the only way to go; that the idea of the bland middle is clearly not what is desirable; that only extremities of opinion make sense these days." Perhaps it gave rise to the Tea Party. Perhaps it gave rise to a stronger left-wing. I don't know that it's really ruining the country, but there is drift... There's lots of structural things. But, it's hard to say this hasn't had some effect on driving people to greater extremes and encouraging it, because they see it all the time. When you get in political discussions with people, a lot of the time it becomes a simulation of a "Crossfire." The Thanksgiving dinner table is like, "oh, I'm going to have to go home and hear Uncle Bob talk about this in the extreme way he just saw on TV."

Farhi went on:

I think people see that, and they see something they disagree with 'cause that's kind of the point, to get people riled up, and they blame the media again. So the link between watching one of these discussions, in which people are throwing opinions at each other, this becomes—in their minds, in the viewer's mind, in a lot of viewers' minds—what the media does. Well, they're right and they're wrong at the same time. Again, that's just one little tiny part of the media, and it's its own little sub-segment; it's not the only thing the media does.

Concern about Incivility *from/perpetuated by* Audiences, Regular People

Journalists' concerns articulated in interviews about incivility on the part of audiences, rather than their colleagues, were consistent with the journalists' views expressed in digital media that were previously discussed.

Mundy (7/30/14) was concerned about the current news environment because of the greater potential for incivility *from audiences* responding, rather than the effect on audiences of public figures' incivility:

I'm sure there are people who, obviously you can turn to the outlet that expresses opinions that you agree with, more easily. So you can read the publications that express your point of view or watch the channels that express your point of view. So I suppose it's easier to immerse yourself in the opinions of people you agree with. I mean, the other more complicated part of the discussion is, the opinions that get expressed back at you, as a reporter, you know, the comments section and the opinions of your writing that get expressed by readers, you know, have become much more vitriolic, and I wonder sometimes what the impact is on reporters. There's been some discussion of this with regard to women writers in particular that there's a lot of hating in the comments. And I've been in journalism for long enough that when readers had to express their opinions by writing a letter, more often than not it would be a letter of praise, or the reader was interested in what you had to say. I got a fair number of letters written in purple ink by elderly women who were interested in you know, my work life challenges as a young parent when I was writing about them for *The Post*. I mean, you never knew what you were gonna get from a handwritten letter, but chances are it was gonna be long and thoughtful. I mean sometimes they would write to point out an error, or to vehemently disagree, but I felt like as commentary moved online, first to, online emails, but then to the comments section in stories, the comments just got much, much more negative. And so, I think that it's hard for writers sometimes to come to terms with that, and so that, I think that's just to me another part of the movement toward opinion. It's not just writers expressing opinions; it's readers expressing opinions of what the writer has written that create sometimes a toxic environment. And sometimes I wonder whether it silences some writers.

Mundy (7/30/14) also described her personal experience being on the receiving end of uncivil comments, and believes that women writers are more likely to encounter hostile responses:

There was a very powerful piece that ran in the *Pacific Standard* magazine, written by Amanda Hess[4] about the level of hatred that she's had expressed to her based on her writing. And I don't know if anybody has ever tried to quantify hateful commentary directed at women writers versus directed at men. I've certainly gotten it. I mean I've gotten tweets that have been very hateful and obscene so, you know, men they get that also but I would be willing to bet that women get it more, and that it's more intense.

Jim Henderson (12/10/14) also discussed uncivil reader comments:

Well, when reader comments first started, they kind of stung. Because a lot of times they'd be attacking the writer of the story even if it was just a straight news story. And then after a while you just start to ignore them, because often they would be just—whatever the story was about, they would go into politics. Unemployment report: it was all Obama's fault, or it was all somebody else's fault.

And then it's not really discussion about anything. And sometimes the comments themselves would be completely off-base and rude to the other commenters. Not off on the story, but to the other commenters. And then that's a forum for what? Drivel. You also get a sense that each comment might represent a lot of other readers, and often they don't. They just don't. It's just that one guy.

When I asked Henderson if he thinks there's a value at all of having those forums online for readers, he said,

I don't think so in a general—in a major publication newspaper. Not with each story. Maybe there's a place for it, certainly on the opinion pages or the opinion pages online, that should be a place for it. But not just attached to any news story about anything.

Journalists' interview comments also affirmed findings from the analysis of published journalistic discourse. Journalists cited anonymity as a main cause of audiences' incivility and discussed tactics for moderating comments on news sites, and also the difficulties of doing so.

Rieder (1/20/15) said,

Comments were considered a key point of the Internet. I think they've been a plague from the beginning. I don't think there is a place for anonymous comments, at all. I've always hated that idea. News outlets would jump through hoops to make sure that their letters to the editors were by actual people and they just let anybody—I think that's been a huge contributor to incivility in digital life. The fact that anybody can get on without identifying themselves, say really vile things, and it's considered a sacred right, and I think it's just bullshit not to be uncivil but, you know, if you are going to take a position, have, make people identify themselves; you won't get rid of all the haters, at all, but it will cut down on it a lot, and I think that kind of took root for so long, it was considered a sacred untouchable right of the digital life, which I thought it was nuts.

Paul Farhi wrote about comments on news sites in May, 2014. In our interview, Farhi (6/4/14) said:

Let me say to start: theoretically, it isn't entirely obvious that civility is a good thing. In other words, why does it matter that people are jerks? Maybe in a free press, free world, Internet world, allowing people to be jerks might be ok. I don't like racism, I don't like sexism, I don't like homophobia—I don't like all of those things—but the fact is, those things exist, and allowing people to express those things might be harmless. Might be. It's an argument worth having. We can't start with the idea that we must have absolute civility in these things.

I said that these ideas of Farhi's didn't make it into the article he wrote. Farhi (6/4/14) responded,

Well, it made it, interestingly, into the comments on the article about comments. People were saying, "Why do we care? Why does *The Washington Post* care that people are jerks?" It's an interesting point. To the extent that we care in so far that it harms our business, then we care If those kinds of comments are driving away people—and there's some evidence that they are—then we do care. Also, you have to ask yourself, do we want to be a forum for that kind of extreme opinion speech done anonymously? I don't know that there's a good argument for that. Maybe we shouldn't. In other words, you wouldn't have that stuff in Letters to the Editor, because Letters to the Editor are edited by someone who says, "this opinion is so far outside the mainstream and so extreme that we won't allow it." The other part about the Letters to the Editor as opposed to the comments on our website is, the Letters to the Editor have a name, also an address and phone number—we don't publish those things, but when they come in you have to have those things for accountability. Whereas, online it's—as I said in my story—it's the unleashed id of people sitting in their basement anonymously saying, "I don't like, fill in the blank." Or, "this particular group of people is bad, wrong, terrible, because." They get to slam whole groups of people with no accountability to it. So, again, back to civility, how do you encourage more of it if you think civility is a good thing to have on your website? And as a business proposition, it may well be. As I said in this story, there have been a few things you filtered through your Facebook page that doesn't eliminate it, but it does cut down on it. It drives the anonymous jackasses to the next site and you refine your things. Or you curate it, you have people actually—like the *New York Times* does—tossing out the extreme ends of the opinions, and you have a much more civilized discussion.

Farhi (6/4/14) went on to say,

> The problem with that is, that kind of stuff costs money. You have to hire people and pay them money to keep things in a more mainstream kind of opinion. And, look, the *New York Times* has 1,100 people working in its newsroom. The XYZ Times does not have 1,100 people or the luxury to curate the incoming bombast. So, it's not necessarily a model that works for everyone. There are others things that people can do to filter a little bit better. *Huffington Post* did this—they got a lot of flak for it, but nevertheless, it has cut down somewhat on the extreme, crazy crap that goes up there. Again, do we want to be the host for that? I don't know, it's not something we're proud of.

Farhi's comments about being concerned because they don't want it to harm their business is consistent with what my analysis of published journalistic discourse, and other scholars, have found as a motivation for moderating or closing comment sections on news web sites.

Not Concerned with Uncivil Comments from Users/Audience

In contrast to these journalists who have expressed concern about uncivil user comments, David Mastio (8/7/14) was not so concerned. He said that *USA Today* requires people to use a real Facebook account to prevent anonymity and to boost civility:

> I think that makes things a lot better, even for people who screw around with the system to create a fake Facebook account so they can comment, at least there's a history that's attached from comment to comment so that, you know, someone can ruin their fake identity by being a jerk. And need to start over. So I think that's really a positive development. I'm glad we did that, but my approach to the comments on our stuff is to just leave them alone. . . . Hopefully the way people interact online will evolve over time, like get evolved over time . . . I don't think we're gonna see big leaps in our lifetime, but I think it will get better over time. I don't think we need to do anything about it.

Mastio (8/7/14) also pointed out that anonymous authorship is not a new development, and it has a long history:

. . . so the big, the big worry back then, you know, this wasn't right in '95, but maybe '96, '97 was just the idea of you know, were we corrupting our product by putting you know, comments on it. It's looks like a ludicrous debate now, but that was taken really seriously in newsrooms and there were people who fought that tooth and nail, and I'm like, it's letters to the editor but faster. You know, there's nothing new about that. You know, only we're not hovering over readers and you know, putting our stamp on their work. But, you know, we weren't supposed to be doing that in the first place. I mean you look at like the Federalist Papers and the things that were written in response to it, and then the contemporary opinion that there was of newspapers at the time, it was not always highbrow, there was lots of low blows and so to the extent that they're analogous, I mean that was the national conversation at that time while we were, you know, when we were, when we had our first few presidential elections. It was, you know, people were writing things anonymously, you know the Federalist Papers were all written anonymously. And we act like anonymous comments today, oh my God, you know, it's the end of the world, well freakin', this country was founded on anonymous comments.

Whether Bad or Good, the Heated and Uncivil Expression of Opinion Has Been Around for a Long Time

Several journalists pointed to the long history of incivility in political discourse as a justification for its presence today. Among them, Erik Wemple (6/12/14) justifies incivility as a successful strategy for gaining attention, while at the same time expressing concern about it. He points out that opinionated news and even the heated or uncivil expression of opinion in news, have been around for a long time. He elaborates on this point about the longstanding tradition:

I think "Agronsky & Company"—I forgot exactly what year it was, but I think the McLaughlin Group is an early '80s sort of thing, '82–'83, and "Agronsky and Company" and the Capital Gang—that's the other one—they would all make sure that their audiences [inaudible] or that their commentators came in with opposing views. And on some level, it's journalistically responsible. In a newspaper article, you want all points of view represented. So, an intelligent format—why not? It just so happens that intelligent format people tend to mug for the camera and carry on, and they want to make a name for themselves so they start shouting. That happens. It's inevitable and sometimes it's even edifying. . . . I think if done properly, it's more educational than . . . intellectual and ideological convergence. . . . it's sometimes good to have someone on the set shaking the shoulders of the other person, saying, "you're in your bubble here."

Jack Shafer (2/11/15) also believes uncivil content is nothing new. Shafer said, "These people are muttonheads. Go back and look at the headlines from the - you can find headlines from practically any era of insulting, uncivil, boisterous, aggressive, attack, it's just nonsense that somehow our era invented incivility. I just don't believe that."

Shafer also equated rhetoric about civility with attempts to censor certain viewpoints. This is consistent with findings from my analysis of what journalists had written about civility online (Meltzer, 2015).

Shafer said,

> Once, again, you're in that problem of it being a much bigger pasture then it used to be. So, maybe the appearances are that there is so much more of it, but (y' know) I'm 63, I remember growing up with Joe Pyne on the radio, this incredibly sarcastic, abusive, wicked talk show host. He was incredibly popular . . . wildly abusive. There is Al Goldstein of *SCREW* magazine . . . He was a sort of pornographer satiric journalist, wild man in New York with a successful smut newspaper in the '60s and '70s. Traditionally, the tabloid newspapers has been abrasive, and combative, and denouncing people . . . The incivility is, I think, calling somebody uncivil is just another way of telling them to shut-up. You don't like their volume. You don't like their style. You don't like the words that they use. But, really, what you don't like is their argument. You just drive that march along and silence them.

Dave Mastio (8/7/14) also cited the long history of incivility in printed news:

> . . . there was no civil age in newspapers . . . Almost everything that people say is wrong with the kind of new media mess that we have today. Everything that they say is wrong with it and that they hate about it, was like true of newspapers in the nineteenth century, you know, you had the partisanship, you had the corruption, you know, you had the owners meddling around. You had angry tirades, you had things that were totally made up.

Everything... There is not a freakin' single thing new in, you know, even if you go back and look at like, there's journalism schools named after newspaper owners, I can't remember whether it's in, the one in Missouri or Kansas is named after a newspaper owner who, he would like hold secret meetings with politicians and then when they agreed to do what he wanted them to do he'd write editorials about, so like, everything that people get mad at Arianna Huffington about, are even done, and if you look into these people's lives and you read biographies of them, they were all you know opinionated, a little bit cracked, a little bit on the ethical edgy side. And you look at the people who created great new media innovations over the last 25 years, it's the very same people. Nothing new is happening here at all.

Back in 1998, writing about the battle between Ken Starr and Bill Clinton for *Time Magazine*'s Men of the Year cover story, Nancy Gibbs wrote, "Civility, long rationed, ran out first. Politicians no longer express opposition: they are expressing hatred. No action, however solemn, is judged on its merits; everyone's got an angle. Even if the fighting ends tomorrow, it will be years before the wreckage is cleared." As Nicco Mele, who introduced Gibbs at the 2017 Theodore White Lecture on Press and Politics, said, "It's almost as if she has anticipated this moment in American politics and media."

Lack of Labeling Content as Opinion Can Be Concerning for Audiences

Even journalists who did not express much concern over mere opinion believe that clearly labeling opinionated content—being transparent—is important for the audience. Following this, Richard Benedetto (3/26/14) was more concerned with mainstream news outlets he believes express views, rather than the outwardly opinionated news channels:

MSNBC has a liberal agenda and Fox News has a conservative agenda, and they're trying to serve that agenda. They know that they've found a way to attract an audience. I mean, the name of the game is ratings. Making money, ratings. Give me advertisers.... If that's your only source of news, you're basically getting a jaundiced view whether you watch the liberal or conservative side. But, you have to understand that that's who they are. I don't want to criticize them, because that's what they do. There's no attempt to say, "We're a mainstream news organization." We know they're conservative, we know they're liberal. I worry more about the mainstream news organizations, which have ideological bents to and they shouldn't have.

Brian Stelter also thinks the risky aspect to opinionated content is labeling:

> That gets back to the filter bubble. The dangers. Like things like, one gripe that I have about Fox and MSNBC and about, well you know, in general the idea of point-of-view television is, they need to be labeled. They use the same. So you know, Bill O'Reilly has the same exact graphic as newscasts on Fox. So there's a labeling failure I think. You might wonder if it's intentional.

Maria Bartiromo (6/19/14) also said labeling of content is problematic:

> If you look at the *New York Times*, I believe that there's a real bias there. If you look at—I mean, Fox News basically tells you who they are. You know that Fox is conservative because the commentators on Fox News are conservative. They're not making believe they're journalists; they are telling you we're conservative commentators. My problem is when someone tells you they are a journalist, and then they put their biases in there. That is when it gets really dangerous. So if you tell me you're left, or if you tell me you're right, then at least I know that I have to take whatever I'm hearing with a grain of salt because there's a lean. But if you tell me you're a straight journalist, I just want the facts. And that's getting harder and harder to find.

But Dave Mastio (8/7/14) disagrees that failing to label opinionated content is concerning for the audience, but believes that pretending to be objective while giving opinionated content is a poor strategy on the part of a news organization:

> I'm not even really, it doesn't worry me that opinion creeps into the news space because I've always thought, you know, the objective, the claim of objectivity was bogus. You know, I can read a news story and you see, you know, you get one party's point of view at the beginning and then there's like five paragraphs backing it up, and then there's like a paragraph or two of rebuttal from the other side, and then the rest of the story is about why that rebuttal is

wrong. And then the final thing is a quote from the same party as at the beginning, and it's all written in perfectly neutral language, you know, the facts are checked, and you know, everything holds together. It's a good story, it tells readers information that they didn't know, it tells them what happened today. It does all the good things that a news story did, but you know, at the core of it, there's an opinion there. There's a judgment that's been reached by the reporter and the editor about what's true.

And you know, I think what, one of the, despite its slogan of you know, we're fair and balanced or whatever, Fox News's great innovation is not that they're conservative, but that they leveled with readers, or with viewers. You know, you know where Fox News is coming from and you can differentiate, you know, you can apply the right lens to that to help you understand better what the facts are, and you can know that you might need to learn more somewhere else to get the full story. I think the fundamental premise of the American objective press is, you know, a little bit dishonest. It's not, you know, it's not that we don't try. And it's not that there's really good people doing their best every day, it's that, you know, just from its nature to write a news story you've gotta make some judgments, and those judgments are based on limited information and mind with your values and perspective and there's no way around that. So, I think that's one of the reasons that Fox is popular is that leveling thing. And I think that's why CNN wallows around. I mean, if you're telling a big chunk of your audience that we're objective. And a big chunk of your audience says, "that's a lie." You know, you can't start your relationship there and expect to be a growing news brand.

Increases in Opinion and Commentary Have Negative Impacts

While some journalists thought opinion itself may have a place, it can negatively impact other parts of news. A TV journalist in Washington (6/18/14) said,

> There are the anchors of opinion shows, you know, I consider them anchors of opinion shows. That said, I still think in my head, they have a responsibility to still, in the same way when you have a conversation with somebody at dinner, just because it's their opinion, doesn't mean they should be saying stuff that's not backed up by fact.

Echoing remarks by Mundy and Rieder, Maria Bartiromo (6/19/14) said that "news is getting squeezed, increasingly."

> ... It feels like the straight, broad news business is being clouded out by opinion and commentators, and also a little entertainment as well. So, I think that journalism today ... is really sitting in a situation where people are not sure what's news and what's opinion ... And that's very dangerous. Journalism is very important. I mean, a free, independent press is critical for any democracy and any economy. And the free and independent press has been impacted by any number of things: divisiveness of this country, the opinions about how to govern in this country, and the idea that—you know, a lot of dumbing down with all the reality shows. And so, unfortunately, straight journalism is becoming harder and harder to find.

Bartiromo said one of the drawbacks to increased commentary and opinion in news is that it decreases the time given for substantive interviews and analysis:

> I'm very aware of it [partisan coverage]. I try to bring both sides of the story into every story that I'm doing. I was at CNBC for 20 years, and I felt like I was very pressured—and this was one of the reasons that I left—very pressured to have 5 people on at once, to do interviews in 5 minutes. I mean, if you turn on CNBC today you've got, like, 6 boxes on screen filled with people talking about the same subject—so the segment is like 6 minutes, everybody gets 30 seconds. Impossible to have a follow-up, it's impossible to have any perspective or analytics because it's so quick. So that is entertainment, and again, it's hard to call that news. So yeah, I'm aware of it, I'm trying very hard to not fall into it. But I think that this is very important for today's journalism students and the emerging journalists of the world to keep in mind, because there are a lot of information portals, and there's just so much information flow today—from the broadcast networks to satellite to the Internet, and print and magazines, etc.—that the onus is on you [the journalist] to make sure that you're playing it straight. And it's more important than ever before.

Bartiromo (6/9/14) also said she thinks it is alright for people to express opinions through media, as long as they are not journalists; journalists should stick to reporting the facts:

> I don't mind. Look, everyone has opinions, and I think it's fine to have opinions and be a commentator. There are certain people who—their opinions I respect and I want to hear what they think about things. And so that's okay. I'm not saying everyone should not have an opinion. But, I think if you are a journalist, you need to play it straight. And if you're writing about something, you need to make sure to look at all sides of the story and ensure that you're giving the public enough information to allow them to make their own decision about it. You know, without putting up misleading headlines, or quotes that support one opinion and not the other opinion. The good news in all of this is that the consumer has access to an enormous amount of information. The good news is that there are experts who have real expertise in certain fields that are giving out their opinions. That's terrific! My biggest problem, again, with this is if you're hiding behind "I'm a journalist," but in fact, you're not. You're giving your opinion. I think going forward, the onus is on the industry and all of us who are journalists to ensure that when you say you are reporting news, you are reporting news and fact. Stick to the facts.

While Dave Mastio (8/7/14) said that opinion in news is nothing new and was not very concerned about it in most ways, he did express concern in the way that opinion today on television can be expressed:

> So, with the TV stuff, you know, I can't watch cable news because I, everybody, what's really, what maybe is different is that, and maybe this is because I'm naïve and I haven't read deeply enough into the history, but you know, I feel like when people were debating a hundred years ago, two hundred years ago, there was an honesty to their debate, but what's different about TV debates is that if you want to succeed on those shows you go in with some cute phrases and some well-thought out points that you want to make. And it does not matter what the other person said. It's not a conversation. And that's what, you know, those conversations never advance to any point of agreement or clarify, you know where they, where exactly they disagree and what they agree on. So they don't do any of the things that conversations are supposed to do, and so that I think maybe is frustrating. I mean, it's just dishonest at its core.

Rem Rieder (1/20/15) expressed similar sentiments about opinionated talking heads on television:

Fox has built an unbelievably successful business and brand by appealing to people with a certain point of view and kind of doing it in a harsh kind of critical way. Now, you've got other people doing it. And, I guess, there is a sense. I don't know. You need to ask the news executives why they do this. I wrote a column when "Crossfire" was briefly brought back to the air, it was as hideous an idea that I could think of. I think one of the worst ideas and television loves this shit is—let's get, somebody is over here (slams hand down) and somebody over here (slams hand down) and just let them beat the shit out of each other. And on "Crossfire," that moment when Jon Stewart went on there and said they were ruining America, I think, again that's one of the reasons why he is one of the best media critics out there. But there is still way too much of it out there. Like I'm a Chuck Todd guy, I'm embarrassed to say, but you watch those shows and they are still too often, I don't want to see Mitch McConnell and somebody and predictably they are going to be taking other positions, they are going to talk over each other and I think that is completely unhelpful and television must think—I guess there is the idea, well, it's fair and balanced . . . But they must think there is an appeal to it, that it sells, and I think it's bad for democracy. Besides being so boring. That's the worst nightmare. It's so intellectually bankrupt and, yet, television loves this. And to this, I mean, people who should know better do this. "Crossfire," that's all it did, but we still have too many places doing that. And somebody should just shake those TV executives and tell them.

Other Reasons for the Decrease in Quality of News

Long-time CBS Justice Department reporter Stephanie Lambidakis left her job of 20 years in 2014 because of changes to journalism for the worse, in her view. She cites two main factors that have contributed to what she sees as a decrease in the quality of news: lack of transparency and access given by the presidential administration, and the hyper-speed, constant news cycle, driven by social media. Lambidakis said,

> The reasons I loved covering the Justice Department, the FBI, Homeland Security, with 9/11 being sort of the most cataclysmic part of the beat . . . was that it's very fact driven. I mean, you have indictments, you have court appearances, you have trials, you have terrorists, alleged terrorists, wannabe terrorists, taken

into custody, charged. I mean these are very cut and dried things, where you can see what the facts are . . . I mean, we operate within a framework of facts as a way to get to the truth, which is always what we are looking for. Journalists. Not just the facts as they present them to us, but ultimately, the truth . . . Which is harder and harder to find on both sides. Those on the journalism side and on the government side.

On the pace of news driven by new technology, Lambidakis said,

So what's evolved, first on the industry side is, when you're an older journalist like myself, the pace of Twitter, Instagram, social media, and the relentless pace of it has made covering the news and writing about the news sort of incoherent because it's all driven now by Twitter. And that's not to say that I don't like Twitter, I see it's important. But now, it's so much more important for everyone to be out there first with their tweets that someone might tweet out, "Justice Department settles with JP Morgan" and we're all at the same news conference for that, and that my editors will call and say, "MSNBC, *New York Times*, *The Washington Post*, have tweeted that out," and I'd say, "well, that's the event." We're all at that same event . . . So the ability on my end to cover, to tell a story, in a coherent fashion in more than one sentence just became very frustrating for me . . . now it's much more difficult for anyone to keep up with that pace and to write and to go through, like tell me a story, which is one of the most fundamental things I learned from some of the greatest correspondents, is, tell me a story. . . . the pace was not every hour, like CNN, it became every five minutes . . . I couldn't keep up with that pace anymore. I mean, I'm happy to admit it as a middle-aged woman in the news business, that just wasn't working for me anymore. So many of my counterparts and my friends, especially women over fifty, and over forty, the layoffs have been just across the board and continue still. Men and women, but that's on the journalism side. And then the flip side is covering the administration.

According to Lambidakis, another negative side effect of the use of new technology is that it can lead to poor reporting practices:

You're eventually gonna get some version of the truth. You're gonna piece it together. But it's much more difficult to do that now . . . The level of control . . . it's hard to get the job. Reporters are lazy now, because we're tethered to the email. You don't go walk the halls anymore. It's hard to develop sources. I mean, shame on reporters, but we've fallen for it.

On the administration's treatment of the press, and media relations efforts, Lambidakis (7/3/14) said,

> I'm just trying to tell the story straight but I don't always have access to the facts, because this administration [Obama], which promised . . . us a transparency that the previous administration for eight years, because I covered the Justice Department for eight years under John Ashcroft, Alberto Gonzalez, Michael Mukasey . . . Because everything was classified then. The torture memos, that we didn't get the full picture. John Ashcroft in the hospital, gave everything after 9/11 especially becomes classified. Grand jury secrecy, and I've always been able to operate in that realm. So when the Obama administration came into office and in the Justice Department in particular, which is the realm I know . . . It stunned me to see that it was even worse than the previous eight years. Because they weren't going to answer the question. And that is another reason why I left this part of the news business, walked away from the news business . . . Because, what this administration has done, in my world, is that they now, and they say this internally, is that they present the, it's not even spin anymore. They prepare the whole package and they present it to you, and they'll give you a little tip, you know, stand by. They'll call you and they give you this package, embargoed, you can't go with it yet. It's all prepared for you in a package. It's all laid out. The Attorney General is going to announce this big settlement with JP Morgan Chase. It's the largest fine ever. The Justice Department prevailed over the bank. And they roll it out. They call it shaping and they call it the contours. They've already shaped what they want to see out there.

The media relations efforts of the government—the complete pre-packaging of stories by a savvy administration who has become good at managing journalists—could be in part what leads to an increase in opinion and commentary. If everyone is being provided with the same information, there has to be a way of differentiating each brand. This reason and the difficulty in being first with a unique story due to social media and mobile technology are points which still go back to a way of distinguishing one journalist's work, and one outlet's from the next.

A Generational Difference?

Lambidakis's comments express and note a generational difference between herself and those of her generation, and younger journalists. She and others have generalized that journalists who, in the first decade of the 2000s, were in the 40 and over age group, are disillusioned and upset by the state of news media today. Their discontent comes from the pace of news, because of the use of the Internet and social media, which they say are responsible for the decline in quality news reporting and storytelling. This is a logical narrative that is easy to tell and seems to make sense, but the evidence from this study—including the interviews with a multigenerational group of journalists—does not paint as clear a divide between old and young journalists. I found younger journalists (under 40), such as the former news producer (6/16/14) and others, who are concerned about the state of news, just as I found older journalists like Bruce Perlmutter and Jack Shafer who are not.

Some older journalists' unhappiness about the changes in news may also stem from an environment where it is increasingly difficult for them to maintain employment and success:

> And I'm not knocking young people, we, gosh, that's the lifeblood. I will say what's different now is when I started out at CBS there was a journeymen system and you started as the lowly person answering the telephones, and then, if you were lucky or you worked hard, you were taught how to cut, you know, to work in radio and cut the tape. And then, I guess I did a good job with that. And then I was taught to be in charge of running the news crews. But somebody taught you at every step of the way. And that does not exist, you're a young person, you're dropped in with a laptop and a camera and you tweet and social media is very paramount. I think that's the most disconcerting. That's the saddest thing for me. And it's not a person who's 25 years old, it's not their fault . . . For the people who work there, it's an enormous amount of pressure because there are fewer and fewer people.
>
> You know all the journalists laid off and put out to pasture . . . There's no place to go so they're going to Aljazeera America, Aljazeera, even people are going to China Television . . . Because the industry doesn't exist anymore if you're over

> a certain age . . . Look who's working, all these great, seasoned journalists with decades of experience, they're, they, they're having to find jobs at China television, with censorship. Because they just want to be in the news, and the news business, and the news business doesn't exist anymore.
>
> I mean the news has always evolved but, God, now, you're just, if you're a certain age you're just holding on to dear life . . . And the ones who are coming up through the ranks, some of them are very good but they don't make any money . . . It was terrible to have to walk out of there. I mean, that is my family . . . I mean, we had an expression, some people said, they're like, CBS doesn't hug you back. But I never found that to be the case. I mean it's sort of dark joke, because you'd slave away, you're working your butt off and you don't ever seem to get rewarded for it, but. And my friends who have been shown the door at other networks. It's, you're just crushed by it. It's just a crushing, devastating experience. (Lambidakis, 2014)

These sentiments are quite different from those of, say, Perlmutter, now Senior Vice President at Conde Nast Entertainment, who has been able to reinvent himself, evolving from news at CNN, MSNBC, then to E!, and RevoltTV, Sean Combs's music network. It seems that the ability to evolve or adapt to the new environment in order to remain successful is the differentiating factor between journalists'—old or young—feelings about changes in the media landscape. Just as there are older journalists who have been able to adapt, there are younger journalists for whom it is proving challenging.

This is consistent with what Usher (2010) found in her analysis, "Goodbye to the news: How out-of-work journalists assess enduring news values and the new media landscape:"

> Findings reveal that these "goodbye" journalists are wedded to an idea of journalism that no longer—and may have never—existed and blame their problems on Wall Street rather than self-reflexively examining the role of their own occupational values and practices in a changing media environment.

Calling It "Point-of-View Journalism" or Similar, rather than Opinion or Commentary

On the August 17, 2014 episode of CNN's "Reliable Sources," host Brian Stelter talked with Frank Sesno, a former CNN bureau chief, now dean of

The George Washington University's School of Media and Public Affairs, and with Jay Rosen, NYU journalism professor and creator of the journalism blog, PressThink. The trio epitomized the range of media critics—from current and former journalists to academics. The trio discussed David Gregory's departure from "Meet the Press," and Chuck Todd's takeover of the program. Stelter had been first to break the news that David Gregory was leaving NBC and "Meet the Press," a Sunday morning competitor to "Reliable Sources." Frank Sesno commented that journalists today need to be having conversations with the audience more and that Gregory wasn't. In addition to connecting with the audience, the three also discussed how program's like Gregory's were perhaps "too inside the beltway" versus appealing to a larger group of audience members.

According to Carroll (2014: 39), as early as 2005, Jay Rosen, at a Harvard conference on blogging, "said that mainstream journalism is 'dying' in part, because it has insisted on objectivity and, in the process, has 'killed the human voice.'" "Blogs," he argued, "marked the return of 'real human voices' and 'real human conversations'" (Rosen, 2005, in Carroll).

When I asked if one of the ways journalists are trying to stay relevant is by having conversations with the audience and more commentary and opinion, Stelter (8/18/14) said,

> I would just make some distinctions first of all off the bat. And I would just say that what I see in national cable television news is exactly what you're describing, I like to use the phrase point-of-view news. Or point-of-view programming, as opposed to opinion. Because I just, on cable news, you know, obviously there's a lot of opinion. But what I think is most striking is that there are an increasing number of programs from a clear point of view, you know, the point of view of the anchor. Whether it's Rachel Maddow or Al Sharpton or Sean Hannity, or even a group of people like . . . "Fox and Friends." I think if, I don't know, I get a little bit lost with the word opinion, as it conjures up to me something different, and it reminds me more of print, like the op-ed pages of the newspaper. But to me, there's this rise of point of view television, and also point-of-view journalism, you know, they kind of go hand in hand although there are some distinctions and differences between them that are important. And I see that in national cable news, particularly in Fox News and MSNBC. It's also visible in CNBC, Fox Business; it's less visible at CNN and Aljazeera America, although it is visible on CNN in some quarters. And, I would say we also see it in some digital news start-ups, I think we do see it at the New York Times in some

corners. So yeah, I would see it out of TV as well but I do think it's a reaction in many ways to the commoditized nature of news, and the desire to add something to it, to add something beyond what's already pervasive, which is the sense of what happened.

Alternately, a CNN digital employee referred to opinion and commentary as "shaping the conflict:

> I will say with respect to sort of like the editorial guidelines, I feel like it's not even worth shaping the conflict; it's more about chasing the gaucho story like I've been sent out with a camera to like, you know, basically ambush a Republican candidate but "yo, how do you feel about vaccines?" or "do you agree with, you know, XYZ crazy-Obama?" and I think that can be a little bit irresponsible at times because we end up serving a story, half that I think is relevant and significant, technically because you know it gets viewers—because everybody wants to know about vaccines and everybody's interested in someone saying something about Obama. I think television news lends itself to that sort of problem.

Amber Phillips (7/23/14) thought that "analysis" is a good term for the type of content we're increasingly seeing. She elaborated:

> [Write] stories with the why and the how and the headline, and more analysis. And that can be tough, because you risk—two pitfalls with that: one, you risk being seen as trying to give opinion, or "this is better as a blog," you know; and the second one is, you risk—with the rest of the media, being seen as falling behind with the daily news. . . . [W]hen you're doing analysis, when you're doing the why and the how and the records, the hamster-wheel kind of reporting, you have to start finding your voice, almost—kind of like a blogger. Because these why-and-how stories are really a product of the Internet, because there are so many sources for readers to find out what's going on in DC, and you have to—you kind of need to: one, speak the language of the Internet for people to read it, but two, like I've been saying, write a story that people will want to invest time to read. So you have to end up developing a voice when you do this analysis, and that's another danger of falling into the opinion and commentary realm. It's a lot of tightrope walking.

Jon Allen (6/9/14) also distinguished between "analysis" as something positive, and "opinion." Allen said:

> I'm encouraged to go out and talk on other media, whether it's being interviewed as a guest on television, radio—I just finished a book tour, and Bloomberg was beyond supportive of it. I haven't really run into that issue. I think all people who are objective news reporters know that they're not supposed to give their opinions in their stories, and they're not supposed to give their opinions as guests. That's not really what we're there to do. But, I think there is some room for analysis. It's not that we're supposed to watch what's going on in front of us and not have a sense that we should be able to tell an audience, not only in our writing but also as a guest on other programs, what it all adds up to.

Rem Rieder (1/20/15) made similar distinctions between "analytic writing" and "conclusionary journalism," which he sees as beneficial, versus opinion and partisan content, but he also noted the slippery slope and blurry boundaries between these.

A TV journalist in Washington (6/18/14) said,

> There's a difference between someone outright saying, "Here's what I believe." And of course there's a difference between that and bias. And just sort of differences in how you cover something . . . I think it's just so much more complex than just opinion. . . .

The TV journalist in Washington (6/18/14) went on to say,

> . . . I get in this type of discussion all the time. And one thing, people are always like, "Oh I can't watch Fox anymore. I can't watch CNN anymore. I can't watch ABC." I'm like, you're totally looking at it completely wrong. It's no . . . you shouldn't choose. It's not that you choose one network to only watch, right? I would argue that you should watch the first half hour. If you're looking for news, the true news. You should watch the first half hour of the morning shows, you should watch the first half hour 6PM on Fox, you should watch, you know, some other. You need to find where the news is. It's not one network that's only gonna offer news and some other network is only gonna offer opinion. I mean that's just, due to the Internet, due to everything, everything's changed.

> In the same way that you go to a website and you're gonna see a bunch of crap. You're not gonna click. If you're searching for straight news [inaudible], if you go to a website, CNN.com, you're gonna go, see a bunch of stuff you're not interested in, but you're gonna go and see a bunch of stuff that you're looking for, so you click on that. You have to do that with TV too. You just have to find where it is.

Richard Benedetto, formerly the White House correspondent for *USA Today*, has made the transition to writing columns for other publications where he expresses his views. Benedetto (3/26/14) said,

> They are columns. They're not news reports. So they're expected to be opinion, but I try, I call it reported columns. If I'm expressing an opinion, I'm just not saying it off the top of my head. This is the way it is. I will say, this is this way because of this. And I'll show evidence. I will use evidence, reported evidence. Here's what *The Washington Post* said about it, here's what the *New York Times* said about it. So that you're using, you're expressing, you're coming to conclusions rather than opinions. You're using evidence to come to conclusions, but you see it based upon your own, through your own eyes. Based upon your own experience with it.

In sum, some journalists prefer to think of opinionated news and commentary in other terms: point-of-view journalism, conversational news, news shaping, news analysis, conclusionary journalism, and reported columns.

How Journalists Who Provide Opinionated Content Think of Themselves and Their Own Work

Partly by design and partly by luck (one critic referred me to another), I interviewed a number of media critics for my study. These critics included Paul Farhi and Erik Wemple of *The Washington Post*, Rem Rieder of *USA Today*, Brian Stelter, host of "Reliable Sources" on CNN, Jack Shafer of *Politico*, and Michael Calderone at *Huffington Post*. Liza Mundy and Frank Sesno additionally act as critics in some of their work and appearances, although that is not their primary role. I reached out to other media critics as well (Dylan Byers at CNN, formerly at *Politico*) but this is the group I spoke with. "While types of media criticism have existed for countless years, media reporting—specifically, having a reporter on the media beat—rose to being a common feature during the media boom of the 1990s" (Fengler 2003, in Bible, 2016). Media beat reporters, or critics, are journalists who cover the media for their respective news organizations. *The Washington Post* also now has Margaret Sullivan, formerly the ombudsman at the *New York Times*. There are a host of other critics including Howard Kurtz, Lisa de Moraes, and others even predating Jack Gould at the *New York Times*. Then there are quasi-academic and academic media critics such as Jim Romenesko, Tom Rosenstiel, Jay Rosen, Michael Schudson, Robert McChesney, and even the writers for *Columbia Journalism Review*, the now-closed *American Journalism Review* and the like.[5]

These different groups of critics occupy similar but different spaces on a spectrum from more journalistic to more academic criticism. And their boundaries seem to be increasingly blurry. The original interview material illustrates the roles of these different groups of critics, or communities of practice, and the ways in which they are increasingly interrelated.

Jack Shafer, Rem Rieder, and David Carr (not interviewed) were part of an informal community of practice of media criticism. They were not formally organized but interacted regularly about professional and social matters (Rieder, 2015; Shafer, 2015). Although they consider other colleagues to have roles that differ somewhat from theirs, other media reporters and critics such as Paul Farhi, Erik Wemple, Michael Calderone, and Brian Stelter are part of a community of practice that acts like a reference group for the journalists (personal interviews in 2014 and 2015). One issue around which this journalistic community of practice interacts is social media use. While some news organizations, like *The Washington Post*, have official policies about their employees' social media use (P. Farhi, personal interview in person at *The Washington Post*, June 4, 2014) and usually encourage them to be active on the platforms, other organizations have no official policies, or their employees do not necessarily know about the policies (Rieder, 2015). So what's appropriate to say through social media is garnered from "common sense" (Rieder, 2015) or looking to one's peers. These journalists provided a perspective different from the others in that they are in the business of opining about, and critiquing, their peers in the media.

When asked how he sees himself versus the other kinds of reporters at *The Washington Post* who are still supposed to be objective, and whether bloggers or columnists are treated differently, Erik Wemple (6/12/14) said:

> I am in the opinions area, so I am fine to write opinions. But I would say that I'm still—objective is kind of a hot-button word—but I would argue that I'm fair to both sides in any dispute, to the extent that I express opinions, generally about the journalism, and not usually about interventionist foreign policy, or abortion or death penalty. It's opinions with a small "o" as far as most of the political discussions go these days.

When asked, Wemple also discussed who he thinks of as his peers, or people who occupy similar roles in other places:

> Sure, Calderone, Byers, Shafer, David Carr; that whole crew. I think that's part of my—depending on the person, maybe that's a little bit aspirational. But that's generally my cohort, I would think. I don't think that many people outside of here, or outside of journalism are really paying that much attention to whether I'm an opinion person or whether I'm a news person, because sometimes I'm reporting news and sometimes I'm opining. So, I think that that is a consideration that's very much within the industry more than it is outside the industry.

Wemple (6/12/14) distinguished between the roles that he and Paul Farhi occupy at *The Post*:

> He's in the newsroom and I am on opinion, so we report up to different people, but obviously we share the same "topical" obsessions, so we'll talk once in a while, but nothing coordinated.

When asked if he considers himself part of the group of media critics and columnists with Wemple, Farhi, Stelter and Shafer, Rem Rieder (1/20/15) said,

> The people you mention do kind of different things. I always thought of Paul Farhi more as a media, when Howie Kurtz was at *The Post* he was a media writer as far as a media critic. Paul does a lot of, very much reported pieces. (And) Eric is kind of a media blogger. Brian does something different. There are more people covering the media than there have ever been, but they do it in very different ways. Paul, who I respect enormously, is more of a media reporter. Shafer is kind of a peer columnist. David Carr does reported columns, but is certainly a media critic. The ultimate challenge, I think, (is) and there are so few of them now, is for "ombudsmen" when you are writing about your own company or own publication all the time. We did a piece in AJR once and the headline was like, "The loneliest job in the newsroom."

When I asked Jack Shafer (2/11/15), who currently writes press criticism for *Politico*, and previously for Slate, Reuters, and the *Washington City Paper*, if he prefers the media critic role to a more traditional objective kind of journalism role, he, to my surprise, said "no":

> Well, as the editor of *City Paper* I was editing columns in news coverage and feature stories as well. I'm like a gastronome who will eat great street food, go to fancy restaurants, and drink Coca-Cola on the side. I'm the ocean that refuses no river. So, I wouldn't say that much has changed, except for the fact that when I wrote press criticism for the *City Paper* it was part-time, it was the wee a.m. hours that I could squeak out and then most of my work was editing and managing a staff.

Shafer characterized his work similarly to how Wemple describes his own work: "I mean the things that I do are reported commentaries. I link to all of the primary sources that I possibly can." Wemple's blog description says that it is a "reported opinion blog." The two writers have similar career trajectories as well. Like Shafer, Wemple was previously editor at *Washington City Paper*, then editor at the now-defunct *TBD*, prior to going to *The Post*. Shafer continued:

> So, that a reader, if I'm saying such and such a thing happened or so and so wrote something, there is a link to it so somebody can independently verify my assertions and argue with me . . . And it varies from column to column. Sometimes I'm making an argument, which is not exactly commentary, it is probably closer to mathematical theorem or a philosophical proof. That there are multiple ways to skin a cat. You can do it with humor, you can do it with sarcasm, you can do it with logic, you can do it with . . . reporting. And so I probably don't sit around and think, "Oh, I'm Walter Lipmann writing my or Eric Sevareid writing my learning thesis in a paneled room." I think I tend to mix it up.

When I mentioned that Shafer is allowed to show more personality, and suggested it is a stylistic matter, he said,

> Well, one of the reasons that you want to be stylistic is that even a daily news reporter has drilled into him some sort of stylistic discipline. You are supposed to write tight leads, you are supposed to have a nutgraf that tells the reader where it is going, you are supposed to have a kicker that sums up and signals a sort of completion of the journalistic mission. But everybody is encouraged, in the business, to develop those talents of conveying information as efficiently and as intelligently as possible. I'm probably that times one and a half, I'm allowed to make juxtapositions and jokes and

say rude things. But [in] a lot of these pieces I could extract from them all the personality and all attempts at cleverness and you'd probably have a very straight news story.

I asked Shafer if he thought that most journalists who previously were doing what we called objective journalism secretly harbor desires to be able to express an opinion or commentary. He said, "It depends. Some people realize that they are not especially good at it or don't have a desire to do it. They want to do straight news . . . I don't think they are wearing civilian clothes and underneath those there is a superhero costume, ready to expose, to express an opinion."

When I asked Shafer's friend Rem Rieder the same question, Rieder said,

> I think there is a mix. (I mean) I've never done a survey on this, but I think there are a lot of people uncomfortable with it, they've been doing what they've been doing for so long that trying so hard not to express opinion, that they . . . I've noticed with some people, they have to write these voices columns, where they are not necessarily supposed to take opinions, but they are supposed to be more personal, and for some it is quite an adjustment, it is uncomfortable at first. For others, it is liberating as hell.

I then asked Rieder if he's ever found his media critic role challenging, critiquing his peers and competitors. He said,

> Yeah. I mean. I guess, it could seem uncomfortable; sometimes you are critiquing your friends. But it just kind of goes with the territory. You have to try not to let the friendships get in the way. I mean, the best person for this—have you talked to Jack Shafer? . . . He is an excellent media critic, but he's just fearless. Mark Lisheron, a terrific writer and a friend of mine, did a piece for me on Shafer at *AJR*,[6] and one of the things people would say about him is that he was just so rigorous, that it didn't matter. If his mother had committed journalistic sin, Jack would be flapping her around . . . And I have a friend who has been in this business a long time who once said, "Ya know, I couldn't do what you do," this is just in terms of running the magazine, as well as a column because I feel comfortable running something that puts friends in a bad light, but I think Shafer is absolutely right. He is uncompromising and that is how it should be.

Michael Calderone (7/2/14) said,

> To a certain extent I can do kind of point of view journalism. I don't offer any straight partisan opinions on the news of the day, but based on my reporting, you know, at the *Huffington Post*, I think we have a little more latitude than say, the *New York Times*, which has a more dispassionate tone in their news coverage. That doesn't necessarily mean our news coverage is slanted in a partisan way, but, we can make a little bit stronger statements about what we're writing about.

Calderone gave an example:

> This week, or the past week, I've been looking back a lot on coverage of the Iraq War and coverage these past few weeks on the unraveling in Iraq, and I think I can make much stronger criticism of the Bush administration's push into war, the faulty intelligence and the media . . . I can make some stronger statements than I could if I was working as a news reporter at the *New York Times*. Doesn't mean that they're necessarily partisan statements. I don't think. I think they're statements based on what happened at the time in 2002 and 2003 and not hiding behind words like you know, critics say the Bush administration, you know presented a bogus case for war. I think they can just say some of these things more straight out. . . . And I think that type of tone does work better online, than, you know, and I think you see even more legacy based outlets, more traditional outlets, you know, having some writers at least adopting a tone that allows them to speak, you know, get right to the heart of the matter. So you know, even places, you know we've seen places like the *New York Times* and *The Washington Post*, you know, employ reporters that are in some ways a hybrid.

When asked about Ezra Klein's reporting and analysis, Calderone called it "explanatory journalism," adding another term to the list:

> It wasn't just that he was kind of spouting opinion. I think his opinions were grounded in facts, and he often presented these opinions with several charts, and you know, independent analysis, and analysis from experts and people at think-tanks, and things

of that nature. So, you know, I think, and that sort of writing has done very well and it's sort of helped foster new kind of explanatory journalism trend over the last couple weeks and months. Where other sites are trying to launch these features to kind of more explain the news or provide data to enhance the news instead of just who, what, when, where, why and how.

When asked which other journalists he would consider his peers, Calderone said:

Umm, less Ezra, I mean he'll do some media stuff but he's more policy focus. Yeah, I mean Eric Wemple is an interesting case, and you know, because he works for the opinion section of *The Washington Post*. Eric has a longtime experience as a reporter and an editor, so he kind of merges the two. He'll do opinion. His posts are opinionated and he works for the opinion section, he works for Fred Hiatt on the editorial, who works for the editorial, who runs the editorial page, but at the same time he'll do independent reporting and so I think his views on media, and when he's especially critical, it's usually grounded in independent reporting and analysis. He's not just kind of riffing, he's not just throwing opinions out there. . . . I would consider Eric somebody I compete with, although in some ways we do different types of stuff. He's running the blog all day; I used to run a blog all day when I was at *Politico*, now I primarily do reported pieces and you know, occasionally more bloggy posts thrown in there.

Then I asked about the spectrum of media critics. Calderone said,

Another one that's, you know, Brian Stelter as well. I think if you want to look at, pretty increased opinion out there. He's been very interesting to watch his evolution. You know Brian, not just that he started a TV blog and was plucked by the *New York Times* when he was 21- or 22-years-old, and Brian for the most part did very straight news reporting on the media for the business section of the *Times*, you know, since he's had his own show over the past year on CNN, he's kind of broken out and given more, offered more point of view on air, which I think you have to do if you're a TV host.

It's sort of what Jay Rosen, the NYU professor always talks about when he talks about the view from nowhere. That too many legacy news organizations have this view from nowhere where it's always, you know, Democrats say this, Republicans say this, and we're just sort of putting it out there. We're not kind of stepping on the scale in some way to say, OK, the Democrats actually have a better point here, the Republicans have a better point here. And if you look at someone like Brian, I think Brian does more media criticism probably than he did at the *New York Times* where he was more of a straight media reporter. I mean it's a strange thing, and as I talked about before, I teach a class on media criticism although my job at *Huffington Post* is media reporter, so I mean sometimes I feel like I'm doing more reporting, sometimes I feel like my pieces are more critical [inaudible] you know, but, in a lot of ways, the two really, to me, complement each other. And you know, I think Dylan Byers at *Politico* as well. He does straight pieces for the *Politico* website on the media, and I think on the blog that he does, he'll often venture more into analysis, or more into criticism of the media. I think you can kind of wear both hats, and you know, do both the reporting or do more commentary. Or do a bit of both.

Richard Benedetto (3/26/14) said he's less comfortable with opinion:

> I used to like to go on C-SPAN because they played straight. And I like to go on and play it straight. I don't like to go on shows like a Chris Matthews show or something like that where you, they're asking you to express your opinion or get into a debate with somebody on an issue. I remember going on one show one time, way back, going way back into the eighties, when Gary Hart had . . . they wanted me to get into the middle of that. It was just not for me. It's not my thing.

Benedetto, however, as previously described, today writes what he describes as "reported columns" from a mostly conservative point of view.

Given that these journalists are in the business of providing opinionated content, it would follow that they think there's a space for both news and opinion in media, and a reason that people like and need both of them. Wemple (6/12/14) said:

> Forever in newspapers, there's been this category of news analysis—like the *New York Times*—forever. I don't know when the first particular branding happened, but you know how when big things

happened they had their straight-up news story and their news analysis story. I would venture that there are only 10 or 15 people who have ever chosen the straight-up news story over the news analysis story. But only because I think the news analysis story uses most of the facts that are in the news story, but puts them in the context. Oftentimes, the news analysis story is basically a Trojan horse—a stalking horse, I guess I should say—for opinion, and allows the reporter to express a little bit of opinion analysis or tilt. And I think that's what makes those stories more readable and more and more edifying, oftentimes, than the straight-up news stories. I could be wrong on that, but that's certainly been my habit over the years. Because news and analysis go together, and they're only a heartbeat away from opinion. My feeling is that if I can report and provide news perspective and a little bit of opinion at the same time, so much the better. There are many times, however, when I feel that just the facts are warranted, if something is new enough and doesn't need a lot of opinion just yet. And there's also times I go straight up the middle of the road simply because I don't feel comfortable yet taking a stand on one side or the other—when there's more to be investigated, and I really need to chew it over. It's a case by case sort of thing . . . It is neat to be able to do both. Here in the opinions, they have no problem if you pursue news on your blog as well as opinion. I'm quite sure that's encouraged.

While some journalists have found the transition from objective news to expressing a point of view difficult, others embrace the voice they're increasingly encouraged to express in their coverage. For example, Amber Phillips (7/23/14) said:

> . . . especially with the politics team, we're kind of leading the way at the *Las Vegas Sun*, and part of that is because we have a magazine that we started, which is also kind of one of the future [trends?] in newspapers in general, is having a website and then a weekly magazine. The *Washington Examiner* does it; we're doing it. And not focus on your daily print product, or drop it all together. So that's another incentive to push toward more of that analysis, that kind of reader-friendly voice, that—you know—I'm the reader's friend in Washington helping them figure out who's kind of talking BS and what's actually working well for their benefit.

I love it. I absolutely love it. It's something I did at Digital First Media, it's something I'm doing at the *Sun*—it's why I took the job at the *Sun*—and I'm hoping—I'm actually banking my career on the fact that this is the future of journalism; and when every other paper in DC, or every publication is finding their model is like paper of records—this happened, so-and-so senator said this—this isn't working anymore, because it's not. I'm hoping that journalists like me will have an opportunity to grow and shine. So, not only do I love it, I'm kind of banking my career on it.

Furthermore, Phillips, who became a writer for *The Washington Post*'s "The Fix" in May 2015, said in December 2015 that her job is to provide a "smart take" on what everybody else is doing. Phillips said that "everything has to be creative, a different look" and that "the best media organizations right now are so difficult to explain" ("The Future of Journalism and Politics," 2015). She reiterated her thoughts from our earlier 2014 interview, and said that what political journalism has to be today is "kind of like analysis, not opinion or editorializing" but "real talk." On *The Washington Post*'s website, when one now hovers over the heading "Analysis" above an article, the description that appears reads, "Interpretation of the news based on evidence, including data, as well as anticipating how events might unfold based on past events."

As a member of the editorial board at *USA Today*, Mastio has a different vantage point from most of the other journalists I spoke with. His job is to write opinion.

Of this role, Mastio (8/7/14) said:

I like to be able to be open, to be myself and so in an age of Facebook and Twitter I want a job where I can say what I think. I think I have an important role here at the editorial board, because I'm the most conservative person on the board and that, it's not just important that *USA Today* have that inside its editorial board, but it's important that you know, that readers know that even if you know, the editorials generally take a liberal stance on things, you know, center left, I should at least give them a little credit. Give us a little credit. That readers know that that voice is represented there. There too, that it's not shut out, that these opinions aren't reached without, you know, somebody hit them over the head with a bat every day.

Mastio said that whereas he's the most conservative member of the editorial board at *USA Today*, he was "actually the liberal of the editorial board at the *Washington Times*." Of his work at the *Washington Times*, Mastio said:

> The opinion staff at the *Times* was great. It's as big as this staff. My boss there was Brett Decker and he was *a Wall Street Journal* alum, so a top notch, a top notch journalist. But, you know, he came from a very Christian conservative background, very traditionalist Catholic, and I'm you know, from the libertarian wing of the party. So, it was actually harder to be myself there than it was, than it is here because you know, I couldn't run things that were pro-gay marriage or you know, that really went far afield from general republican orthodoxy. And here you know, I can run as far afield to the left or as far afield to the right as I want to go. But you know, I grew up here, I came here at 25 . . . this is home.

While Op-Ed sections of newspapers have existed since the earliest partisan presses in the United States, perhaps the views previously expressed in the Op-Ed sections are being replaced by that content throughout news outlets. In former editorial board editor Chris Satullo's view of editorial boards and their endorsements in presidential elections (3/14/16), "nobody cares anymore." In those races, people feel they get ample information to make up their own minds. Endorsements only retain influence, he believes, in local elections where information on candidates and their views is scarce.

Examining journalistic discourse about opinion and civility in news brings to light the wide range of views journalists hold. Journalists' divergent views of opinion, commentary, and incivility in news reflect the communities of practice in which they have membership and operate. Whether journalists think it's important or not, there are examples—few though they may be—that show that the mere existence of opinion in political news discourse does not necessitate incivility. Civility in opinionated news discourse is possible. One well-known example serves as a case study which will be discussed in the following chapter.

5

Opinion ≠ Incivility

The Case of PBS's Brooks and Shields*

In a political environment viewed as containing much uncivil discourse, and in which opinion journalism is often blamed, Mark Shields and David Brooks give their disparate political views on the PBS "NewsHour" with exemplary civility. Early in 2012, the first annual Allegheny College Prize for Civility in Public Life[1] was awarded to Mark Shields and David Brooks, regular Friday night political commentators on the PBS "NewsHour." Shields, the resident liberal, and Brooks, the conservative, give their views in response to the various moderators' questions and, as noted in *The Christian Science Monitor*, "though they may disagree with each other on issues, they do so with good-natured civility" (Hughes, 2012). For the past 10 years, a national representative survey has found that "PBS and its member stations are ranked first in trust among nationally known institutions and are considered an 'excellent' use of tax dollars by the American public. The yearly study has also called PBS the most fair network for news and public affairs 10 consecutive times" (PBS, 2013).

What various definitions of civility make clear is that there is a line—albeit at times a blurry one—between opinion journalism and disagreement, and incivility. Throughout the history of American journalism, "expressions of opinion have been readily accepted by the journalistic community when they are demarcated as such. Traditional journalistic norms have condoned op-ed sections of newspapers and opinion columns for decades, so long as they are clearly cordoned off from the rest of the paper. Movements such as new journalism and advocacy journalism entailed the insertion of the journalist's

---

*Passages included with permission from SAGE Journals. doi: 10.1177/1931243114557598.

perspective and opinions in stories" (Meltzer, 2010: 116). Therefore, what is really at issue is not that these are journalists expressing their opinions, but that they are doing so under the label of "objective news" and not commentary. Another factor in the distaste for opinion journalism on TV in particular may be that TV visually exploits the spectacle of bombastic sounding off. "So something journalistically unattractive is visually interesting to viewers, benefiting network ratings, and making it even more distasteful to traditional journalistic values" (Meltzer, 2010: 116). As Gutmann and Thompson (2012) write, "compromisers do not make the most compelling television." Some people believe that giving news with opinion is actually more realistic and honest than seeking to achieve the ideal of objectivity which may be strived for but never reached.

Mediated Political Discourse

Central to idealizations of the public sphere is that those who participate do so with informed and reasoned opinions, not emotional and knee-jerk reactions. But many people's cultural experience of public life is not one that encourages or motivates civic participation. Mutz's (2002) and others' research on political crosstalk and cross-cutting networks has found that people tend to avoid talking about politics with others who think differently from themselves. They avoid talking politics in order to preserve social relationships and to avoid feelings of cognitive dissonance when faced with ideas contrary to their own. When people do become involved in cross-cutting political discussion, it decreases the likelihood that they will participate in politics in the future. This is at odds with ideals of discussion and debate thought crucial to the health of the public sphere. Instead, research shows that it is homogeneous political networks and interactions that increase the likelihood of political participation (Mutz, 2006). Mutz (2006) aptly describes this dilemma pitting deliberative democracy against participatory democracy. What are we to do if selectively paying attention to only the affirming niche media outlets spurs us to participate? People must not be fearful of engaging with diverging viewpoints. Mere disagreement does not have to be unpleasant. It only becomes that way when it devolves into nasty shouting matches. Disagreement could in fact be invigorating and thought-provoking if carried out in a polite, rational way. Perhaps we are just lacking sufficient models.

Some hope lies in Mutz's findings that it may be more palatable to have politically cross-cutting experiences with people with whom we have weak ties, such as in the workplace (Mutz, 2006), or through mediated communication, as on TV (Mutz & Martin, 2001). In fact, Mutz (2007) suggests that it is precisely through TV that people are most likely to be exposed to divergent political views, and her study found that the civil delivery of opposing political views through TV is more likely to lead viewers to consider the rationale for the opposing views legitimate. Conversely, uncivil and "in-your-face" televised political discourse is likely to lead viewers to evaluate the opposing views as illegitimate (Mutz, 2007). Other research finds that uncivil televised political discourse adversely affects people's trust in government (Mutz & Reeves, 2005). On the other end of the spectrum, Barber (1999: 40) points out the tendency for civility to be thought of as boring, interpreted to mean "docility or tranquility, a kind of politeness that evades the central conflicts that are the real stuff of politics." This, too, is a misconception according to Barber: ". . . though deliberative discourse may be something less than riveting entertainment, it is neither conflict-avoiding nor soporific." Herbst (2010) underscores the importance of argument and debate in democratic politics and recommends that Americans, especially young Americans, need to become accustomed to and learn techniques for a productive culture of argument. Taken together, these research findings point to the need for examples of what productive, mediated, opinionated political talk can look like. A conversation analysis of the Shields/Brooks weekly political discussions during 2012 on the PBS "NewsHour" reveals ways each frames his position without resorting to accusations, polemics, name-calling, or other such tactics—indeed, while maintaining civility.

Method

The exchanges discussed in this chapter were examined using conversation analysis with the goal of revealing ways Brooks and Shields each frame their positions without resorting to uncivil tactics and carry on a productive conversation containing divergent viewpoints. According to Goodwin and Heritage (1990: 283), conversation analysis "seeks to describe the underlying social organization—conceived as an institutionalized substratum of interactional rules, procedures, and conventions—through which orderly and intelligible social interaction is made possible."

It requires "an integrated analysis of action, mutual knowledge, and social context" (Goodwin & Heritage, 1990: 284). In discourse analysis, and particularly conversation analysis, a basic construct is that of a "cooperative principle" by which those engaged in discourse may be considered competent if they communicate adequately, honestly, relevantly, and clearly (Grice, 1975). Jacobs and Jackson (1983) add a "reason rule" to this construct, by which participants in conversation are able to adjust their responses to the statements or perspectives of the other participants. They are not required to agree, only to be reasonable; however, the situation itself may provide some encouragement to agree.

A total of 35 programs from January 6 through November 2, 2012, were analyzed. The PBS website gives access to both the video versions and the printed transcripts of each program. Both versions were consulted for this analysis. The conversation topics, agreements, and disagreements from Shields and from Brooks and from both, memorable phrases, quotes, jokes, laughter, and crosstalk or interruptions were all noted in the analysis. Most sessions were moderated by Judy Woodruff, but some by Jeffrey Brown or Gwen Ifill. Early in the year, most segments featured references to those engaging in the Republican primary campaigns and debates. Once Mitt Romney became the "last person standing," the discussions centered on Romney and President Obama, along with topics not related to the election. In terms of the third party to these discussions, the transcripts revealed what the moderator asked them to do and what they were not invited to do, along with the moderator's demeanor.

Findings

Use of Humor

One of the most interesting factors in the process of analyzing 10 months of news analysis was the humor found on the part of both Shields and Brooks. Although Shields was much more likely, by a count of 61 to 22, to make a joke or to use an unusual and humorous phrase, a narrowed use of their quotations during the entire 10 months resulted in 50 for Shields and 44 for Brooks, he being the more stoic or perhaps serious of the pair. For example, by February, when the unemployment rate declined, Shields noted that Republicans almost seemed saddened by the news. His response was that "You almost wanted to say, cheer up, fellows. Eventually, things will get worse" (PBS "NewsHour," February 3, 2012). When Romney said, "I'm not concerned about the very poor" and their safety net, Brooks said, "People who are in touch or see the electorate as human beings, those words would not come out of your mouth" ("PBS "NewsHour," February 3, 2012). To Shields it meant that Romney comes across as "a guy who was born in a log cabin in Grosse Point, Michigan, with silver earplugs," as a guy who is "really tone deaf" (PBS "NewsHour," February 3, 2012). During the Michigan primary, Romney said that perhaps if he were "to light my hair on fire, I might be doing better," to which Brooks responded, "You don't say, oh, these Republican voters are so crazy, if I would light my hair on fire, they would be impressed" (PBS "NewsHour," February 28, 2012).

Additional exchanges in the conversations on the program in March displayed Brooks's and Shields's humorous style. Romney's foremost opponent was Rick Santorum, whom Shields described as having "a two-by-four" on his shoulder rather than a chip, and who had done the "unthinkable" by saying that John Kennedy's Houston minister's speech "made him throw up." Meanwhile, according to Shields, Romney was coming across as "Don Draper out of Mad Men," or as a would-be "white knight" out to defeat those who would raid the "public treasury" (PBS "NewsHour," March 2, 2012). Romney's problem of authenticity came to the fore as he tried to be "Southern" in Mississippi by saying "Hello, y'all" and talking about eating "cheesy grits," not a term in vogue in the south. Instead, Brooks advised, he should stop "doing the same things over and over again, not controlling the discussion with something you are actually offering" (PBS "NewsHour," March 9, 2012).

In August, the issue of sequestration, or letting the Bush tax cuts expire among other dire things, brought out the gallows humor in Brooks. He said, "They said to themselves, we're going to force ourselves to cut a budget deal with each other. And if we don't do it, we will hit ourselves in the face with a hammer. And that will be so bad, we will do it. The problem is, suppose you don't do it. Then you end up hitting yourself in the face with a hammer." Shields responded, "I think the Republicans are trying to make the case, which is a hard one to make, that sequestration is this terrible plot foisted upon them. Seventy percent of congressional Republicans voted for it." Though Brooks had lamented that Pentagon planners would not know what to do, Shields noted that "half the cuts come out of school lunches and Head Start" (PBS "NewsHour," August 3, 2012). The use of humor by both men about what could be a highly emotionally and politically charged subject enables them to converse with good will, positive spirits, and productive speech. In addition to quick wits, the clever remarks are made possible by grounded knowledge of the subject and the facts.

Willingness to Listen to Others and Exercising Self-Control

Among the definitions reviewed for civility are the "willingness to listen to others and a fair-mindedness in deciding when accommodations to their views should reasonably be made" (Rawls, 1993: 217, as cited in Ben-Porath, 2007); and "an agreement on how to disagree and the exercise of self-control" (Peck, 1996, as cited in Ben-Porath, 2007: 4). In the following conversations, although Shields and Brooks do not agree with several of each other's comments, they listen, acknowledge the other, and exercise self-control in their responses. Rather than spending much time discussing the third presidential debate on October 26, Shields and Brooks talked about the importance of Ohio to the election. Brooks mentioned the "pretty broad prosperity" in Eastern Ohio due to the production of shale gas. Shields agreed, noting that this year you can "forget the Big Apple and Big D and LA. It is Chillicothe, Zanesville and Steubenville that is—this is the big casino of this election." With the importance of the auto bailout that "Romney . . . is still trying to explain," Obama is "running better with whites and white males in Ohio," Shields said. Brooks pointed out, however, and Shields agreed, that "it's not a slam-dunk for Obama." When Brooks said that Romney was going "big, with big change," Shields retorted that "I have heard Romney talk about big change, big change. I know he is large bills, but I didn't know he was big change" (PBS "NewsHour," October 26, 2012). At that point, the discussion dissolved into laughter. The only mentions of the third debate came from Shields, who decried the differences between the "old Mitt, who said, Iraq war, I was for it, I supported it then, I support it now." Then came the new Mitt with his talk of "peace, peace, peace." In terms of Iran, "as recently as months ago," Romney was "talking about an aerial strike, and now he is saying, no, I'm all for sanctions. We have to do it peacefully and diplomatically." Brooks agreed (PBS "NewsHour," October 26, 2012).

In another example when Shields and Brooks discussed the second presidential debate, according to Shields, Romney became "peevish, he became waspish, . . . petulant, and . . . hectoring," which led to a "solid Obama victory." Brooks agreed that "people liked Obama's presence, his forcefulness," but in his view the two had reached "equilibrium." On the issue of women, Shields claimed that with his five mentions of Planned Parenthood, Obama seemed to be playing to the issues of abortion and contraception. Romney, however, Brooks said, seemed more concerned with the so-called "waitress moms," who may be most interested in the economy (PBS "NewsHour," October 19, 2012). Although Shields and Brooks align themselves with different political ideologies and parties, their mutual respect, interest in furthering their own and others' understanding, and ability to exercise self-control lead them to listen and consider the other's comments and position. Part of exercising self-control entails responding to the other's comment with disagreement about the merits of the point made, or aspects neglected, but not personal attack.

Use of Bolstering

In the exchanges between Brooks and Shields, each is not embarrassed or afraid to agree with the other, and they are even frequently seen to use bolstering in their conversations. Bolstering validates the other's statement and extends it by adding further evidence or examples (Stiff & Mongeau, 2003). One example of their use of bolstering was in the discussion of Romney's trip abroad in July 2012. In London, Romney seemed to wish to tell the British how to organize the Olympic Games based on his own experience in Salt Lake City. For Brooks, Romney should not have even gone to London, indeed, the "little gaffe was just icing on the cake to a deep anxiety that they are not running a coherent, effective campaign, and it's the candidate who is overruling a lot of the things that need to be done." Shields summed it all up saying, "You expect somebody to go to the United Kingdom and to praise Judi Dench and the royal family. . . . I think it draws attention, quite frankly, to the dressage factor." Soon after London, Romney went to Israel and attended fundraisers, which perplexed both of these commentators (PBS "NewsHour," July 27, 2012).

In another example of bolstering, in September Shields and Brooks compared and contrasted Romney and Obama, agreeing that to Romney growth comes through tax cuts and to Obama growth comes through stimulus spending. Brooks claimed that Romney is a "good person if he knows you," and Shields agreed that Romney has a "personal ethic, but not a public policy." The 47% comments had become public by then and Shields and Brooks agreed that they not only "played into the stereotype," but also showed "contempt and disdain" for the poor, piling on top of Romney's earlier comments about his wife's driving a "couple of Cadillacs," and his US$10,000 bet during the primary campaign (PBS "NewsHour," September 28, 2012). Here again, we can see the men building on and extending each other's comments.

Agreements and Disagreements

During these 35 episodes of the "NewsHour," 55 sources of agreement were counted, with Shields agreeing with Brooks 25 times, Brooks agreeing with Shields 20 times, and each mutually agreeing 10 times. Of the 18 examples of disagreement, Shields disagreed with Brooks 13 times; Brooks disagreed with Shields 2 times, and each mutually disagreed 3 times. Shields was much more likely to say immediately that he either agreed or disagreed, whereas Brooks often had to be asked by the moderator and his agreements were often of the "yes, but" variety. So, considering their opposite political and philosophical viewpoints, what did they find to agree and disagree about? They agreed on the facts, or what Jamieson, Fallis, and Darr call "consensual facts" necessary for grounding engaged arguments in political debates (Jamieson, Fallis, & Darr, 2013).

Pure job numbers would be difficult to disagree upon, but implications of those numbers became more problematic over the 10-month period. However, in January, Shields "didn't question David's analysis of the long-term implications" of a good jobs report. Still, he said, "good news is really intoxicating. Americans are starved for good news" (PBS "NewsHour," January 6, 2012). He also agreed with Brooks in regard to Romney's need to "tell his story," but disagreed that the Bain Capital story could ever be a positive for Romney (PBS "NewsHour," January 13, 2012). With unemployment even lower by February, Brooks claimed that presidents "do not control the economy under their watch," but Shields countered that the president "did take dramatic, bold, controversial steps . . . and that there were major policy changes . . . at the outset of his administration" (PBS "NewsHour," February 3, 2012).

Shields and Brooks agreed that the contraception portion of the Affordable Care Act had been a mistake, Shields calling it "indefensible," and Brooks saying it was "enormous" (PBS "NewsHour," February 3, 2012). They further agreed that the compromise reached on this issue had been successful, Shields saying that on the issue of "religious liberty," the administration "had stepped back from the brink," and Brooks going even further saying that it "shows deference, it shows respect" (PBS "NewsHour," February 10, 2012).

In June, Romney averred that he would "repeal and rescind" the Dream Act. When Congress denied passage of the Act, Obama put it into effect with what Brooks called "a stroke of the pen," calling it a "good policy" accomplished by "bad means." At that point, Shields said that he "emphatically" disagreed with that criticism, in that it was a "fair and reasonable policy for people who came here, were brought here by their parents" early in their lives (PBS "NewsHour," June 22, 2012).

The issue of a nuclear Iran found Shields and Brooks in agreement that the president had made a very strong statement indicating that the United States would not tolerate such a move. Brooks said that part of the purpose was to "hold the Israelis off from doing anything rash," and Shields thought the president "was just sending a message to both sides that we're serious about this . . . Israel, don't act. And, Iran, you better be very careful" (PBS "NewsHour," March 2, 2012). Agreement could also be found in March regarding good job numbers, which Shields called "sand in the gears" of Republicans "expecting to run on the economy," and which Brooks called "without question, good news" (PBS "NewsHour," March 9, 2012).

In a discussion about Afghanistan, Shields claimed that the situation there was now being influenced by the "iron rule of history" in that "armies of occupation throughout human history are unpopular." Besides that, he said, "nobody can define what the mission is now." Brooks disagreed, saying that the mission is to "create an Afghan army that can defend the country, so it doesn't descend back into civil war." Shields countered that it is a "failed mission" because "we are propping up a corrupt regime." Brooks agreed that

Hamid Karzai is neither "admirable nor [a] reliable ally" but said that what the United States needs is a "basic level of stability" rather than a "civil war, which will be a breeding ground for Taliban" (PBS "NewsHour," March 16, 2012).

In a discussion about Paul Ryan's budget proposal, Shields called it "science fiction" that "favors the rich over the middle class by 65% to 28%," in that all the "advantages go, in terms of the tax side of it, to the best-off." Brooks also had his "doubts about it," but saw it as a "step" that could help avoid "a fiscal catastrophe" even though it "doesn't balance the budget," it "increases spending 3 percent a year," and "it doesn't shrink government" (PBS "NewsHour," March 23, 2012). Once the House had rejected the president's budget proposal and adopted the Ryan budget, Brooks once again called it a "step," and yet nothing could really be done until after the election since the Simpson-Bowles bill had been defeated. Shields called the failure of Simpson-Bowles "proof that bipartisanship is no longer possible." He said that the "indefensible" Ryan budget is "the blueprint that House Republicans are laying down right now for the lame-duck session" following the election (PBS "NewsHour," March 30, 2012).

Discussion: How Do We Account for Civility?

We began with the question: How do they, one liberal and one conservative, manage to engage in civil conversations about sensitive issues week after week for nearly a year, or actually for year after year? Our observations from the analysis include factors based on the "NewsHour" format and factors based on the men themselves.

Factors Based on the "NewsHour" Format

In almost all cases, Brooks and Shields were addressed by first name and generally asked for their "take" or their view on very specific matters. The topics themselves were introduced by the moderator and, of course, were based on events of the week. They were never encouraged to contend with each other or with the moderator's questions and they never did so. The scene in which the two of them sit side-by-side and right across a narrow table from the moderator would seem to promote a nonconfrontational atmosphere. The usual moderator, Judy Woodruff, generally leads off with a gentle introduction and/or humor. For instance, on November 2, she said, "Welcome gentlemen. It's just another Friday night. Not much going on." The response, of course, was laughter. Most episodes feature laughter, some at her comments, but some generated by either Shields or Brooks. Certainly, humor and laughter can take the edge off disagreement and foster a convivial rather than a tense atmosphere.

When asked about the civility award, Shields insisted that they were the "beneficiaries of the standards laid down by Robert MacNeil and Jim Lehrer," the founders of the PBS "NewsHour." Brooks agreed, saying, "When you come on this show, there are certain expectations. And you—it is easy to fall into the expectations of civility and intelligence. And so it's just a pleasure to be part of the show." However, before that accommodating response, Brooks said, "I want to apologize for punching Mark at the end of the . . . Unfortunately, I lost my temper and I . . ." Judy Woodruff bantered back, "And maybe you will never come to blows on the "NewsHour." Is that right?" Shields replied, "If he pushes that corporate tax thing . . ." (PBS "NewsHour," February, 24, 2012). Joking aside, the expectations of the program are that all present will conduct themselves with civility and intelligence, exemplifying the principles of willingness to listen to others, exercising self-control, and fair-mindedness.

Factors Based on Brooks and Shields Themselves

These two people are so comfortable with themselves and with each other, they both seem able to lob insults at the other without becoming insulting. For instance, when Brooks claimed that immigration would not play a large part in the election, Shields disagreed, saying, "David's presentation is, as always, thoughtful and reflective. Unfortunately, it's divorced from political reality." Laughter was the only response (PBS "NewsHour," April 27, 2012). Again, when Brooks said that money would not affect the outcome of the Wisconsin gubernatorial recall, Judy Woodruff said, "Let it be noted. Mark just deeply sighed." Brooks said, "He just deeply sighed. It's a sign of deep disrespect," to which Shields replied, "Respect, but sympathy." Brooks concluded, "Sympathy. Oh, good. He's sympathizing for my ignorance" (PBS "NewsHour," June 8, 2012).

Sometimes the humorous barbs were directed at others. On one occasion, a previous guest on the "NewsHour" was a professor who thought that whoever won Ohio would win the election. When the moderator asked for their opinion on the matter, Shields said, "I never argue with a tenured professor." Brooks retorted, "I often argue with tenured professors, but this one happens to have stumbled upon the truth" (PBS "NewsHour," October 26, 2012). Brooks's attitude toward civility, however, emerged in their discussion of the vice presidential debate. As noted earlier, Shields claimed that "Joe Biden's default facial expression is a smile," whereas Brooks referred to Biden's behavior as "weird smiling." Indeed, he continued, "If I had interrupted Mark—or if anybody came on the "NewsHour" and behaved the way Biden did, we would kick them off in the middle of the set. It is just not what discussions should be like. And not only the "NewsHour." You could go on Hardball, and you don't talk that way" (PBS "NewsHour," October 12, 2012).

Looking at the comportment of both Shields and Brooks on other broadcast events, although neither is a "fighter," each displays on occasion a somewhat more assertive demeanor than we ever find on the "NewsHour." Shields regularly appears on "Inside Washington" on ABC where he had been known to spar with Charles Krauthammer, and Brooks may be found occasionally on "Meet the Press" on NBC, both of which feature strong efforts at persuasion. It's also not just PBS that is responsible for their civility. Other PBS programs, from the truly belligerent "McLaughlin Group," to the more genteel but still highly competitive "To the Contrary," feature arguments, interruptions, and sometimes real disdain for one's opponents. Thus, we may conclude that the combination of the setting of the "NewsHour" and the friendships of the participants along with the precedents determined early on and expected of all have allowed and encouraged civility to prevail.

Conclusion

The factors described earlier help to explain the civility practiced by these two participants on the PBS "Newshour." However, we may be able to go further in our understanding of civility itself by viewing their behaviors through the lens of conversation analysis. Revisiting Grice's (1975) "cooperative principle" and Jacobs and Jackson's (1983) "reason rule," they are not required to agree, only to be reasonable; however, the situation itself may provide some encouragement to agree. Certainly, both Brooks and Shields strive to be considered competent. They are, after all, called upon each week to explain complex political and social issues from either a conservative or a liberal point of view. Yet, the context of the program also demands that they be reasonable with each other and with the moderator. Failure to cooperate followed by complete disagreement would render these Friday night conversations more like the typical political discourse of the day which only results in anger and gridlock.

This analysis illustrates that opinion or point of view in journalism has a potentially useful role to play within the public sphere. Partisan journalism that reflexively and transparently describes itself as such may also make useful contributions to public discourse. Key to each of these is the moderation, the reflexivity, and the transparency; maintaining a civil tenor of conversation and actually listening to and considering views that diverge from one's own. Another requirement for effectiveness is that the individual news host and news organization disclose the point of view from which stories are being reported. Under these conditions, a hybrid media sphere where multiple models of journalism coexist could be productive.

6

Symbolic or Just Coincidence?

How Journalists Made Sense of Katie's, Anderson's, and Brian's Talk Show Experiments

On May 25, 2011, Oprah Winfrey, the longest-running, and arguably most successful, host of a daytime television talk show ever, signed off from network television after 25 years, ending her syndicated talk show. A slew of TV personalities rushed to try to take her place. Among these were the daytime talk shows "Katie," "Anderson Live," and the evening magazine program "Rock Center with Brian Williams." Why did three famous TV news anchors try and fail at magazine and talk shows within two years' time? Why did one of those anchors, Brian Williams, exaggerate or misstate his experiences reporting in Iraq and elsewhere? And prior to those exaggerations, why was Brian Williams a frequent guest on late-night comedy and satire programs? This chapter tracks, through the published journalistic discourse and personal interviews with journalists, how journalists made sense of these events, whether journalists viewed these events as emblematic of the increasing fluidity of journalistic boundaries, and the struggle that television news and its personalities experience as they try to find their place in the fast-changing media landscape. As discussed, the strategy by CNN to broaden its definition of news (Gold, 2014; Byers, 2014; Stelter, 2014) is also indicative of this struggle.

Recent journalistic discourse about changes in television formats has spiked and coalesced around these notable events. Four of these events may be best understood when viewed together: the end of Oprah's syndicated talk show in 2011 (CBS, 2011), and the ushering in of three high-profile talk shows in its place—"Katie," "Anderson Live!," and "Rock Center with Brian Williams." What punctuates these events is the rather quick failing of all three talk show programs within a two-year window of time. Taken together, the end of "Oprah" and the rise and fall of the three programs form a revealing phase. The suspension and subsequent permanent demotion of Brian Williams from the NBC Nightly News anchor position in February 2015, after an internal investigation found he misreported or conflated his own role in several stories, is another aspect of this phase.

Many scholars have documented the histories of TV news and talk shows (Nerone, 2012; Meltzer, 2010; Barnett, 2011; Timberg et al., 2002; Grindstaff, 2002; Manga, 2003; Scott, 2008; Wood, 2009; Shattuc, 1997). Since the beginning of television, many strategies have been, and are being, tried out to maintain the place of news and news personalities on television: the move to talk shows, or to a talk format in news; to have more dramatic displays of news, including more heated debates (i.e., shouting talking heads) (Mutz, 2015); opinionated news (Stroud, 2011; Feldman, 2011; St. John & Johnson, 2012); to broaden/hybridize/soften (or some would say water down) news content (Williams & Delli Carpini, 2011; Baum, 2002; 2003; 2006; Moy, 2005; Prior, 2003; Baym, 2005; 2010); to satirize news (Vraga et al., 2012); to jump ship altogether (like Katie going to Yahoo news); or to keep doing the same old thing and hope the decline will stabilize or level off. This chapter analyzes the published discourse and interview material by journalists about Katie Couric's move from CBS Evening News anchor to her own syndicated talk show on ABC in September 2012, the announcement in November 2013 that she would become the new face of Yahoo news, and news of the cancellation of her talk show, also in 2013. The analysis includes discussion of the expectations of the show and Couric (such as that she'd fare better in the talk show format than she had on the evening news), whether those expectations were met, and reasons for the new venture. The chapter also analyzes the published discourse and interview material about Anderson Cooper's dual roles as anchor of "360" news on CNN and host of his eponymous talk show. In addition, it analyzes the published journalistic discourse and interview material about Brian Williams's "Rock Center" program which he began in October 2011 while continuing to anchor the NBC Nightly News. Some of "Rock Center's" key moments were the first episode with Jon Stewart, the Jerry Sandusky interview, and the announcement of its cancellation in May 2013 after a year and a half of poor ratings and changing time slots (Mirkinson, 2013a; 2013b).

Because American journalists tend to engage in conversations about their norms, values, and boundaries through articles published in the popular and trade press, at organizational proceedings and organizational blogs and on their broadcasts, these are the materials that were analyzed for evidence of their thoughts about the three cases, in addition to the interviews personally conducted.

Analysis

What have journalists written and said about these cases, and what they mean for the future of televised news? Looking across these cases of Katie Couric's, Anderson Cooper's and Brian Williams's talk and hybrid programs—television stars trying to do these alternate types of shows with all three cases that didn't work out—makes one wonder whether it could be just a coincidence or if there is a pattern. On the side of not believing the cases signify anything about the status of TV news, some journalists said that these cases are just part of the trajectory of a TV journalist's career, that they go through these phases of wanting to do news and then wanting to try something different. The rules of career progression are arbitrary.
Jack Shafer (2/11/15) said:

> But, newsmen and newswomen sometimes like to put on different hats. In Katie Couric's case, she needed a job, she was being eased out of CBS because she was not being successful.

However, Shafer went on to say,

> In terms of beating an audience, I think she is a fine newsreader . . . and she has a backstory of really good journalism. She was a great Pentagon reporter, everyone says. So, I wouldn't make it too big a deal about people trying different things, trying on different hats.
>
> When Anderson Cooper goes on and has a talk show, he's doing kind of what he does on the network and that is talking into a camera to somebody else. So, much of what is both cable news and network are two ways, the anchor talking to the reporter. In the case of his talk show, the people he was largely talking to were not other newsmen but civilians. So, I wouldn't make too big a thing out of it.
>
> Walter Cronkite, while being the anchor of the CBS Evening News, also had other projects at CBS. There was one called "The Twentieth Century." He did—at the beginning of his career, he did this show called "You Are There." So, it would be a dramatization, let's say, I can't remember a specific episode, let's say the signing of the Declaration of Independence, and, if I am remembering this correctly, he's interviewing actors who are portraying the founding fathers or he is providing commentary to a kind of docudrama. So—the fabric—I just think that there

is a lot more versatility and fewer walls and rules then your question would imply.

Paul Farhi (6/4/14) didn't think the moves by Couric, Cooper, and Williams signaled anything new:

> And as far as the talk shows go, Katie Couric's talk show was never about the news, Anderson Cooper's really isn't about the news, and if it is about the news, or it comes off of some news event, I don't know that you could tell what Katie Couric thinks about that . . . I think we've always had infotainment and this hybrid of news and entertainment, and—I mean the "Today Show" is a perfect example. It wasn't always about telling you what the president said yesterday. It's about cooking and books and movies and culture and things like that—all good. Not everything has to be hard news. It's a big world and different flavors can coexist.

Or, as another journalist suggested, maybe it's because these people become famous and for any journalist, the more space and time you can get to be seen and present your work, the better. These are all plausible explanations. Still, other journalists have suggested that the cases are symbolic of real shifts in the news media environment. How did journalists view the cases—as mere coincidence or representative of a pattern? Is the shift related to the audience decline for TV news that has been occurring for decades and is likely to continue despite the TV companies' efforts to disseminate their news more and more through other types of devices and platforms? Are TV news personalities trying to do something else because they know that this form of news is going away.

Three themes emerged as reasons posited for why the three stars (Couric, Cooper, and Williams) embarked on the talk and magazine programs. These are: (1) The new news/media environment requires/expects/demands that journalists, and all public figures for that matter, be present in multiple venues/platforms; and journalists are hedging their bets/making multiple bets, as reason for appearing in multiple venues, both across and within types of media (for example, TV print and online, or on more than one TV program at a time); (2) Hubris of the journalist-star: already well-known personalities want to expand their brand, get in front of the largest audience possible; show another side of themselves, have another forum for their work; and (3) corporate strategy and business interests on the part of the networks and hosts (synergy, financial incentives).

(1) *The new news/media environment requires/expects/demands that journalists, and all public figures for that matter, be present in multiple venues/platforms (show a personal side—parasocial interaction between viewers and journalists, be everywhere audiences are); and journalists are hedging their bets/making multiple bets, as reason for appearing in multiple venues, both across and within types of media (for example, TV print and online, or on more than one TV program at a time).*

Asked if the timing of Katie's, Anderson's, and Brian's forays into talk shows and newsmagazine programs was a coincidence or reflects something larger happening in television and journalism, Brian Stelter (8/18/14) said,

> I do think it's a time of experimentation, so maybe that's what it reflects. That it's a time of experimentation and people making. You know what we keep seeing? We keep seeing people making multiple bets. You know, when "GMA" wanted to add a cast member, they went to "Live with Kelly and Michael," and brought over Michael. So now Michael has multiple bets on the table about what's gonna matter.

Stelter continued,

> Anderson Cooper is at "60 Minutes" and he's at CNN, you know, so I think we're seeing a lot of that. And part of that is, I would think it's hedging in a rapidly changing media environment . . . that's what I think they're doing. I mean when you see, I mean look at the propensity for anchors to have two or three jobs, George Stephanopoulos with "This Week" and "GMA" and now chief anchor. Part of that is a network that's making a choice to elevate a star. Part of that is a choice to save money by having one person do two jobs. Part of it is, who knows where we're going? [laughter]. So, that's what it feels like to me anyway.

Asked about the fact that Stelter, himself, has all of these different roles at CNN, and that it was reported that one of the reasons Stelter agreed to the move from the *New York Times* to CNN was because he wouldn't just be anchoring or hosting a single show, he would get to report from across their site, Stelter confirmed this:

> Well yes, for me the key was, I think of the job as having three parts or three components. One is writing for the website all week with news and commentary. The second is going on television shows during the week to report. And the third is having the show on the weekend. I think of it as a three-legged stool and it was appealing to me because of all three. Just a television show, frankly, would not be enough because it wouldn't give me the reporting outlet that I need. The writing outlet that I need. So, I kinda had to have all three.

In one episode of "Reliable Sources" (7/6/14), Stelter focused on David Muir taking over for Diane Sawyer on ABC's evening news, and on the ascendance of morning shows on television. The continued strength of the morning shows seems evidenced by the announcement that George Stephanopoulos would also have a chief anchor title. Stelter (8/18/14) surmised that things are becoming "If not more point of view driven, at least more personality driven." So in different variations, TV programs are becoming either more "point of view," more commentary-based, more opinionated, or more personality-driven.

Further supporting the point that journalists today have the desire and need to appear in multiple venues, less than two years later, David Muir, anchor of "ABC World News," fills in on "Good Morning America" and guest co-hosted on ABC's "Live with Kelly Ripa" as she searched to find a co-host to replace Michael Strahan (Sblendorio, 2016).

> If you look at who's been promoted on these shows lately, on morning shows, they're getting hired probably because of their personalities, because of their backgrounds, in some cases because of their celebrity. And, I think that's all part of the same trend, which is, to be something other than just a news reader. (Stelter, 8/8/14)

(2) *Hubris of the journalist-star: already well-known personalities want to expand their brand, get in front of the largest audience possible; show another side of themselves, have another forum for their work.*

Some believe that the choices by Couric, Williams and Cooper to do talk and magazine programs in addition to their evening news programs were not motivated by fear that their newscasts were going under. Rather, that's simply what "talent" does—they want to do more, and their contracts allowed it. However, a confidential source who formerly worked in TV news also said that very few journalists actually want to do a talk show and for those who do show an affinity to broaden beyond what they're doing, if they test well, will give it a shot.

From the perspective of the networks, the same confidential source said, there are few good talented hosts out there and that's why they resorted to their news divisions [to pull existing hosts for these new programs].

Erik Wemple (6/12/14) said:

> And I also think you can't disregard the ego of these people behind it too. They want to grow their own name. And so Brian Williams wants—he gets 20 minutes every night, right? He gets 20 minutes. Anderson is a different matter, but he gets more exposure because he's on cable. But, especially in the case of Brian Williams, I mean, really. You're on that show for 20 extremely polished and over-produced minutes. Think about that. I mean, that's nothing. And all these other guys out there, everybody's talking about the cable guys 'cause they're on the air all day long. You know, only when the biggest of news breaks does Brian Williams get to sit there all day long and direct traffic. Just think about how life-sucking that's gotta be. You work all day long, and you read from a script for 20 minutes. You would be miserable.

Frank Sesno (10/9/14) suggested a similar reason:

> One thing it [that Couric, Cooper, and Williams all tried new shows] also says is anybody who has ever been in front of a camera has never met a camera they didn't like. Trust me on this, one of the other reasons I left the business (and I loved being on TV and doing television), but it's an "all about me" business. And that can become very distorting. So that's one thing.

Asked about the reason for the decisions of Anderson, Katie, and Brian—that they were making these multiple bets, and that there's a natural appeal in getting to try different things, Stelter (8/8/14) said,

> I would think so, yeah. I would think so. I would think that, though there are oftentimes, you see from these second or third outlets is a chance to be more personable and more loose. And that was Anderson's talk show, and Katie's talk show, the chance to show more of yourself.

Jon Allen of *Sidewire* (6/9/14) said:

> Opinion is a lot easier than news, to be honest with you. I think that might be part of it. I mean, if you could be a big personality and not have to worry about the constraints of being objective or not showing what you really think, which is very difficult to do whether you're a newscaster or an umpire at a baseball game, I think it's attractive to be able to try to do that—to just say what you think. I'm sure there is some jealousy in watching guests go on television, and say increasingly . . . personalities who have their own talk shows go out and say [things] that are increasingly inflammatory and watching them be successful and get ratings. If you're a news person and you're in this environment where not that many people are watching the network nightly news as used to, my guess is that there's an allure to try something new. But that doesn't mean people won't be able to do it in the future, it doesn't mean it's not the right thing to try to do; it just means it might not have worked out in those particular cases.

But some cautionary tales of hosts who left the programs that made them stars for greener pastures might give pause to some current celebrity anchors. For example, one article by Joe Scarborough warns Megyn Kelly about leaving Fox News and remembers what befell Glenn Beck when he left the network (Scarborough, 2016).

(3) *Corporate strategy and business interests on the part of the networks and hosts (synergy, financial incentives).*

Several journalists pointed to corporate strategy or business interests as reasons for the three new programs. For example, a confidential source who currently works in TV news suggested that one reason why Brian Williams did "Rock Center" was that it was right when Comcast was taking over NBC and they [Comcast] promised to do more news programming and wanted to do Rock Center. Here, this source thinks of Rock Center as a news program; Bruce Perlmutter referred to "Rock Center" as a newsmagazine show.

A former news producer (6/16/14) also suggests the same reasons:

> I think it's a dollar sign type of thing. There's a lot of money in the talk shows and very little time for them. I think it also fills their brand more, in a way. It brings these people who—you know, if you're the evening news anchor, the type of people who are seeing you are older, whiter, or whatever. And the daytime talk blockers are totally different people. And—I don't know what you're selling;

if you're selling your brand, if you're selling your—you know, some people are selling brand and they actually just want to sell things, other people just want their name to be bigger, other people just want to do interesting things. Also, I think someone like Katie Couric, she's had a lot of success in different areas, she's not going to retire—she's not old enough, she wants to try new things—but, from what I heard, she didn't seem to be too keen on doing the traditional talk show, daytime talk and stuff, which is a lot of fluff. She doesn't like a lot of fluff, but that's what daytime viewers are expecting. They're not expecting hard news at 1:00 p.m. while they're doing the laundry, or whatever people do.

David Mastio (8/7/14) also cited the financial incentive and desire to increase one's celebrity:

I think what is happening is that people are trying to take the fame that they earned through journalism and turn themselves into a celebrity, you know and that's the way I guess you go from 5 million a year to 10 million to 20 million a year.

Erik Wemple said:

Why did they make that move to talk shows? My feeling is that the reason is—I think in both of those cases, both of those networks have a huge amount of costs and expenses sunk into these fellows, into the individuals. So, in other words, they pay these people enormous contracts. So, I think the first thing is that they want to get their full money's worth out of these guys. So that's one notion. Two, there is—Williams and Cooper, as you know in both cases, are already pretty established brands, and so why not give them a shot at a slightly different format. They're both very versatile, and why not give it a shot in another format . . . why would they try to do "Rock Center," why would they try to do Anderson's talk thing. And I think they're trying to stretch their buck on these guys.

Wemple continued:

Well, network news—you know there's the "Dateline," there's the "60 Minutes"—they've been trying to extend their brand forever, in that way. I think they've been trying to prevent their extinction that way for a long time. The "Rock Center" was just another attempt in that direction, I suppose . . . I think there's NBC News, and there's NBC network, and they get into some crossover there. So it's not just the news; it's an entire network consideration at that point.

Why Didn't Katie's, Anderson's, and Brian's New Programs Work?

As for why the three programs all failed, journalistic discourse pointed to lack of fit of the personality with the genre and poor timing. Some believe Cooper was not the right fit for daytime. For Williams's magazine show, perhaps the timing just wasn't right and the landscape wouldn't support another evening news magazine. Williams was said to have been frustrated with the "numerous schedule moves and lack of promotion" for the program (Goldberg & O'Connell, 2013). And most critics and observers believe that Couric excelled at the morning show format on "Today," but not in other formats.

For example, Stelter (8/8/14) said, "So, I don't know the lesson from all the talk shows. I do think, with Couric, you know, there's a series of career steps that may have been missteps. You gotta know what you're good at, and, in this case, she was good at the "Today Show."

The former news producer said (6/16/14):

> I don't know why all their daytime talk shows failed. Maybe people are looking for a different voice. Like, Steve Harvey's show does well, Wendy Williams's show does well, Ellen DeGeneres. Maybe it's just the more kind of natural, funnier personalities. I don't know, maybe it's that. Ellen DeGeneres is really funny and she's goofy and she's likeable and she's a comedian. Wendy Williams is a talk show host, but she's really very real. Her whole thing is about, like, being your girlfriend and telling you what's what. And I think Harvey is very funny. These are clearly different people than warm, empathetic, likeable, smart reporters. They're all smart, obviously, they're all doing something right, but I think it's just a different personality mix. But Oprah sat somewhere in the middle. People trusted her like an anchor, but they also thought she was their girlfriend. I mean, there is that middle. I think media like Brian Williams, Anderson Cooper, Katie Couric didn't hit it. It might just be overdone. Anderson Cooper is great, but I don't know that people want to watch 3 hours of him every

day. I guess they're assuming that it's different people who are watching different shows.

Others, like Erik Wemple (6/12/14), say it's just the luck of the draw, that there's no great explanation for why some shows make it and others don't:

> The fact that it didn't work out was—I don't know what it says, because it's so hard, I think, to create a viable and new news product and show. I mean, look at how many of these things flame out. The list is just so long; it goes from [Parker Spitzer] CNN to the "Rock Center" to just about everything MSNBC has tried in recent times. The only ones that are really able to plug in new shows appear to be Fox, which leads me to believe that they're the plug-in network. And I read about this before; they have this base audience, and they can do anything they want with it, and they can put whoever it is—a decent broadcaster—they can plug him into a spot and they will win. Otherwise, how do you explain "Fox and Friends," which goes from 6 to 9 in the morning for Fox News. It is easily, objectively the worst, dumbest program on the air, yet it just destroys everyone else. It just absolutely kicks the shit out of every other show. Who knows why any show works or not. You know, Megyn Kelly is a great talent, but Sean Hannity did just fine at 9 o'clock before she moved there; he was really strong. I have a feeling that if Megyn Kelly moves to 8 o'clock, Bill Hemmer could do 9 o'clock—and Bill Hemmer is not under consideration for any such thing, but I have a feeling he would be just fine. They have an audience, not necessarily a set of programs.

Jack Shafer (2/11/15) said,

> In Couric's case, she went into an incredibly competitive environment. There is a lot of talent, there is a lot of audience loyalty, there are a lot of time slots that are already occupied by Queen Latifah and Ellen and Oprah and all these other people. I wouldn't draw any too big of a conclusion from the fact she went out and failed. Conan O'Brien, who is an incredibly funny guy, went to the [Tonight Show] and sort of failed and had to go down to the minor leagues on TBS. So, I think that the—I wouldn't make—a lot of news magazines have failed. No one has ever at any of the other networks has created anything as successful

as "60 Minutes." Including, CBS tried it with "60 minutes II." It was never the powerhouse of the original. I wouldn't make too big a thing out of failure. Failures, you know, are important to journalism, it indicated someone is trying, someone is stretching, somebody is trying something new, sometimes. I wouldn't draw huge conclusions from it.

Upon the news that Couric would become Yahoo's Global Anchor, many critics thought the Couric-Yahoo match a poor one. In *Variety*, Wallenstein (2013) wrote:

> After stints at CNN, NBC, CBS and ABC, maybe Katie Couric is going to Yahoo because there is simply nowhere else to go.
> Couric has always been admirably aggressive about experimenting with online video and social media, so this is no neophyte putting a toe in new waters. But the problem is she is still a fixture of the old media world. Regardless of how willing she is to shed her skin and embrace new ways, the world still mostly sees her in the over-familiar constructs of "anchor" and "talk show host."
> In fairness to Couric, there may not be a news personality on planet Earth that any digital property can bring in that will truly move the needle in terms of traffic and revenues . . . Still, you can't help but root for Couric to finally figure out how to reinvent herself. It's downright courageous of her to make a headfirst dive into a very uncertain future, not just at Yahoo but in any part of the digital landscape. Many of her cohorts would probably sooner retire than risk being seen as slumming it.

In 2015, it was reported that Couric had renewed her contract at Yahoo (Carson, 2015). In 2016, there were reports that she could be on her way out at the struggling company (Huddleston, 2016), but after the sale of Yahoo to Verizon, questions continued about where Couric would find a place at the new company (Wallenstein, 2016).

Frank Sesno (10/9/14) said:

> . . . people watch people, but not all people are going to be watchable all the time. You know, every major Hollywood star has made a Hollywood flop. So what you have to be careful about is that you don't sacrifice quality on the road to quantity. And so I think what Anderson and Brian and Katie all discovered was that just

because you're in one format that works, doesn't mean you're in another. The fact of the matter in my opinion is that yes, it's all about people, but people in the right place. Bill O'Reilly works really, really well as an opinionated talk show host, he's great at that, but would probably be dreadful as a newscaster. Brian Williams works really well as a newscaster, but he didn't have a very good time as a quasi-talk show host, although I think he'd actually be a terrific talk show host because he's got a great personality.

When I asked Jon Allen (6/9/14) why he thought all three shows failed, and if it means anything that three high-profile people who were doing the news—or said to be doing the news—all wanted to have talk shows, but those haven't worked out, he said:

[To me that means that] it's hard to make it in television, and it's really hard to make it twice. I think the public gets to know a particular personality as somebody who delivers them the hard news, or somebody who brings them entertainment, and there are very few people who are able to do that in both realms successfully. I mean, they're newscasters; that's what people want from them. Even on the "Today Show," Katie Couric was not doing a show that was entirely talk show. I mean, it is a talk show, but there is a fair amount of news involved in it, and she had come from a news background—I remember when she was a local reporter here in Washington. That's somebody who is seen as a serious newscaster, and I think her brand is there; it was a difficult transition.

The Brian Williams Scandal

In February 2015, Brian Williams was suspended for six months, and then permanently demoted from the "NBC Nightly News" anchor chair after charges that he misremembered or conflated wartime incidents he reported on from Iraq and Israel. He also came under scrutiny for possible conflations in reporting from New Orleans after Hurricane Katrina (Parker, 2015). Many speculated why Williams did it. Jack Shafer, in his *Politico* article of February 6, 2015, "Brian Williams' Slow Jam," was probably the first person to talk about Williams's ego and how perhaps the fact he was already appearing in many entertainment venues signaled there was something else, that he had other "desires." According to Shafer (2015),

In 2011, a *New York* magazine feature applauded the comic gifts he'd demonstrated on *30 Rock, Late Night With Jimmy Fallon* (slow jammin' the news), *The Jay Leno Show, The Tonight Show, The Daily Show, Ellen,* Conan O'Brien's *Late Night* (where he appeared 25 times), *The Late Show With David Letterman,* various comic *Today Show* spots and as a host of *Saturday Night Live.*

Wrote Shafer (2015):

Williams' insistence on playing for laughs—and his talent at garnering them—points to the compulsive desire to please often seen in the behaviors of salesmen, teachers, confidence men and political candidates. As long as the comedian has the crowd chuckling, he can sell them something, teach them something, pick their pocket or otherwise bamboozle them. The comic arts should not be banned from journalism—god forbid that should happen! But journalists who work overtime on entertaining you or making you laugh deserve your suspicion. In journalism, the story is supposed to be king. That doesn't mean the cleverness or emotive writing has no place, only that the narrow bandwidth comedy offers can carry only so much journalistic information.

Likewise, journalism shouldn't be all vegetables. But if a news writer or TV anchor elevates entertainment values over news values, journalism tends to suffer. The examples of Williams' exaggeration or embellishment advanced by his critics capture Williams speaking at his most entertaining best. He appears to be milking the anecdotes of his Iraq tour and of his Katrina days for maximum emotive impact on his audience when his real job is to tell his stories in the straightest possible way.

There's nothing wrong with a journalist making a few visits to the late night couches, but the frequency of Williams' appearances on entertainment programs indicate he's forgotten what business he's in. Nobody is big enough to slow jam the news and broadcast the news at the same time.

Alluding to the same tendencies Shafer described, Terrence McCoy, in a *Washington Post* article (2015), "Why Jon Stewart and Brian Williams should just switch jobs," endorsed the suggestion of Williams for Stewart's spot upon Stewart's announcement he'd be stepping down from "The Daily Show:"

It wasn't long before the murmurs started—through Twitter, through Facebook, through the nether reaches of the Internet. They called for something that at first seemed totally insane but, as it sank in, began to make sense: Jon Stewart, now as much a newsman as a comedian, and Brian Williams, now as much a comedian as a newsman, should just switch chairs.

In another article, "Williams undone by his gift for storytelling," the subhead read, "Anchor's love of a good yarn played a role in his downfall" (Roig-Franzia, Higham & Brittain, 2015).

The Williams scandal, which occurred after his magazine program had already been canceled, was attributed by many journalists to reasons (1), (2), and (3) identified above, which implies that Williams's behavior—his aggrandizing and misstating—were by-products of his individual character, but also symptomatic of behaviors/phenomena not unique to Williams, but instead ones many famous personalities might be susceptible and prone to.

In summary, journalistic discourse about the three cases were divided. Some believed there were systemic reasons for the ventures (i.e., the media environment requires being present in multiple venues; hedging bets; hubris of the journalist-star; and corporate strategy and business interests) and some believe the three cases are coincidental and don't mark anything larger.

7

Journalists' Thoughts about the Future of News

Across their discourse about civility, opinion, talk in news, and moving from news to talk, what have journalists revealed about the future of news? What are their predictions about where news online, on television, in newspapers, and elsewhere, is headed? This chapter's discussion of journalistic discourse on the future of news pays special attention to what journalists have said about the future of opinion in news, personalization of the news, focus on brand creation and the individual notoriety of journalists and other personalities, and their predictions about the success and survival of different news mediums.

Opinion Is Here to Stay

In June 2017, Fox News announced that it would abandon its "Fair and Balanced" slogan that had been mocked (Grynbaum, 2017b). "'The shift has nothing to do with programming or editorial decisions,' the network said in a statement. Instead, the slogan was dropped in part because of its close association with Roger Ailes, a network founder, former chairman and the originator of the phrase, who was fired in August in a sexual harassment scandal" (Grynbaum, 2017b). Onlookers will watch and see whether the dropping of the motto will lead the network to make its viewpoints more transparent. In October 2017, former ESPN "SportsCenter" host Lindsay Czarniak described how ESPN had changed the format of her show "to inject more opinion and voice into the 6 p.m. program" (Steinberg, 2017).

Journalists predict that opinion in news will continue to increase, while they still believe there's a place for "mainstream" straight news. Brian Stelter (8/18/14) spoke about opinion on television news in particular:

> [W]e will continue to move toward a more opinionated American journalism landscape. I don't know, I don't think there's any stopping that. People in some ways, having more of a point of view is a way to regain trust of the audience. Telling people where you're coming from, not all the time, but in certain cases, helps. It's really tricky isn't it? It's really tricky because the audience craves facts and information, and yet, so many people don't think they're getting that right now from the media.

As Stelter observed,

> [R]ight now you're on the air on CNN, Don Lemon is on from Ferguson. Don Lemon has opinions and he expresses them, and in some ways he is, he's leading. I don't know, I'm afraid, I don't want to say lead the way, but he's leading the way because he's showing that it's acceptable and accepted to do so on CNN when you're an anchor. So, there's all these forces I think moving us in that direction.
> ... David Muir will have to not take, like I take a political position. But I think that he will stand up for s[tuff]. I think he will not give commentaries, but you know, make choices, editorial choices. And express where he comes from sometimes. I mean Brian Williams already does that. So, I think we will see more of that gradually over time.

A former news producer (6/16/14) also thinks opinion is here to stay:

> It's definitely not going anywhere. I don't think opinion news is going anywhere at all, as long as it's offering something different and not something vanilla. I think that's what the usual problem was. And I think that in the morning news, you see that too. Like, the "Today Show" is going downhill. They have the same quality producers and anchors, it's just too vanilla. They're not introducing enough personality or flavor or opinion or personality. Everyone wants something that's more entertaining or more interesting, more informative, but not bland.

Jim Henderson (12/10/14) also thinks we'll see more opinion in the future:

> People talking to each other a lot. Yeah, I think it'll continue. I mean, they've got to fill the air for 24 hours, and it certainly doesn't cost much to have people talking to each other, and then the ultimate journalists interviewing journalists. Ugh! So, yeah, it'll continue, but unless it gets to the point where the viewership is just so small that the advertisement just shrivels up completely. I mean, that's the other side of the whole thing: the Internet didn't hurt newspapers because of online journalism; the Internet hurt newspapers because of Craig's list. And if advertising just completely evaporates from cable news, then I don't know what happens. Although, it's not very expensive to produce that stuff. It's a lot cheaper than killing trees and printing newspapers, and shipping them out.

And Paul Farhi (6/4/14) agreed that opinion news will continue:

> Oh no, we'll always have this. As long as there's an economic rationale for this—and there certainly is—it's cheap to produce—I can call up a couple people and sit them down in a studio—and it gets a relatively decent rating, having a host who gives lots of opinions—Bill O'Reilly has been doing it for years—this is always going to be a stock-in-trade. Again, this is the marketplace of ideas. There are certain ideas I don't like or don't agree with, but that's ok, it's not about what I want. It's driven by an economic basis. But to the extent that it drives the polls, the extremism in politics, I think that's not so great. I think we need to figure out a way to solve our problems without going off to opposite corners. It might be a good idea. There are moderates in this country— there's lots of them. You have to appeal to them to win national elections. You still sort of do in some state-wide elections, but less and less. I think our direct elected representatives can play to these extremes more and more, and win elections.

Although he said that he believes opinion news will continue, Farhi (6/4/14) also said he believes there will continue to be a role for the mainstream media:

> I don't think we are going to move to a world in which every publication is of a particular ideological stripe. There will be plenty

of that—left, right, and center—but there is still going to be a role for the mainstream media. If you look at the opinion shows on the cable networks, the opinion shows are in primetime, and that's a clue because during the day, they will attempt—maybe not always successfully—but they will attempt to cover the news in a more or less straight forward fashion. MSNBC has kind of blurred that line. But nevertheless, CNN's daytime programming tends to be news-driven. Same with Fox, more or less. The point is, people come to the opinion shows at night, after they've had that, more or less, one clean shot at the facts. They've gotten the news, now they want a take on the news. They want to know what to think about the news. That tells you there is still going to be a role for people who play it straight, who don't give you an opinion before they even tell you what the facts are. There will be a *New York Times*, there will be a *Washington Post*, there will be an NBC News, there will be, CBS, etc. But there's going to be this expanding market for opinion journalism, and we will see if . . . more of it or more of the same. I don't think you'll see this disappearance and this devolvement into: are you a left-wing publication, are you a right-wing publication. As the British have always had as their model, we will still have a mainstream, non-ideological—although you could argue about what's non-ideological—but, nevertheless, an attempt to play it straight, as well as this additional thing of opinion journalism.

Personalization of News Will Continue

Some journalists predict that personalized news, niche news, and news that caters to particular interests will continue. Jon Allen (6/9/14) said:

> I don't think it's [news] going to change that much from the essential idea that we're all hungry to get information that we didn't have before. I always describe the most noble principle behind journalism as taking information from a small number of people and giving it to a larger number of people, and hoping that improves society through transparency. I think we're doing that right now. I said before, it doesn't matter whether it's—in terms of the value of news—it doesn't matter what the motivation is behind doing a story if you put something out there that is true, that people didn't know about, and that people would be interested

about. By and large, you've done a service. So, do I like objective news reporting better than the partisan news organizations? Sure, absolutely. I've done that for my entire career. Am I worried that society is falling apart because we have partisan media? No, not at all. If you go back in our history, the tradition is for somebody to buy a newspaper because they have a political viewpoint to advance. That may not have been true as much in the last 30 or 40 years, but generally speaking, as a historical study, the idea of having partisan media is nothing new.

. . . The rapid dissemination of information is always going to have value. And the question is: what form does that take? It's who owns the media or the tools to disseminate that information and collect payment for it. . . . I think that, by and large, the more directly—if you get information to people's devices that is stuff that they want, the better you're going to do. My personal view is, I think you're going to see more mixed media going directly to people's devices. That is to say, people, news organizations, whatever, that provide information on the very specified set of things that a particular person is interested in. So, you're interested in botany and lacrosse, you're going to get something that provides botany and lacrosse news to you, twice a day, for 25 cents a day, or 20 dollars a month, or whatever it is.

Amber Phillips ("The Future of Journalism and Politics," 2015) said,

The Post doesn't control the dissemination [whether it's shared on Facebook, etc.] so it doesn't know the answer to the problem of echo chambers.

Paul Farhi (6/4/14) similarly described the demand-supply cycle of news that is likely to persist:

Well, this is an interesting topic because now we know what people want, we can see it minute by minute as a result of our server logs telling us. It's neat and it's dangerous. It's dangerous because, if all you want to do is give people what they want at any given minute, there'll be a lot of Kardashian stories in the paper. That's again, a little bit of an oversimplification, but nevertheless it is true that being popular is—look, the point is, we do want to sell newspapers, and people say things like, "all you're trying to do is sell newspapers," and I say, "yes, that's exactly what we're trying to do," but there's a responsible way to do it and an irresponsible way to do it. You can say sensationalized things, or you can cover the news that's interesting. We don't want to do boring stories.

But, as it turns out—here's the good news—there is a niche for hard news reporting about topics that are vital for people to know about: politics, government, the military, the news media, on and on and on. Every time I think I'm going to predict how well one of my stories is going to do, I am utterly wrong, and I love that because no one has figured out exactly what popular taste is. If they had, they would dominate the world, and no one can figure out at any given time what story is going to be a huge hit. And you can't entirely engineer it; you can make certain assumptions, but you can't entirely engineer it, and that's wonderful because that means there is a big, wide open territory for creating something that you didn't know was going to take off and capture public interest. One of the things that we're doing is throwing a lot up there and a lot against the wall. It's not just whatever is trending now, we do things that come out of nowhere.

Some of the most popular stories have been the kind of in-depth journalism that is not a superficial hit about what Rihanna's dress looked like, or Kim Kardashian's wedding. I'm not putting it down. It's a big tent—we can do a lot of different things. There's still a lot of room for great journalism here. And there's also a lot of room for popular journalism. Is there anything wrong with having on the same site Rhianna's dress and the primary battle in Iowa? No, there's nothing wrong with that. They can coexist. If you look at our most popular, most read list at any given time, it's a grab bag: lots of serious stuff, some breaking news—the Bergdahl prisoner thing is big, people want to know about that. So, again, it's not like one thing crowds out another thing. But I think we're all at risk if all we want to do is chase clicks, because then it would be self-defeating. We've got to have the serious stuff there because people want serious stuff as much as they want superficial stuff. Think about your own life, think about any student you teach. We can contain worlds. I mean, you're interested in the high and the low at any given moment, as am I.

Farhi (6/4/14) also addressed funding models for news going forward:

The Internet has destroyed the old model and hasn't really given us a true direction of a new model . . . The only paper that seems to have figured out paywalls is the *New York Times*. *The Washington Post* really hasn't. I guess the *Journal* and the *Financial Times*, they've had paywalls going way back to the beginning, and I would guess it's worked pretty well for them. But the only general-interest newspaper that's gotten somewhere with this is the *New York Times*, at this point—maybe not the only one, but strikingly few. And there's real question as to whether paywalls are going to be the answer.

In response to my mentioning that some of the newer models of funding so far include foundations helping to sponsor news endeavors or new owners who have deep pockets, Farhi said,

> It's absolutely life-saving for *The Washington Post* to have a multi, multi billionaire. It is very, very comforting to know there is a person who has the money and the interest—I mean, those two things go hand in hand—to allow us to experiment. Because, again, no one's figured it out; we have to experiment, we have to fail, we have to lose money doing so. It takes a lot of money to do it, and thank God, this is someone who is willing to invest in the future of our journalism, if not journalism per se. But then you have Pierre Omidyar who's doing "First Look," you have the ProPublica model, I mean you've all these different experiments. I'd say at this point they're not really experiments—they're continuing models—but we're still in trouble. We, journalism, is still in trouble financially, because, again, I don't know that anyone has truly figured out how to be an on-going, successful, financially self-sustaining publication in a world in which there is a race to the bottom, in terms of the advertiser model. Advertisers pay pennies—pennies—for the clicks that we attract. So, one idea is, we've got to get lots, and lots, and lots of clicks to get those pennies to add up, and that's just a boulder going uphill. It's really, really hard to keep pushing it up, because again, the price per thousand advertising keeps going down. It's almost like we give this away to attract readers. The Internet is a bottomless pit; you could start a website, you could start a news site at any given moment, and people do. And at some point, it's just an exhausting, self-defeating kind of race. So again, it helps to have someone who's going to invest the money and give us the time to attempt to get to a place—if we can get to a place—that will be a self-sustaining business enterprise. Look how much hasn't

worked. We're 20 years into this; it's not like the Internet is new at this point, and we're still struggling. It's very, very discouraging.

Farhi (6/4/14) said that although there are many sources of news today,

> I still think we [newspapers like *The Post*] have some agenda-setting capability, and the news cycle gets shorter and shorter, so there's a lot of instantaneous stuff. By the way, one of the things that was said long ago was that people don't—because there were so many news sources, and people have many different options to choose from—that we will all not have the same frame of reference. In other words, you'll have your news sources, and you'll understand the news . . . But it's not true. It's true on the margins, but if I said to you, or I said to anybody here, "what are the 3 news stories you're following today?" We pretty much get to a fairly common news agenda. It's true that you may have seen a story that I haven't seen because you went to a website that I didn't go to, or a news source that I didn't pay attention to, but the big stories are still pretty much the big stories. It's just that the news agenda has gotten so much bigger and wider.

Here, Farhi disagrees with fears about segmentation of audiences and news when it comes to a general news agenda. He doesn't, however, go so far as to try to contradict concern over the potential selective exposure, or echo chambers of versions of opinionated news.

Liza Mundy (7/30/14) said,

> . . . we seem to be moving in this golden age of verticals and really deep wonky dives into any number of topics, and who really would have predicted that? And so, I don't, and that just seems to be sort of unfolding right now, so in five or ten years, right and I guess the other, we're in the midst of a time, as I understand it where fewer readers are going to sort of a news entity like the *New York Times* or *The Atlantic*, you know specifically [inaudible] and more and more readers are reading things from *The Atlantic* or the *New York Times* that have been shared with them, so they're reading it more in nuggets, or you know, stand alone as opposed to part of a publication. So those seem to be trends that are happening right now, sort of I guess the disaggregation of news that would typically be presented as part of a newspaper or part of a magazine but it's now being consumed in

discrete chunks or nuggets, and that's all I can see from where we are now, and I would be perfectly willing to predict the future or to hazard a guess if I could think of a prediction, but I don't really, I don't have a prediction for what will be the kind of new trend five years from now.

Amber Phillips ("The Future of Journalism and Politics," 2015) said the "old business model to think people care where they get the 'what' from—they care where they get the 'why' and 'how.'" Phillips believes that the role of legacy media going forward is editing, curating, and filtering; cutting through the noise and creating a narrative.

The Notoriety and Brand of Individual Journalists

Sesno (10/12/14) predicts that,

> Yes, personality will persist. We are creatures that have always been drawn to compelling people. That is being magnified by the web, which is a personal branding opportunity for those who have the talent and the tenacity to make it happen. Ask Andrew Sullivan, Zach Galafianakis, Maureen Dowd or, God forbid, Kim Kardashian!

Major anchor changes continue. As of May 2017, Scott Pelley is no longer CBS News anchor (Koblin & Rutenberg, 2017). Bill O'Reilly's sexual harassment lawsuits finally led to his firing in April 2017; shortly thereafter, Roger Ailes, former Fox News chairman who had been forced to resign after Gretchen Carlson's harassment suit, died in May. Megyn Kelly, who also alleged harassment by Ailes, left Fox News in January for NBC where her new duties began in June 2017, including on the "Today" show (Koblin, 2017). Kelly was fired in October 2018 after making controversial comments on air. After these major anchor departures and Fox News' lineup in disarray, MSNBC began winning some nights in the ratings against Fox News (Koblin, 2017). Earlier, Greta Van Susteren had left Fox News in September 2016 for MSNBC. Before Fox News, Van Susteren had been at CNN.

These changes on both news and entertainment programs and choices of new hosts reinforces the argument that it's all becoming about individual brand and all interchangeable. The shuffling and interchangeable nature of TV hosts and personalities has always gone on throughout the history of TV in the United States. (Meltzer, 2010). And these particular changes highlight the fact that moves can be made even across ideological divides, such as from

Fox to NBC, or CNN to Fox to MSNBC. Although a Pew Research Center report from January 2014 found that most Americans could not recognize then-"NBC Nightly News" anchor Brian Williams (Suls, 2014), some journalists still believe the signature (Meltzer, 2010) of individual hosts matters. I asked Maria Bartiromo (6/19/14) why she thinks viewers watch her when they have so many choices. She said,

> Well I would like to believe I'm trusted. I have my own brand. I've been doing this 25 years. So I would like to think that I have a following and that I'm trusted. But I'm not in this illusion that I'm just going to have it just because; I have to continue doing a good job.

When asked if it matters who is giving the news, Brian Stelter (8/18/14) said,

> I think it matters for a bunch of reasons. I think it reflects the priorities of the United States, it reflects the, because those shows reflect what is in the news. They still have, 22, 23 million viewers combined a night. And, not every viewer is watching every night. So over the course of a month, you're getting many tens of millions of people that are interacting with those shows, and seeing what they have. They, those anchors are still there for us in times of crisis. And will be. And they provide a sense of stability and a sense of prioritization of news.

Of course, Stelter and Bartiromo are on TV themselves so they have a vested interest in the success of the genre. But a former news producer (6/16/14) also believes that the appeal with audiences of a specific person—the reporter or anchor—matters:

> Anderson Cooper really became a star, not just the news . . . he's likeable and empathetic. People just like him; he's very likable, he's very intelligent. And morning show hosts have personality but not necessarily opinion, but a lot of TV show hosts . . . a lot of the ones who are doing well . . . have louder voices, balancing being annoying and being opinionated. And the ones that are striking the right balance are the ones that are succeeding. Like Megyn Kelly on Fox News, she's smart and she's pretty and she is educated, so she's not just some person spouting her viewpoint. She's a lawyer. She has experience in the professional law world,

and she gets her opinions across . . . and she has charisma. There are a lot of attractive, smart reporters out there, but not all of them are going to be stars. And I think in the cable news world, if you're opinionated, but you're striking the balance between not being annoying with being opinionated, and also sprinkling in some charisma, that's kind of how to succeed right now.

While Frank Sesno (10/9/14) expressed that the personality of the individual journalist is important today, he also said that the journalist's personality alone, without regard for the audience, is not enough in today's media environment:

> The audience expects to be brought into a conversation now . . . And even if people aren't participating in the conversation, they want to feel that there is access to a conversation. More than anything, it needs to be part of the mindset of the journalist. It's less about every member of the audience participating in the conversation, it's the journalist knowing that they—he or she—is part of a conversation. Which drives, I believe, a greater responsiveness to the audience, a greater accountability to the audience, and a higher real-world quotient for the audience. The idea of the Washington-inside-the-beltway types talking to Washington-inside-the-beltway types and people thinking that that's going to be fascinating forever is a complete misnomer. The idea that overpaid network correspondents can talk to overpaid beltway bandits you know, whatever, that that is somehow going to be compelling news is not the case. That's one of the reasons why the public is angry and so distrustful about the media and political institutions. And we have to go about talking about a conversation to actually having a conversation. And there are almost no news organizations that I can really point to that I think are doing this well.

While Sesno (10/9/14) believes bringing the audience in is crucial, exactly how to do that successfully is still being figured out:

> You bring the audience into the conversation by helping to crowdsource stories that you cover. You bring the audience into the conversation looking very hard to make sure you have the right voices in the stories you're reporting, in the way you're reporting the stories. You've got diversity in the newsroom, so you actually know what the audience is because part of that audience is

working for you or with you. You use the media tools that are out there today to engage the audience around the stories that you do and actually let them—I think there are very interesting ways to let the audience buy the story.

You know, what was Al Gore's thing he sold off to Al Jazeera, Current TV. Plenty of folks have experimented with this, but no one has delivered on it. The idea that user-generated is going to be news, forget it. User-generated content is unbearable because most people are not trained storytellers. I'm not insulting them, it's just a reality. I've done it with my students and it's really, really hard, even when we're training them. Getting the audio right, getting the video right, getting the lighting right, getting the composition right, getting the character right, getting the information right, getting the story arc right. Those are hard things for someone who's even done this all their lives . . . So it's naïve to think that you can just open the doors and say, "OK audience, come on in and drive the news." But, we've got to find the right barrier to entry if you will that still allows that process. People have tried it, Obama held a Google town hall meeting and CNN tried to pull questions from the audience into the debate. And the presidential debates commission tried to figure out very hard how. I'm not saying it's not working at all. I'm saying it's a work in progress. These are new technologies and new expectations.

Richard Benedetto (3/26/14) said,

Maybe they won't use anchors but you know, day time anchor, evening anchor. And you'll be bringing the news more often, in smaller bites. I can see that coming. It's a good way of force feeding news onto people who are watching TV for entertainment. News breaks rather than news programs.

The shift in prestige and sheer numbers from the traditional news anchor/reporter to opinionated commentators and talk show hosts on television affects the role of women on TV. The trend toward the deprofessionalization of journalism, including on TV journalism, with more "citizen journalists" and people not trained as television journalists appearing on-screen, the proliferation of talking heads and the need for commentators may open up more space and positions for women, but at the same time, with so many talking heads, these roles seem interchangeable, easily replaceable and lacking the gravitas or importance of the traditional anchors.

The Success and Survival of Different News Mediums

Will Traditional Network TV News Broadcasts Go Away, or Will Digital Efforts to Expand on Other Platforms Keep Them Afloat?

Is the TV news of the past half-century a hopelessly sinking ship? For years, some network news executives have predicted that their companies will get out of the news business altogether (Wurtzel, in Meltzer, 2010). Alternately, I and others have hypothesized that TV news would evolve in several ways, including that the same TV content creators will produce content for newer modes of distribution. I reasoned that the special quality of hearing the news from a familiar human being (the newscaster), the parasocial relationships audiences form with TV newspeople, and the visual aspect of viewing the news and its accompanying imagery on a large television screen, would be enough to preserve at least some TV news in some form (Meltzer, 2010). As Tsukayama (2014b) reported around the launch of Amazon's Fire TV in 2014, a streaming video device, TV still attracts the greatest number of users:

> For all the talk of drones, wearables, homes of the future, and flying Internet networks, the truth is that tech companies are still keenly interested in the consumer electronics device that's been a fixture in the American living room for decades: the television.
>
> Amazon.com . . . is one of an increasingly crowded group of firms who want to control your time on the couch. Speculation has been flying for years that Amazon will release a streaming video device—similar to Apple's Apple TV or Google's Chromecast—that brings online video content, and potentially Android-based games, to the largest screen in your house. Why? Despite what you may think, the TV is still where people turn for the bulk of their screen time, and Amazon wants to be a main portal for all of your entertainment . . . According to the data from Nielsen published in February, Americans still spend an average of 185 hours per month with their televisions, as opposed to 34 hours and 21 minutes with their smartphones.

But what have journalists written and said about the move from news to talk on TV, and what it means for the future of televised news?

TV News Should Have Already Gone Away or Will

Several journalists are doubtful or predict the demise of the traditional television newscast. "Well, if you would've asked me five years ago, if there still would've been evening newscasts on major over the air television, I probably would've said no. I mean, they're still there because they still earn a profit, and it's also the prestige factor," said Bruce Perlmutter (8/7/14).

A CNN employee who works on CNN's digital content (4/14/15) said there is a need to rethink the point of video and investing in these name brands, and doesn't think TV news will be around in five or ten years; those formats will be inefficient. The same CNN employee (4/14/15) suggested that because TV executives were never involved in print and web journalism, and they don't get news that way, that's why they continue to invest in and focus on TV and video.

When asked about the broadcast networks who haven't changed their news formats very much, Bruce Perlmutter (8/7/14) replied that:

> Yes, the broadcast networks still do 22 minutes in between, sometime between six and seven o'clock at night, with a single anchor, whether it's a man or a woman, delivering what they believe to be the top stories of the day. And there's a reason why, even though they still get an audience, the broadcast networks' nightly news or evening news shows' audience has dwindled. For more than any other reason, the same thing. You have an appointment to watch at 6:30, to watch contextual or to watch the nuts and bolts of the top stories of the day. People already know those stories by the time they tune in, which is why the broadcast networks' news shows' audiences have dwindled. And that's been a chronic problem for years, and that's why on all the broadcast networks they have franchises which deliver a more in-depth component of the stories of the day.

Amber Phillips (7/23/14) is pessimistic about the future of TV news:

> I am a news junkie; my job is to spend all day on Twitter, all day on the Internet. And by the time I get home, the last thing I want to do is turn on the TV and watch all over again news that, to me, in Internet years, is 100 years old cause it happened at noon that day. And I don't think it's just because I'm a journalist; I think it part of Millennials, I want to say. So, I worry a lot—I don't see a point at all for evening news broadcasts, local news broadcasts at all. And the only use I could see for cable news broadcasts is: (1) breaking news—they do it better than anyone else in the world; and (2) the Youtube clip the next day. So I'm pretty pessimistic—more pessimistic, I should say—about

the future of TV news. Like, the Sunday morning talk shows, right? There's a huge conversation here in Washington about their decline in usefulness. That used to be something you had to do if you wanted to be here in DC, and now it's more the super, hardcore political junkies. And the rest of us, Sunday afternoon or Monday morning, just read what *Politico* writes up if anyone said anything interesting.

On the Sunday talk shows, Phillips said she was referring to "Meet the Press," "Face the Nation with Pat Schaffer," and "This Week." Of the decline in usefulness of Sunday talk shows, Phillips referenced *Politico*'s media blog by Dylan Byers who has written on the topic (Byers, 2014) and said that's "one example of how the news . . . doesn't matter anymore if we've already read it on Twitter."

Phillips predicted that in 5 or 10 years, at least some local news channels will get out of the business, and that the content that is left will be digital for other platforms:

> . . . I would say the same prediction for local news, too. Like, it would be disseminated in 3-minute video clips that I could go to their website and watch. Or livestreaming. I was thinking, and this goes to Millennials' TV use, too, right? The only time I turn on my actual TV and surf the channels is to watch C-SPAN or CNN when there's breaking news. The rest of it I'm streaming on my computer.

Jim Henderson (12/10/14) was also pessimistic about the future of TV news:

> It is kind of remarkable; you watch the clock and it's a half hour and twelve minutes into it you're starting to get the soft stuff. And some of it of course seems like it's playing to the audience, it's an older audience who get a lot of health care and things like that. But a lot of it is just—I'm sure it's just a lack of resources committed by the companies that own them to hire more journalists, and also to bureaus overseas and different bureaus here. Not just regionally, but beat-wise. You see the same poor reporters there who we all know by name, and everything. And my God, they're just flipping around from one story to another as opposed to going deeper. So I'm not sure it will survive. I mean, I'm sure it'll make it through the baby boomer generation retiring, because that's . . . but I don't know.

TV News Will Survive

On the health and future of television news, Brian Stelter said,

> I wouldn't want to speak for CNN, but from my perspective, television news is a remarkably healthy sector of the industry, and there will, I believe there will be pretty traditional television newscasts ten years from now, but, increasingly those will be accessed online, so I don't know how much of those you'll find on linear cable television.

Stelter believes that making use of new technology will help keep TV news in some form afloat:

> . . . CNN has an amazing app called CNN X . . . So it's this, it's their TV everywhere app and it solves all the problems I have with cable news. For example, you can, in the future, you can imagine a situation where every business report that aired on CNN within 24 hours can be lumped together into a list and you could watch them all at once. And suddenly, you know, that reshapes what we think of when we think of CNN. So I think there'll be those sorts of innovations that'll change what we mean when we say TV news.

Jon Allen (6/9/14) said,

> I don't think anyone's worried about TV news going away. If anything, people want news on television now more than ever. It's just that it's a more diffuse market. The networks used to really reign, and they no longer do that. I can get my news on television from a dozen different sources [much less] [inaudible]. It's not just CNN, Fox, MSNBC anymore, I can get Bloomberg TV, I can get CNBC, I can get CNN Headline News, I can probably watch HuffPost TV either on some channel somewhere or on the web. So there are a lot of choices for the consumer, and as a result, you don't have as much power as you used to as a broadcaster for one of the major networks.

Lambidakis (7/314) said,

> I think they'll [the networks] still be able to keep the thirty-minute slots. At CBS, I'm told they're creating a digital network. For it to

be only online so everyone can keep it on their mobile devices. They will always exist in some form.

Several journalists remarked that the morning shows have become very strong. "They're big profit centers. A lot of the resources are being shifted to the morning shows. That two-hour block in the morning where the audiences have grown . . . And there will be nothing that will replace turning on your television when something happens" (Lambidakis, 2014).

Maria Bartiromo (6/19/14) also thought that TV news will survive:

Oh sure. I think right now, even though the growth is going toward digital, the bulk of the ad dollars and the bulk of the content—the bulk of the business is really coming from—I mean certainly advertising dollars are going to TV. I think it's all merging. I mean, you see Comcast acquiring Time Warner Cable right now; we're in the midst of really an important period for information flow, because it's all converging. I think what's converging is the distribution, and I think it will be on TV, it will be on your computer, you might have one screen that fits the bill for both. But I don't think TV goes away.

I asked Bartiromo if she still considers it TV even if you're watching it on your tablet or on your phone, and whether that is because it's the same content producer—the people creating the content for whichever device it's viewed on.

Bartiromo said:

Well, it depends. There's a lot of . . . content . . . blogs. But I think it's all converging. I mean, I think news has already changed so much. Years ago it would be you would wait until 6:30 at night to get the evening news; no one's waiting until 6:30 at night anymore to get the evening news. You know the news by the time it happens. So, I think it will be all of the above. I think it's a journalist's franchise to lose. But if you have a franchise name, and if you have the credibility in terms of your journalistic practices, then I think you'll probably keep it, provided that you do a good job, and that it's an accurate job. But it is yours to lose in an environment where, you know, you have a lot of news sources and you have a lot of distribution methods. So, I think there are certain franchises—the *Wall Street Journal*, the *New York Times*—that are trusted, and I think that they will continue to be trusted if, in fact, they continue to do a good job. So I'm not worried in NBC,

ABC, CBS—I mean I'm not worried, but I think that we are at a moment in time right now where people are deciding. They have choices, and they don't have to listen to one news organization. There are a lot of them, and they don't have to watch TV or listen to the radio; they'll choose.

Jack Shafer (2/11/15) also thinks TV news will survive:

Network news will be around as long there are old people who buy the medicines that are advertised on the nightly news. The audience has shrunk and gotten smaller and smaller because of changes in what drugs can be advertised on television. That audience is reaching that demographic (that) has become incredibly lucrative. There is a statistic that I cited from a *New York Times* story from two days ago in a tweet that the three nightly newscasts in 2013 were collecting something like five hundred and forty million dollars in revenues each year; that is a lot of money. And, as long as there is the money and an audience to monetize, network news will be around. It might be shrinking like a lot of media assets today, they are shrinking, but they are still incredibly profitable.

A TV journalist in Washington (6/18/14) cited several reasons why he believes TV news will continue, including that it filters the noise from all of the different sources of the day, that straight or hard news is still important and people still watch it, and that there will always be a special impact of watching and hearing people through the medium of television. He said,

the reason I sit down and still watch the nightly news is because I know there's been a whole day of them sort of sifting through everything. On cable news, you get the like, the development . . . So you're actually following the story as it's unfolding on cable news or on the Internet or on Twitter.

The correspondent sees the nightly news as a place to "sift through what's real." On the future of TV news, the same TV journalist in Washington (6/18/14) said,

And I do think that there is this viewpoint . . . that real news or hard news or straight news is dying. If I thought that were the case, I would be very sad to be working in the industry I'm working in, or doing what I do on a daily basis. I am surrounded at [my network] and elsewhere by people who take this stuff extremely seriously . . . and strive every day to do the right thing. And I think, empirically speaking and even . . . the numbers, I mean the first half hour of the morning shows, which is the hardest of the[m], they do very well. You know and some of the Sunday shows, they're doing well. The 6 p.m. show on Fox News, the first half hour, which is more of the hard news on Fox, is . . . You know? . . . so that's not to say that the others aren't doing amazingly well too. It's just, it's not, in my view, it's not dying.

Forget the journalists, talk to the people who are getting covered. They will say that if you want to make an impact, you have to do it on TV. One thing that will never get lost is the power of actually being able to see someone and see how they talk and see what they're [saying].

The correspondent said,

I think it is possible and likely that news and Internet sort of intersect more, overlap more . . . Would you count news on television as if you go to CNN.com and you sit there for a half hour and watch a video. Is that news on television? In my head, yes, that's still, you know, it's just that's truly where things are headed. The *Wall Street Journal*, *The Washington Post*, all of them have these from online TV programs. And the opposite is true, right? All the TV networks have their websites.

Michael Calderone (7/2/14) also believes TV news will survive and will in the future continue to meld digital and mobile content services with television programs:

I think, you know, five, ten years from now you'll still see the morning shows and you'll still see the nightly news, because there is an audience for that. There is an audience each morning. Millions of people still are tuning in, but there is increasingly, you know, broadcast news divisions need to figure out how to reach potential viewers who are only going to be accessing their network news online, or increasingly on mobile devices. And you've seen CBS and ABC and others, you know, looking at doing 24-hour digital news services. You're gonna [get] more and more of a push to digital, because, you know, a young viewer isn't going to watch a news segment that isn't necessarily, you know, at 6:30

every evening. But that same twenty-year-old may watch it on NBCnews.com or on their phone or share it in some other way. You know, I think "Vice News" has been really savvy in reaching millennial viewers by doing a different type of news program, and that might be something that legacy news organizations, your CBSs and NBCs and ABCs may look to emulate.

Josh Altman also believes TV news will survive, but provided a different reason—the cable infrastructure:

> TV is going to continue to exist because the cable companies aren't—we're not getting rid of cable companies. We're going to deliver cable. People aren't ditching their cable TVs at any rate, despite what you hear about cord cutters. There is a regulatory framework because we subsidize these low-income people partly because there is no other way—same thing we did with electrification . . . The same thing we did with electrification, we did with telephones because getting those things to everyone in the country is important. Getting those things to everyone is important. We just decided as a country that is something that we want to do. Which having everyone have power and phones is good. And there are subsidizes for the companies to help pay for some of that. We're not getting rid of it, especially after we paid so much to put it in. People aren't ditching televisions.

TV News Might Survive

According to Erik Wemple (6/12/14),

> Network news has been in decline, but cable news, their audience has maxed-out too. I think May [2014] was one of the lowest audience nets for the cable news operations that has ever existed. So, the cable news audience is maxed-out, and it's pretty small. But the network news audience is bigger—probably maxed-out, but it's also a very short window. In other words, you get those 7, 8, 9 million people for a half hour. But when you strip it of the commercials and stuff and throw it on the internet, it's like 20 minutes of content. So you get that bigger audience for a smaller window, and I think that bigger audience is also pretty old. It's just so depressing . . . you know, what's the medium age of the Fox News audience? It's like the mid- to late-fifties. I think

MSNBC is just 5 or 6 years younger, as is CNN . . . It's depressing that no one—I mean, maybe I should change the language a little bit—it's dismaying how hard it is to reach young people with news products. It is. It's difficult. And I'm not saying that it ever hadn't been, but I would just love it if one week the medium age for Fox News showed up to be 35. It would be awesome. But maybe it wouldn't be, too, because do you really want the whole country watching TV all the time? I root for the continued financial prosperity of all news organizations. Someone from CNN told me that the future—trying to get the young people involved—is mobile social videos. So, in other words, video news chunks distributed on Vine and Instagram and Twitter, and so on and so forth. But that's the way you want to get your audience.

The former news producer (6/16/14) thinks that opinion will be at least partly what keeps TV news relevant, along with convergence:

Well, I think the concept of TV will change. We're currently watching Netflix on my "TV box," but I have cancelled TV and I'm going on to—I'm trying to think of what app I use. I think people will still watch in some way, shape, or form. I think Nielsen ratings will have to over time represent the truth of how we're watching. I think the standard—the "overnights"—if I DVR something and watch it days later, I'm still a viewer, I'm still watching that show. So, I think that the rating system will have to be updated. I think there will definitely be news because people want opinion because they want to help . . . people aren't in school anymore but it doesn't mean their education is over. People want to be guided to stronger opinions about things. So, I think that's why people are watching this. I think that everyone—you know, news is a water cooler thing, and you talk about it over your dinner table, you talk about it at the water cooler at work. I think people already have their own opinions but want to figure out more and understand more, perhaps try to figure out their argument while watching other people fight it out.

I think opinion will not go anywhere. I think opinion won't go away; I think where it will end up might be different, and I think it's also an age thing. You know, is opinion programming going to seep in to demo in millennial viewing things? I don't know. I don't know what younger people want to watch. But I think it will continue—opinion news, opinion programming will continue; it might be in a web format, you might be watching it on your TV, you might be watching it on some screen that's connected to your Internet. I don't know who's going to own the space, I don't know who's going to run TV news in five years. I don't think any of these websites are going to own it for the next two years or so. But I think in four or five years, we're going to see a completely different being take over different outlets; be in control of our media consumption. I don't know what that is. Otherwise, I would be a millionaire, billionaire.

Frank Sesno (10/12/14) also believes convergence is the key to TV news' survival:

> The future of TV news is cloudy at best. That's because TV news won't stay TV for long. The future of video is digital and mobile. TV News has already suffered major ratings declines—local, network, and cable news—because people are getting their information online and on their own time. When CNN went on the air, it was a revolution because it was news on demand, 24/7. But now all news is on demand. All news is 24/7. Just ask the newsweeklies. So the future of TV news? It will have to be more accessible, more mobile and ever-less dependent on appointment viewing. Will nightly newscasts go away? Not anytime soon. But they will become ever more multi-platform presentations, I believe, that debut on television but have larger audiences online.

David Mastio (8/7/14) said of network broadcast news in particular that "it changed less than almost any medium." The large caveat he included, as some other journalists I spoke with also did, was "I think, but, just to put any comments I may make on this in context, I haven't watched a complete evening newscast in fifteen years at least."

Mastio said,

> I think that decline got really underway with generation X stuck with newspapers a lot longer than we stuck with the evening news. Especially with the rise of cable and that whole idea of, if I were gonna imagine one real change that's gonna have to come to cable, or to broadcast news, is give it to me now when I want it, you know if you can get your entertainment shows anytime you want, why on earth should you not be able to get the evening news whenever you want? I think they're gonna have to do four,

five or [inaudible] editions a day if they're gonna keep people's attention. That's the ridiculous thing that has changed. I mean, who's home at 5:30 anymore?

Taking a more pessimistic view, according to a CNN digital employee, the only reason people might continue to watch TV news is if it was just a personality or for some other purpose, entertainment value, versus really getting information.

I mean like if there's, I don't know, a protest or a sudden weather event and you want to see it, then you turn on the news. But then it gets to be four hours of the same clips over and over again, and—I'm sure you've been reading about like [the move toward web content] and how that stuff's really going to change things. I mean I don't think we can say that they're going to revolutionize reporting yet. . . . [B]ut if that is sort of a trend that we're going in, then can we trust it anymore? I mean like just because I'm seeing it, I don't trust it, because I know that the people talking to me about it don't actually have all the expert-level knowledge about it; they went to a binder for a bunch of information and hope to synthesize it. So I don't blame people for not trusting too many anchors.

Predictions about the Future of Newspapers

Jim Henderson (12/10/14) is somewhat optimistic about the future of newspapers, citing new ownership and convergence as positive trends:

I mean, I think it's good, because we have a lot more people doing journalism now, and they will get better and better, because a lot of those people are Millennials who are very sharp and smart, and they're gaining a lot of experience very quickly. And they also have the technological savvy. And it's sort of going a little bit back to the future, too, where as far as newspaper legacy models, you're getting more ownership by non-media companies or non-media people. Bezos with *The Washington Post*, and there are a bunch of others. And that's good. Because in the old days, we had all those great newspapers, a lot of them were supported by some rich guy who was taking a flyer on it. Some of them made a lot of money, but a lot of them went out of business. The other side is television, of course. Local ownership of TV has become very profitable. Whether that will remain so—certainly with political advertising, the huge surge in revenue every two years—God, it's a windfall. So if those companies decide to put their revenue and earnings toward journalism, that could change things. You could have situations where a local TV station starts to take over, becoming the main news outlet over what was once a metro newspaper because they've got their own line. It's just that the company that owns that local TV station would have to commit to that. . . . You've got your TV journalists, but if they've got print journalists, online journalists there as well, writing more in-depth stories—you see it now. You go online to some of the TV stations, and they have written news reports, local news reports . . . And they've got the video to go with it, of course, which is very powerful. So, you can see that happening.

On the future of newspapers, Rem Rieder (1/20/15) said,

> to me, the most fascinating will be the continuing evolution of newspaper companies and newspaper properties. And, now, we have this wave of spin offs coming and that's going to . . . the newspapers are not going to be there with all those fabulously wealthy TV stations. And you've got the same thing happening at *The Tribune*, Rupert Murdoch has done it, *Time* has done it, and the deal with Scripps, and the Milwaukee paper. So the really significant story to follow will be spin offs, the Gannett spin off will probably be happening in July or something.[1] What will happen to the newspapers? Whatever their shortcoming, still so much of the reporting power, fire power, is the newspaper companies, a lot of network is digital, but how they evolve and how they both in terms of revenue and editorially is to me that is the most fascinating question out there.

Amber Phillips thinks that more analysis, more of the journalism that walks the line between analysis and opinion, is what will keep newspaper journalism—in print and online—going:

> I'm still optimistic about the future for newspaper journalism. I do think this is kind of the way of the future for it, because there's so much news through the Internet, which is kind of what everyone said hurt newspapers—there's so much information, why would you read your own paper?—but it's an opportunity for us

as newspapers to provide analysis—specific, dedicated, focused analysis—for our readers. It says, "Hey, we know there's a lot of information out there, we know you're not reading us for what happened, but we can tell you why this happened or how this happened." So I think it's an opportunity for us.

However, she cautions that if all print journalism moves this way, it could lead to the oversaturation of similar types of content, like she sees on TV:

TV news moves so much more quickly to be distinguishing themselves toward opinion and commentary. It certainly helps the brands of the channels they were on. But I almost wonder if there's not an oversaturation—that's such a clichéd term, I apologize—but I almost wonder if viewers [think] cable news, blah blah blah. And I've seen CNN in the past 5 years trying to distinguish itself as almost the opposite of print journalism. "We're going to cut through the noise by providing you with objective, here's what happened news with thoughtful analysis." And so I'm—maybe that's a cautionary tale for print journalism, like do we run the risk of having so many Voxes—you know, Vox.com—that readers are kinds of sick of the BuzzFeeds and the Vox.com "listicles" and analyses, and then we revert back to the AP style with just the facts, like I've seen CNN try and make its name.

By December 2018, several of these digital news sites, including Vox and Buzzfeed, had begun to struggle financially (Pompeo, 2018). Phillips made similar comments about "explanatory journalism" in a Brookings Institution project (Hudak, 2016). In a different Brookings Institution paper (Dionne, 2016), E. J. Dionne wrote about the rise of opinion journalism which he sees as potentially positive, as long as measures are taken to preserve objective reporting.

In summary, journalists think opinion in news will continue to increase, but could reach a saturation point. They think personalization of news will be key in its usage and popularity. They think the brand and notoriety of the individual journalist will matter more in the future, and that television news might survive because it makes use of the human element—the individual journalist's brand. Journalists think that TV news has a greater chance of survival if convergence between television and mobile and other devices is effective. Television news also performs a sifting and summarizing function. Convergence was also cited as the essential ingredient in keeping newspapers afloat.

The following concluding chapter will discuss the predictions and recommendations made by journalists, and the implications of their perspectives.

8

Where We Go from Here

At the beginning of this book, I wrote that the title of the book, *From News to Talk*, describes two phenomena in news: the first, a spectrum ranging from news to talk, gradients in formats, content, and delivery/hosts; the second, a movement from news to talk (news to entertainment, "objective"/traditional to opinion/commentary). There is a third phenomenon that the title alludes to: that news leads people to talk, in all sorts of ways (i.e., water cooler, social media, in and on other news venues). While beyond the parameters of this book's research, other scholars are pursuing research on the sharing of, reacting to, and discussion of news in social media. Since the November 2016 elections, much work has begun and advanced on ways to solve the problems of echo chambers, particularly on social media—especially Facebook. Mark Zuckerberg and Facebook are experimenting with ways to expose users to different points of view and news sources, and to detect and delete "fake news" (Kosoff, 2016). Facebook and Twitter both joined the First Draft Coalition, a network of partners whose goals are "to raise awareness and address challenges relating to trust and truth in the digital age. Partners work together to tackle common issues, including ways to streamline the verification process, improve the experience of eyewitnesses and increase news literacy" (First Draft News). Partners include social platforms, news organizations, other industry projects, associations, research labs, and universities. Other researchers (Bode, 2017[1]; Porter, 2017) are examining and looking for strategies to improve the quality and veracity of the information shared through social media. Facebook also changed its algorithm to reprioritize users' news feeds to focus on posts from friends and family rather than businesses and publishers which is having an effect on news organizations who use the site to promote their content (Bromwich & Haag, 2018).

One thing we know is that we can no longer say categorically that journalists are resistant to change. We've witnessed journalistic invention and adaptation in response to the changes of the past decade. These changes include the decreasing relevance of form or author: who the author is/who does "journalism," (i.e., professional, non-professional journalists), what kind of "journalism" (straight/traditional, opinion/point of view/commentary, personality-driven, entertainment elements), or on which platforms, devices, or venues content is made available and seen. In the current era of journalism, Tom Rosenstiel (2015) suggested that perhaps what matters are enduring principles such as transparency, evidence-based assertions, trustworthiness, and credibility. In a 2016 Brookings report, Rosenstiel wrote, "The answer for journalism is not going to be found in chucking all the old notions or in clinging to them, but in a blend of embracing some revolutionary methods while keeping faith with some key fundamental principles."

The findings across the previous five chapters are a range of responses and thoughts about journalism, as varied as journalists themselves, but they reflect certain themes. Chapter 2 revealed that most journalists agree that there's been an increase in opinion and commentary in news over the past ten years. The reasons journalists cite for the increase are competition from more outlets and the fight for the audience's attention, the low cost of opinion and commentary, the expression of opinion through social media, the polarization of the audience who desires to have their views reflected, the rise of cable news, and the 24-hour news cycle. Of Jeff Zucker's strategy to "broaden" CNN's definition of news with new programming, some journalists defend and justify the strategy as a practical necessity for a network that has always thrived during breaking news but struggled at slower times, and recall that "news" has always meant varied formats and content. Other journalists think the strategy disappointing and one that will weaken the news provider. Most journalists said that journalistic self-branding is also a practical necessity today, and while a few were uncomfortable with the trend, they don't fault journalists who pursue it.

Chapter 3 examined journalists' views about opinion and incivility in news discourse through analyses of what journalists have said and written in published digital news media since the '90s. Some journalists blame their peers for contributing to an uncivil media climate, but most believe journalists and their organizations have merely reflected or catered to a less civil culture. In chapter 4, through what the more than thirty journalists expressed in our personal interactions over the past several years, we can garner that the views of journalists with regard to incivility are not monolithic. They don't cohere to a single theme. While some journalists are concerned for audiences and their field due to incivility, others have confidence in the audience's ability, or don't assume that incivility is undesirable to start. The different journalistic views about opinion and incivility didn't break down neatly by variables such as the journalist's age or time in the field. Generational differences did not appear to be linked in any consistent way with journalistic perspective.

Chapter 5 sought to tease apart the distinct ideas of opinionated news and uncivil exchanges in political news to show that they are not equivalent or automatically linked, through a case study. The PBS "NewsHour" with Brooks and Shields provides a model of heated political exchange that remains civil and informative. The Brooks and Shields case study enables the suggestion of conditions under which opinion/point-of-view and partisan journalism could make useful contributions to the United States' current political and cultural climate. Although the discourse of Brooks and Shields on the "NewsHour" has a particular context, we believe that these examples of civil discourse can be applied in other contexts and that it is important for our society that principles of civil discourse be applied in other contexts. PBS, as a public broadcaster, has a special situation, being free from the same commercial pressures as network and cable news programs, and also attracting far fewer viewers (Pew, 2013). Yet it is still considered the most trusted source in news for 10 years running (PBS, 2013). According to the reports, the PBS "NewsHour" "differs in its agenda from other television news programs," offering "more than a third more coverage of international news," a third more time covering government than the commercial network newscasts, and much less time on crime, disasters, and lifestyle (Pew, 2012). Consequently, almost "one-third of the respondents (31%) have deserted a news outlet because it no longer provides the news and information they had grown accustomed to" (Overview; Pew, 2013). Although its audience is significantly smaller than its broadcast and cable counterparts, the "NewsHour" still attracts nearly one million people (Pew, 2013).

In trying to extract our findings about civil discourse on the "NewsHour" to commercial programs, we know that more civil news discourse translates to more trust of particular journalists and programs, and TV news as an institution. People can still learn from opinionated news, and there will be more opinionated talk on TV "news." But fewer people watch civil political news commentary. Why is this and can it be changed? People's reasons for watching civil versus uncivil news may be different (uses and gratifications they seek—affirming already held opinions vs. seeking out new information; information vs. entertainment). But another possible reason why fewer people watch civil political news commentary on TV might be simply because there is not much of it around. In addition to Brooks and Shields, one other notable example of the opposing political commentary duo on TV was the "Hannity & Colmes" show which ran on Fox News for 12 years from 1996 to 2008. It featured Sean Hannity, the conservative, and Alan Colmes, the liberal, and although Hannity, in interviews about Colmes's departure from the show in 2008, highlighted the friendship between the two "sparring" partners, the show was never recognized as a bastion of civil discourse (Calderone, 2008). Even so, the "Hannity & Colmes" show stands as an example of a successful pairing of politically opposite commentators on commercial TV news. If given more of these types of options, might audiences watch? It would be a worthwhile experiment (albeit at someone's financial risk) to see whether the principles and examples of civility in political news discourse exhibited by Brooks and Shields could be successfully implemented in a commercial context. If so, it could pave the way for more civil news discourse on TV, and if not, it could justify the need for more alternative venues and modes of funding to foster and sustain news enterprises valuing civil discourse.

Chapter 6 analyzed journalistic perspectives about Katie's, Anderson's, and Brian's ill-fated talk show attempts. Journalists' comments cohered around three themes regarding why Couric, Cooper, and Williams embarked on the talk and magazine programs. These were that (1) The new news/media environment requires/expects/demands that journalists, and all public figures for that matter, be present in multiple venues/platforms; and journalists are hedging their bets/making multiple bets; (2) Hubris of the journalist-star: already well-known personalities want to expand their brand, get in front of the largest audience possible; show another side of themselves, have another forum for their work; and (3) Corporate strategy and financial interests on the part of the networks and hosts. Journalistic discourse about the three cases was divided. Some believed there were systemic reasons for the ventures and some believed the three cases was coincidental and don't mark anything larger.

How journalists expect the new news landscape to continue to evolve (i.e., hybridity, genre blurring, the larger context of the info-tainment environment, "the daily me," citizen journalism, online news, alternative news providers) was the subject of Chapter 7. Journalists were split in their predictions about whether television news will continue to exist and thrive, but their views on whether opinion and commentary in news will continue were unanimous: a resounding "Yes."

Avenues for Future Research, and Implications

The research in this book was unable to determine exactly what definition of civility was being used by journalists who expressed the views examined here. As discussed, definitions of civility and incivility are many and varied. Future research could complement the work of Stryker et al. (2014) and Muddiman

(2014a) and investigate the interpretation of civility and incivility by journalists to further move toward a standardized understanding of civility. As Stryker and Muddiman suggest, it would be useful for research, measurement, and evaluation purposes to have a more unified understanding of civility. It would also be useful in discussions about public political discourse to have a more common understanding of the meaning. In terms of what journalists think, it is less important whether the definition is consistent than knowing what definitions and understandings they have and are using.

While this book provided evidence that some journalists are aware of academic research about opinion and civility in mediated discourse, academic research in this area is quickly expanding, and journalistic knowledge is not likely to keep pace with the latest findings. Equally, academic research should continue to consider it important to take into account the perceptions and practices of journalists. Several resources are trying to bridge these different communities, such as Nieman's *Journalist's Resource*, the National Institute for Civil Discourse, which has already held sessions with journalists and plans more, the Association for Education in Journalism and Mass Communication, and others.

A third community that belongs to this conversation is that of educators and news and media literacy proponents. Going forward, it makes sense to consider the different conversations about opinion and civility taking place and to endeavor to bring them together. Finally, future work can envision and plan steps toward action. As Stryker et al. (2014: 2) wrote, "Constitutional protection for free speech precludes establishing legal rules requiring civility, but it does not hinder the adoption of strong social norms favoring civility." Although regulation is unlikely, social norms can be powerful and influential. What this study can offer is evidence that journalists, too, share in the concern about uncivil mediated discourse in many cases, which may strengthen the arguments put forth by advocates for interventions to improve the quality of public political discourse.

Of the new media environment, termed by Williams and Delli Carpini (2011) as a "media regime," they state:

> Assuring this regime is a democratic one requires serious consideration of what was most beneficial and most problematic about past regimes and what is potentially most beneficial and most problematic about today's new information environment.

This book has not sought to be prescriptive or normative. It has described and analyzed journalists' perspectives. Others are involved in filling in gaps where, in their view, journalism has faltered, or is faltering, with foci on local news, investigative journalism, fact-checking, and civility.[2] The three types of responses suggested as remedies to concern over the state of news most often have to do with the audience (media or news literacy education, and technological interventions such as changes to Facebook news feeds), government/policy, and the media themselves.

Focusing on the audience, initiatives such as the News Literacy Project seek to make education and news literacy training part of the school curriculum. Nancy Gibbs (2017) said, "I do think we're going to have a massive, to the extent that it's possible, education campaign in news literacy, really making us all mindful of what we consume and what we share." Chris Satullo, former VP News and Civic Engagement, WHYY; former editorial page editor at Philadelphia Inquirer (3/14/16), thinks media/news literacy is very important, but Satullo also said that we "need journalists to parse it out and tell us what's true and important." Among the efforts focusing on the media themselves, in September 2015, the Council on Foundations hosted an event and released a two-year status report on its Nonprofit Media Project (2013; 2015). The intermediate outcome of the 2009–2010 future of media sessions was the Aspen Institute–Knight Commission and report on The Information Needs of Communities in a Democracy (2009). That, in part, led to the funding and launching of many of the news initiatives we've seen over the past several years. The 2015 Nonprofit Media event brought together panelists from non-profit online, print and television journalism organizations, and representatives from foundations who support nonprofit media. They, along with other supporters such as McChesney, Pickard, and Rosenstiel, feel that commercial media are not completely satisfying the public's needs for information. The report on "The IRS and Nonprofit Media" explains that the fact that an organization may advocate a particular viewpoint does not prevent it from being granted nonprofit status by the IRS if it "presents a sufficiently full and fair exposition of the pertinent facts as to permit an individual or the public to form an independent opinion or conclusion" (2015: 7). A 2013 Pew Research Center Report (Mitchell, Jurkowitz, Holcomb et al., 2013) found that while the nonprofit news sector is growing, "many of these organizations face substantial challenges to their long-term financial well-being . . . large, often one-time seed grants from foundations help many of these nonprofit news outlets get up and running. But as those grants expire, many organizations do not have the resources or expertise necessary for the business tasks needed to broaden the funding base."

Pickard (2015) and others also believe that while these nonprofit media endeavors are essential and important, they alone are still not sufficient for providing the information the public needs, and so they call on government policy intervention and reform to help support particular types of news (namely local and investigative). These types of reform are much less likely in the Trump era and Republican-controlled agencies. Many policies enacted by the FCC and FTC under the Obama administration were already repealed during the first six months of the new Presidency. Still others will continue to argue that a market approach is best—if the public demands new types of news, organizations will rise up to produce the supply. And as this research has shown, not all journalists or industry professionals are dissatisfied or concerned about the state of news.

Journalistic views about their craft and peers amidst the changes of the past decade are complex and not always unified. While certain similarities in their perspectives have been detectable as themes, the disparities reflect the different communities of practice with which journalists today identify. The journalistic field has become so varied that journalists look to those whose positions are most like their own as reference points, whether that means the community of media critics, self-branders, opiners, journalist-hackers, or those facing obsolescence for unwillingness or inability to adapt to new practices. Under an all-journalism umbrella network of weak ties, many journalistic communities of practice coalesce, mature, and disperse. The evidence in this book, through the focus on journalists' perspectives about opinion and commentary—or "talk"—in news, has provided a window into this cyclical phenomenon.

Notes

Chapter 2

1. The Commission on Freedom of the Press was also known as the Hutchins Commission.
2. Shafer was referring to: "The Needlers: Our Journalistic Satirists." Henry Ladd Smith and James Knox. *Journalism & Mass Communication Quarterly*, September 1962, vol. 39, no. 3, 309–316. http://jmq.sagepub.com/content/39/3/309.short
3. Lack had previously been President and COO of NBC before leaving in 2003, was chief executive and chairman of Sony Music Entertainment; spent six years at the helm of Bloomberg Media Group; then had a tenure as chief executive of the Broadcasting Board of Governors, and is now News Chairman at NBC.
4. Allen was referring to Jonathan Martin at the *New York Times*—"Jay Mart" or "J. Mart."

Chapter 3

1. York (2013) suggests that perceptions of political incivility are a function of viewing distinct genres of television news media: "hostile" cable news versus network news. His research attempts to explain the discrepancy between public perceptions of incivility and the Annenberg Public Policy Center's (APPC) baseline measure of political incivility in Congress which had been relatively flat, as of 2011. York's (2013) study found that cable news outlets provide more coverage of elite political incivility than do network news outlets, and cable news viewers perceive politics to be more uncivil than do network news viewers. York suggests that cable news viewers may perceive more incivility in national politics overall than actually exists, but concedes nonetheless that incivility is conveyed on cable news and that the public's perception of incivility itself is concerning.
2. *The Financial Times*, along with other media outlets, published articles blaming their media peers for perpetuating a "viciously partisan tone" of political coverage that some argue set the stage for such violence (Edgecliffe-Johnson, Andrew, & David Gelles. January 11, 2011, "America: Vanquished by Vitriol"). Some of the resulting

civility initiatives are the University of Arizona's National Institute for Civil Discourse; The 2014 Harvard Negotiation Law Review Symposium: Political Dialogue and Civility in an Age of Polarization; A National Symposium on Civility in Public Discourse at Bradley University; a two-day event at DePauw University.

3. The oldest articles returned from the organizational sites were from the early nineties. The decision to include items older than ten years was made to show that journalistic conversation about opinion and civility stretches farther back. We considered all items returned in searches of the *AJR*, *CJR*, Nieman Lab, and Poynter sites, through Google News searches using the terms "civility in news discourse," and through Google blogs. The regular Google search for "civility in news discourse" returned thousands of results, so relevant items were retrieved from links in the first ten pages of Google search results.

4. Liu, the author of the *Time* article, may not be considered a journalist by all; the author bio on Time.com says he is the author of several books, was a speechwriter and policy adviser to President Clinton, and that the views expressed are solely his own. His piece appeared in the Viewpoint section.

5. This serves to complete the circle of former journalists-turned-academics who frequently appear on journalism sites.

6. A *CJR* article (Rose, 2008) and The Engaging News Project also provide a list of many of these same strategies used by journalists for moderating online reader comments.

7. Dave Mastio (8/7/14) was the interviewee who originally told me about the case of Froma Harrop.

Chapter 4

1. Pew Research Center (2014, 12 June). "Political Polarization in the American Public." http://www.people-press.org/2014/06/12/political-polarization-in-the-american-public/ as discussed by D. Balz (2014, 12 June). *The Washington Post*. https://www.washingtonpost.com/politics/pew-poll-in-polarized-america-we-live-as-we-vote/2014/06/12/0b149fec-f196-11e3-914c-1fbd0614e2d4_story.html?utm_term=.7df9d82b2040

2. Samuelson, R. (2014, 23 April). "Media Bias Explained in two studies." *The Washington Post*. https://www.washingtonpost.com/opinions/robert-samuelson-media-bias-explained-in-two-studies/2014/04/23/9dccdcf6-cafd-11e3-93eb-6c0037dde2ad_story.html?utm_term=.181f14c8e18d. The study referred to is by Gentzkow & Shapiro (2014).

3. http://thehill.com/blogs/floor-action/senate/213003-hatch-senate-has-emasculated-itself

4. Mundy was referring to this piece: Hess, A. (2014, 6 January). "Why Women Aren't Welcome on the Internet." Pacific Standard. https://psmag.com/social-justice/women-arent-welcome-internet-72170. Scholarly research has found gender bias against women in journalism (Steiner, 2012; Chambers, Steiner & Fleming, 2004). Usher, Holcomb & Littman (2018) found that on Twitter, "male journalists amplify and engage male peers almost exclusively, while female journalists tend to engage most with each other."

5. AJR ceased online publication in July 2015. Hoyt, M. "The end of American Journalism Review and what it means for media criticism." (2015, 24 August). https://www.cjr.org/analysis/american_journalism_review_no_more.php

6. Lisheron, M. (2011, 24 August). "A Fearless Media Critic." *AJR*: http://ajrarchive.org/article.asp?id=5133

Chapter 5

1. The Allegheny College Prize for Civility in Public Life each year "will honor two winners, one from each side of the ideological spectrum, who show noteworthy civility while continuing to fight passionately for their beliefs" (Allegheny College, February 21, 2012). http://sites.allegheny.edu/news/2012/02/21/david-brooks-and-mark-shields-honored-with-inaugural-prize-for-civility-in-public-life/

Chapter 7

1. At my interview with Dave Mastio of *USA Today* on August 7, 2014, two days prior, Gannett had announced the split of the company with one new company composed of 2/3 digital and broadcast stations, and the other company keeping the Gannett name to include the rest of digital and the newspapers. The 8/6/14 *USA Today* article in the Money section discussed the split.

Chapter 8

1. Bode presented on research she and E. Vraga have co-authored, including the article, "In Related News, That Was Wrong: The Correction of Information through Related Stories Functionality in Social Media," in the August 2015 *Journal of Communication*, 65 (4); and the 2017 article, "Using Expert Sources to Correct Health Misinformation in Social Media," in *Science Communication*, 39 (5).

2. See the FCC's (2011) report, The Information Needs of Communities: The Changing Media Landscape in a Broadband Age: http://www.fcc.gov/info-needs-communities, which contains its findings and recommendations from its "Future of Media" project: http://www.fcc.gov/events/serving-public-interest-digital-era-0; the white papers discussing ways to implement recommendations from the Knight/FCC report: http://www.knightcomm.org/implementing-the-recommendations-of-the-knight-commission/; the FTC's "How Will Journalism Survive the Internet Age?" project archives; or the New America Foundation's project, "Making Media Work": http://www.newamerica.net/events/2010/making_media_work; the website of Free Press: http://www.freepress.net; or books such as *The death and life of American journalism: The media revolution that will begin the World again* (2010), or *Venomous speech: Problems with American political discourse on the right and left* (2013), and *Will the last reporter please turn out the lights: The collapse of journalism and what can be done to fix it* (2011).

Bibliography

Adler, B. (2014, 21 April). "The rise of internet video news." *Columbia Journalism Review.* http://archives.cjr.org/news_literacy/kids_these_days.php

Allee, V. (2000). "Knowledge networks and communities of practice." *OD Practitioner.*

Alvarez-Monzoncillo, J. M. (2013). *Watching the Internet: The future of TV?* Formalpress.

Amanpour, C. (2016, 23 November). "Journalism faces an 'existential crisis' in Trump era." http://www.cnn.com/2016/11/23/opinions/christiane-amanpour-journalism-in-trump-era/index.html

American Press Institute. (2016). "About us." Retrieved from https://www.americanpressinstitute.org/about/about-us/

American University Center for Media & Social Impact. (2013). *Set of principles in fair use for journalism.* Retrieved from http://www.cmsimpact.org/journalism

Anderson, A. A., Yeo, S. K., Brossard, D., Scheufele, D. A., Xenos, M. A. (2016, August). "Toxic Talk: How Online Incivility Can Undermine Perceptions of Media." *International Journal of Public Opinion Research.* https://doi.org/10.1093/ijpor/edw022

Anderson, A. A., Brossard, D., Scheufele, D. A., Xenos, M. A., & Ladwig, P. (2014). "The 'Nasty Effect': Online Incivility and Risk Perceptions of Emerging Technologies." *Journal of Computer-Mediated Communication* 19(3): 373–387. doi: 10.1111/jcc4.12009.

Anderson, C. W. (2013). *Rebuilding the News: Metropolitan Journalism in the Digital Age.* Philadelphia: Temple University Press.

Andrews, T. M. (2017, 13 June). "Megyn Kelly dropped as host for Sandy Hook group's gala over Alex Jones interview." *The Washington Post.* https://www.washingtonpost.com/news/morning-mix/wp/2017/06/13/megyn-kelly-dropped-as-host-for-sandy-hook-groups-gala-over-alex-jones-interview/?utm_term=.19aeb8264293

Arceneaux, K., & Johnson, M. (2015). "More a Symptom than a Cause: Polarization and Partisan News Media in America." In James A. Thurber and Antoine Yoshinaka (Eds.) *American Gridlock: The Sources, Character, and Impact of Political Polarization.* Ch. 14, pp. 309–336. Cambridge University Press.

Associated Press. (2013, 7 October). "Government Shutdown Timeline: A Look at Congress' Battle." http://www.huffingtonpost.com/2013/10/07/government-shutdown-timeline_n_4058471.html

Association of Opinion Journalists. (2016). Retrieved from https://www.asne.org/aoj-asne-merger
Barber, B. (1999). "The discourse of civility." In S. L. Elkin & K. E. Sołtan (Eds.), *Citizen competence and democratic institutions* (pp. 39–47). University Park: The Pennsylvania State University Press.
Barnes. R. (2017, 19 June). "Supreme Court to hear potentially landmark case on partisan gerrymandering." *The Washington Post.* https://www.washingtonpost.com/politics/courts_law/supreme-court-to-hear-potentially-landmark-case-on-partisan-gerrymandering/2017/06/19/d525237e-5435-11e7-b38e-35fd8e0c288f_story.html?tid=notifi_push_breaking-news&pushid=5947d3dbf07ec1380000000a
Barnett, S. (2011). *The Rise and Fall of Television Journalism.* London: Bloomsbury Academic.
Baron, M. (2016, 30 November). "Washington Post Editor Marty Baron's message to journalists." http://www.vanityfair.com/news/2016/11/washington-post-editor-marty-baron-message-to-journalists
Bauder, D. (2013, 25 November). "Martin Bashir's Sarah Palin Comments Haunting Him Weeks Later." The Associated Press. http://www.huffingtonpost.com/2013/11/26/martinbashir-sarah-palin-msnbc_n_4342846.html?ir=Politics
Baum, M. A., & Jamison, A. S. (2006). "The Oprah effect: How soft news helps inattentive citizens vote consistently." *Journal of Politics,* Vol. 68, Is. 4, pp. 946–959, November.
Baum, M. A. (2003). "Soft news and political knowledge: Evidence of absence or absence of evidence?" *Political Communication,* Vol. 20, Is. 2.
Baum, M. A. (2002). "Sex, lies, and war: How soft news brings foreign policy to the inattentive public." *American Political Science Review,* March, Vol. 96, No. 1.
Baumard, P. (1999). *Tacit knowledge in organizations.* Thousand Oaks, CA: Sage.
Baym, G. (2005). "The Daily Show: Discursive Integration and the Reinvention of Political Journalism." *Political Communication,* Vol. 22, No. 3.
Baym, G. (2010). *From Cronkite to Colbert. The Evolution of Broadcast News.* Paradigm Publishers.
Becker, L. B., Fruit, J., & Caudill, S. (1987). *The training and hiring of journalists.* Norwood, NJ: Ablex Publishing Corporation.
Beaujon, A. (2012, 22 June). "Politico Suspends Joe Williams for Racially Tinged Remarks about Romney." *Poynter.* http://www.poynter.org/mediawire/topstories/178226/politicosuspends-joe-williams-for-racially-tinged-remarks-about-romney/
Ben-Porath, E. N. (2007, 23 April). "Internal Fragmentation of the News: Television news in dialogical format and its consequences for journalism." *Journalism Studies,* Vol. 8, Is. 3, pp. 414–431. doi: 10.1080/14616700701276166.
Ben-Porath, E. N. (2010). "Interview effects: Theory and evidence for the impact of televised political interviews on viewer attitudes." *Communication Theory,* 20, 323–347. doi: 10.1111/j.1468-2885.2010.01365.x.
Ben-Porath, E. N. (2007, May). "The Watchdog's Bite: Viewer Reactions to Uncivil News Interviews." Conference Paper, International Communication Association Annual Meeting, San Francisco, CA.

Bennett, W. L. (2011, 28–29 March). "What's Wrong with Incivility? Civility as the New Censorship in American Politics." Paper delivered at the 2011 John Breaux Symposium: "In the Name of Democracy: Leadership, Civility, and Governing in a Polarized Media Environment," Manship School of Mass Communication, Louisiana State University, Baton Rouge.

Bennett, W. L, Gressett, L. A., & Haltom, W. (1985). "Repairing the News: A Case Study of the News Paradigm." *Journal of Communication* 35:50–68.

Benoit, W. L. (1995). *Accounts, Excuses, Apologies: A Theory of Image Restoration Strategies*. Albany: State University of New York Press.

Benoit, W. L. (1997). "Hugh Grant's image restoration discourse: An actor apologizes." *Communication Quarterly*, 45(3): 251–267.

Berkowitz, D. (2000, August). "Doing Double Duty: Paradigm Repair and the Princess Diana What-a-Story." *Journalism* 1(2): 125–43.

Berkowitz, D., & TerKuerst, J. V. (1999). "Community as interpretive community: Rethinking the journalist-source relationship." *Journal of Communication*, 49(3): 125–136.

Bible, G. (2016). "Are we our own harshest critics? A case study of media criticism across different platforms." Unpublished paper, 2016, Georgetown University.

Bishop, R. (1999). "From Behind the Walls: Boundary Work by News Organizations in Their Coverage of Princess Diana's Death." *Journal of Communication Inquiry* 23:91–113.

Bishop, R. (2001). "New Media, Heal Thyselves: Sourcing Patterns in News Stories about Media Performance." *Journal of Communication Inquiry* 25:22–37.

Bishop, R. (1999). "From behind the walls: Boundary work by news organizations in their coverage of Princess Diana's Death." *Journal of Communication Inquiry*, 23:91–113.

Bivens, R. (2014). *Digital Currents: How Technology and the Public are Shaping TV News*. University of Toronto Press.

Blau, P. M., & Scott, W. R. (1962). *Formal organizations, a comparative approach*. San Francisco, CA: Chandler Publishing Co.

Bluhm, W. (2004). Originally Appeared in *Green Bay News-Chronicle* as "It Turns Out That Hate Works." Reposted in "Blame '60M' Point/Counterpoint Segment for Loss of Civility" on Poynter.org by Jim Romenesko, *Poynter*, July 13. http://www.poynter.org/latest-news/mediawire/24178/blame-60m-pointcounterpoint-segment-for-loss-of-civility/

Boczkowski, P. (2010). *News at Work: Imitation in an Age of Information Abundance*. University of Chicago Press.

Bode, L. (2017, 21 October). Presentation at 2017 Journalism/Interactive conference on panel, "Researching Misinformation." Philip Merrill College of Journalism, University of Maryland.

Bond, M. (2012). "An Online Political Venue for Conservatives and Liberals." *American Journalism Review*, August/September. http://ajrarchive.org/Article.asp?id=5371

Borchers, C. (2015, 8 December). "Donald Trump was on Morning Joe Tuesday. It didn't go so well." Washington Post.com. https://www.washingtonpost.com/news/

the-fix/wp/2015/12/08/donald-trump-was-on-morning-joe-on-tuesday-it-didnt-go-so-well/?postshare=5551449600518376&tid=ss_mail

Borchers, C. (2017, 24 February). "White House blocks CNN, *New York Times* from press briefing hours after Trump slams media." *The Washington Post*. https://www.washingtonpost.com/news/the-fix/wp/2017/02/24/white-house-blocks-cnn-new-york-times-from-press-briefing-hours-after-trump-slams-media/?utm_term=.65a5083d73b6

Born, G. (2004). *Uncertain vision: Birt, Dyke and the Reinvention of the BBC*. London, England: Secker and Warburg.

Boylan, J. (2009). "Brief Encounters." Review of *Scandal & Civility: Journalism and the Birth of American Democracy* by Marcus Daniel, Oxford University Press. *Columbia Journalism Review*. http://www.cjr.org/review/brief_encounters_11.php?page=all

Bradshaw, P. (2011). "Communities of practice: Teaching students to learn in net-works." Retrieved from http://onlinejournalismblog.com/2011/04/01/communities-of-practiceteaching-students-to-learn-in-networks/

Brazile, D. (2010). "Twelve things the world should toss out: Pundits." *The Washington Post*. http://www.washingtonpost.com/wp-srv/special/opinions/outlook/spring cleaning/pundits.html

Breed, W. (1955). "Social control in the newsroom: A functional analysis." *Social Forces*, 33, 326–335.

Brewin, M. (1999). "The interpretive community and reform: Public journalism plays out in North Carolina." *Journal of Communication Inquiry*, 23(3): 222–238.

Bromwich, J. E., & Haag, M. (2018, 12 January). "Facebook is Changing. What Does That Mean for Your News Feed?" *New York Times*. https://www.nytimes.com/2018/01/12/technology/facebook-news-feed-changes.html

Brooks, D. J., & Geer, J. G. (2007). "Beyond Negativity: The Effects of Incivility on the Electorate." *American Journal of Political Science* 51:1–16.

Byers, D. (2014, 21 April). "The death of the Sunday shows." *Politico*. http://www.politico.com/story/2014/04/the-sunday-shows-105876

Byers, D. (2015, 5 October). "MSNBC has new roles for Steve Kornacki and Alex Wagner." http://money.cnn.com/2015/10/05/media/msnbc-steve-kornacki-alex-wagner/

Byers, D. (2014, 12 November). "CNN ratings blow vindicates Zucker." http://www.politico.com/blogs/media/2014/11/cnn-ratings-blow-vindicates-zucker-198669.html

Cain, S. (2012, January 13). "The rise of the new groupthink." *New York Times*. Retrieved from http://www.nytimes.com/2012/01/15/opinion/sunday/the-rise-of-the-new-groupthink.html

Calderone, M. (2008, November 24). "Hannity and Colmes split up." Politico.com. Retrieved from http://www.politico.com/blogs/michaelcalderone/1108/Hannity_and_Colmes_split_up.html

Calhoun, C. (Ed.). (1993). *Habermas and the public sphere*. Cambridge, MA:MIT Press.

Carlson, M. (2017). *Journalistic Authority: Legitimating News in the Digital Era*. Columbia University Press.

Carlson, M., & Peifer, J. T. (2013). "The Impudence of Being Earnest: Jon Stewart and the Boundaries of Discursive Responsibility." *Journal of Communication* 63(2): 333–350.

Carlson, M. (2015). "Metajournalistic discourse and the meanings of journalism: Definitional control, boundary work, and legitimation." *Communication Theory*. Advance online publication. doi: 10.1111/comt.12088.

Carlson, M., & Lewis, S. C. (Eds.) (2015). *Boundaries of Journalism: Professionalism, Practices and Participation*. London and New York: Routledge.

Carpignano, P., R. Andersen, S. Aronowitz, & W. Difazio. (1990). "Chatter in the Age of Electronic Reproduction: Talk Television and the "Public Mind." *Social Text*, No. 25/26, pp. 33–55.

Carr, D. (2014, 23 February). "Piers Morgan and CNN Plan End to his Prime-time Show." *New York Times*.

Carroll, B. (2014). *Writing & Editing for Digital Media*, 2nd Edition. New York: Routledge.

CBS News. (2013, 26 November). "CBS asks Lara Logan to take leave after flawed Benghazi report." http://www.cbsnews.com/news/cbs-asks-lara-logan-to-take-leave-after-flawed-benghazi-report/

Carson, B. (2015, 12 June). "Katie Couric gets a pay raise as she re-signs with Yahoo." Businessinsider.com. http://www.businessinsider.com/katie-couric-gets-a-pay-raise-as-she-re-signs-with-yahoo-2015-6

CBS (2011, 25 May). "The Early Show." CBS News Transcripts.

Cecil, M. (2002). "Bad apples: Paradigm overhaul and the CNN/Time 'Tailwind' story." *Journal of Communication Inquiry*, 26, 46–58.

Chalif, R. S. (2011). Selective politics: The fragmentation and polarization of news on cable TV (Master's thesis). Washington, DC: Georgetown University.

Chambers, D., Steiner, L. and Fleming, C. (2004). *Women and Journalism*. London and New York: Routledge.

Chariton, J. (2015, 3 August). "The State of MSNBC: When One Lean Forward becomes two steps backward." http://www.thewrap.com/the-state-of-msnbc-when-one-lean-forward-becomes-two-steps-backward/

Chariton, J. (2015, 28 August). "MSNBC Turmoil: High Profile Anchors Oppose Network's Hard News Pivot." http://www.thewrap.com/msnbc-turmoil-high-profile-anchors-are-against-networks-hard-news-pivot-exclusive/

Chavez, P., Stracqualursi, V., & Keneally, M. (2016, 26 October). "A History of the Donald Trump–Megyn Kelly Feud." http://abcnews.go.com/Politics/history-donald-trump-megyn-kelly-feud/story?id=36526503

Clark, R. P. (2007). "The Frames of Incivility." *Poynter*. http://www.poynter.org/how-tos/community-engagement/dialogue-or-diatribe/82374/the-frames-of-incivility/

Cleghorn, R. (1993). "The Public Looks at the Press with *AJR*." *American Journalism Review*, October. http://ajrarchive.org/Article.asp?id=951

Cleghorn, R. (1994). "Beyond Opinions: Setting the Stage." *American Journalism Review*, May. http://ajrarchive.org/Article.asp?id=1253

Coe, K., Kenski, K., & Rains, S. A. (2014). "Online and Uncivil? Patterns and Determinants of Incivility in Newspaper Website Comments." *Journal of Communication*. http://nicd.arizona.edu/sites/default/files/Online%20and%20Uncivil.pdf

Cohn, A. M. (2012). "Lawmakers Re-launch Civility Caucus in Time for Election Day." *The Hill*, September 21. http://thehill.com/blogs/twitter-room/other-news/250897-reps-cleavercapito-want-congress-to-make-nice-with-civility-caucus#ixzz2zYbZNdYm.

Collins, S. (2013, December 4). "Martin Bashir exits MSNBC in wake of Sarah Palin outburst." *Los Angeles Times*. Retrieved from http://www.latimes.com/entertainment/tv/showtracker/la-et-st-martin-bashir-exits-msnbc-in-wake-of-sarah-palin-outburst-20131204,0,3269678.story#ixzz2mdWXrKIG

Columbia Journalism Review. (2004). "A Summer of Lies." 43(2): 3.

Cooper, H., & Zeleny, J. (2011, 12 January). "Obama Calls for a New Era of Civility in U.S. Politics." *New York Times*. http://www.nytimes.com/2011/01/13/us/13obama.html?_r=0

Copps, M. (2014, March/April). "From the desk of a former FCC Commissioner: Journalists need to generate a national discussion on the future of the internet." *Columbia Journalism Review*. http://www.cjr.org/essay/from_the_desk_of_a_former_fcc.php?page=all#sthash.GP0mlbfq.dpuf

Council on Foundations. (2015). "The IRS and Nonprofit Media: A Step Forward Toward Creating a More Informed Public."

Council on Foundations. (2013). "The IRS and Nonprofit Media: Toward Creating a More Informed Public."

Cushion, S. (2015). *News and Politics: The Rise of Live and Interpretive Journalism*. Routledge.

Dalton, P., & Kramer, M. (2012). *Coarseness in U.S. public communication*. Madison, NJ: The Farleigh Dickinson University Press.

Davenport, E., & Hall, H. (2002). "Organizational knowledge and communities of practice." *Annual Review of Information Science and Technology*, 36, 170–227.

Diakopoulos, N., & Naaman, M. (2011). "Towards Quality Discourse in Online News Comments." In *Proceedings of the ACM 2011 Conference on Computer Supported Cooperative Work*, Hangzhou, China, ACM, 133–142.

Dionne, E. J. (2016, January). "The media democracy needs—and deserves: A response to 'Seven trends in old and new media.'" The Brookings Institution. https://www.brookings.edu/wp-content/uploads/2016/07/dionne.pdf

Ebner, T. (December 2011/January 2012). "Is Facebook the Solution to the Obnoxious Comment Plague?" *American Journalism Review*. http://ajrarchive.org/Article.asp?id=5213

Edgar, D. (2011 10 June). "Online Comments: 'Our Goal of Civility Is Falling Short.'" *Reader's Representative Journal, Los Angeles Times*. http://latimesblogs.latimes.com/readers/2011/06/online-comments-our-goal-of-civility-is-falling-short.html

Edgecliffe-Johnson, A., & Gelles, D. (2011, January 11). "America: Vanquished by vitriol. Financial Times." Retrieved from http://www.ft.com/cms/s/0/30bf2658-1dce-11e0-badd-00144feab49a.html#axzz3GGkvVVQ2

Ellis, J. (2010). "No Comment: The Portland Press Herald's About Face." *Nieman Journalism Lab*, October 21. http://www.niemanlab.org/2010/10/no-comments-lessons-from-the-portland-press-herald/

Ellison, S. (2017, March). "Megyn Kelly, Matt Lauer, and the Battle for the Future of NBC." *Vanity Fair Hive*. http://www.vanityfair.com/news/2017/02/megyn-kelly-matt-lauer-and-the-battle-for-the-future-of-nbc

Ekdale, B., Singer, J. B., Tully, M., & Harmsen, S. (2015, July). "Making change: diffusion of technological, relational, and cultural innovation in the newsroom." *Journalism & Mass Communication Quarterly*, Vol. 92, Is. 4.

Epstein, E. J. (1973). *News from nowhere: Television and the news*. New York: Random House.

Esser, F., & Umbricht, A. (2014). "The Evolution of Objective and Interpretative Journalism in the Western Press. Comparing Six News Systems since the 1960s." *Journalism & Mass Communication Quarterly*, 91(2): 229–249.

Fabian, J. (2017, 24 February). "White House hand-picks select media outlets for briefing." *The Hill*. http://thehill.com/homenews/administration/321049-white-house-hand-picks-select-media-for-briefing

Farhi, P. (2012, March 18). "A conundrum for conservative talk radio." *The Washington Post*. Retrieved from http://www.washingtonpost.com/lifestyle/style/a-conundrum-for-conservative-talk-radio/2012/03/15/gIQAVbAQLS_story.html

Farhi, P. (2014, 24 January). "Can the Dish show the way for breakaway journalists?" *The Washington Post*, C1.

Farhi, P. (2017, 10 March). "What's a legitimate news outlet? A new face in the White House press pool raises questions." *The Washington Post*. https://www.washingtonpost.com/lifestyle/style/whats-a-legitimate-news-outlet-a-new-face-in-the-white-house-press-pool-raises-questions/2017/03/10/2c7a6922-050d-11e7-b9fa-ed727b644a0b_story.html?hpid=hp_rhp-top-table-main_presspool-6pm%3Ahomepage%2Fstory&utm_term=.970a0adddd67

Farhi, P. (2016, 2 June). "Breaking News: We have reached peak punditry." *The Washington Post*. http://www.washingtonpost.com/sf/style/wp/2016/06/02/2016/06/02/pundits/?wpmm=1&wpisrc=nl_wemost-draw5

Farhi, P. (2016b, 28 February). "MSNBC severs ties with Melissa Harris-Perry after host's critical email." *The Washington Post*. https://www.washingtonpost.com/lifestyle/style/msnbc-will-cut-ties-with-show-host-who-wrote-critical-email-to-colleagues/2016/02/27/bce30c8e-dd82-11e5-891a-4ed04f4213e8_story.html?hpid=hp_no-name_hp-in-the-news%3Apage%2Fin-the-news

Farhi, P. (2014, 7 May). "Some news sites cracking down on over-the-top comments." *The Washington Post*. https://www.washingtonpost.com/lifestyle/style/some-news-sites-cracking-down-on-over-the-top-comments/2014/05/07/4bc90958-d619-11e3-95d3-3bcd77cd4e11_story.html?utm_term=.a95eba927871

Feldman, L. (2011). "The Effects of Journalist Opinionation on Learning from the News." *Journal of Communication*, 61(6): 1183–1201.

First Draft News (n.d.). https://firstdraftnews.com/about/

Fish, S. (1976). "Interpreting the 'Variorum.'" *Critical Inquiry*, 2(3): 465–485. Retrieved from JSTOR.

Fish, S. (1980). *Is there a text in this class? The authority of interpretive communities*. Cambridge, MA: Harvard University Press.

Fishman, M. (1980/1999). *Manufacturing the News*. Austin: University of Texas Press. In H. Tumber (Ed.), *News: A reader* (pp. 102–111). Oxford: Oxford University Press.

Flaherty, M. (2009, 23 January). "The rise of CNN's Don Lemon." *Variety*.

Folkenflik, D. (2016, 2 November). "Donna Brazile's Resignation Illustrates Cable TV's Pundit Problem." NPR. *All Things Considered*. http://www.npr.org/2016/11/02/500407470/donna-braziles-resignation-illustrates-cable-tvs-pundit-problem

Folkenflik, D. (2017, 24 February). "Lashing Out Against Critical Reports, White House Bars Outlets From Briefing." NPR. http://www.npr.org/2017/02/24/517112555/lashing-out-against-critical-reports-white-house-bars-outlets-from-briefing

Fraser, N. (1999). "Rethinking the public sphere: A contribution to the Critique of Actually Existing Democracy." In C. Calhoun (Ed.), *Habermas and the Public Sphere* (pp. 109–142). Cambridge, MA: The MIT Press.

Freidson, E. (1984). "The changing nature of professional control." *Annual Review of Sociology*, 10(1), 1–20.

"The Future of Journalism and Politics" (2015, 9 December). Speaker panel with Andy Carvin, the founder of reported.ly who is now with the social video publisher NowThis, and Amber Phillips, staff writer for "The Fix" at *The Washington Post*. In conjunction with Monash University's (Australia) master's program in journalism. Washington, DC: Georgetown University.

Gans, H. (1979). *Deciding What's News*. New York: Pantheon.

Gans, H. J. (2003). *Democracy and the News*. Oxford, England: Oxford University Press.

Gertz, M. (2017, 9 January). "Why We Should Keep Using The Term 'Fake News.'" *Media Matters for America*. https://www.mediamatters.org/blog/2017/01/09/why-we-should-keep-using-term-fake-news/214957

Gibbs, N. (2017, 15 November). Twenty-eighth Annual Theodore H. White Lecture on Press and Politics. Harvard Kennedy School Shorenstein Center on Media, Politics, and Public Policy.

Gibbs, N. (1998, 28 December). "Bill Clinton and Kenneth Star." *Time Magazine*. http://content.time.com/time/world/article/0,8599,2054146,00.html

Gieryn, T. F. (1983, December). "Boundary-Work and the Demarcation of Science from Non-Science: Strains and Interests in Professional Ideologies of Scientists." *American Sociological Review*, Vol. 48, No. 6, pp. 781–795.

Gitlin, T. (2016, 12 May). "Donald Trump's secret for avoiding hard questions: too many interviewers aren't asking the follow-up." https://www.washingtonpost.com/posteverything/wp/2016/05/12/trump-cracked-the-tv-interviewers-code-its-time-to-change-tactics-before-its-too-late/?utm_term=.10009277d8e8

Glaser, B. G, & Strauss, A. L. (1967). *The Discovery of Grounded Theory: Strategies for Qualitative Research*. Chicago: Aldine.

Glass, I. (2010). As reported by J. Hamer (2010, August 23) "Ira Glass on Broadcasting's 'Failure of Craft.'" *Washington News Council*. http://wanewscouncil.org/2010/08/23/iraglass-on-broadcastings-failure-of-craft/. Also featured on Jim Romanesko's blog on the Poynter site, August 24, 2010. http://www.poynter.org/latest-news/mediawire/105196/opinion-in-all-its-forms-is-kicking-the-ass-of-journalism/

Gold, H. (2014, 10 April). "CNN reveals new prime-time series." http://www.politico.com/blogs/media/2014/04/cnn-reveals-new-prime-time-series-186652

Goldberg, L., & O'Connell, M. (2013, 10 May). "NBC Cancels 'Rock Center with Brian Williams.'" *The Hollywood Reporter*. http://www.hollywoodreporter.com/live-feed/nbc-cancels-rock-center-brian-520842

Goodwin, C., & Heritage, J. (1990). "Conversation analysis." *Annual Review of Anthropology*, 19, 283–307.

Gretawire. (2012). "The Self Delusion of Broadcast News and the Danger of 'Quiet' Bias." September 21. http://gretawire.foxnewsinsider.com/2012/09/21/the-self-delusion-ofbroadcast-news-and-the-danger-of-quiet-bias-am-i-wrong/

Grice, H. P. (1975). "Logic and conversation." In P. Cole & J. Morgan (Eds.), *Syntax and semantics* (Vol. 3, pp. 41–58). New York: Academic Press.

Grindstaff, L. (2002). *The Money Shot: Trash, Class, and the Making of TV Talk Shows*. University of Chicago Press.

Grynbaum, M. M. (2017a, 17 February). "Trump Calls the News Media the 'Enemy of the American People.'" *New York Times*. https://www.nytimes.com/2017/02/17/business/trump-calls-the-news-media-the-enemy-of-the-people.html

Grynbaum, M. M. (2017b, 14 June). "Fox News Drops 'Fair and Balanced' Motto." *New York Times*. https://www.nytimes.com/2017/06/14/business/media/fox-news-fair-and-balanced.html?_r=0

Gutmann, A., & Thompson, D. (2012*). The spirit of compromise: Why governing demands it and campaigning undermines it*. Princeton, NJ: Princeton University Press.

Haas, T. (2006). "Critical Forum: Mainstream News Media Self-criticism: A Proposal for Future Research." *Critical Studies in Media Communication* 23(4): 350–355.

Haas, T. (2006). "Critical forum: Mainstream news media self-criticism: A proposal for future research." *Critical Studies in Media Communication*, 23(4): 350–355.

Hagan, J. (2014, 4 May). "Benghazi and the Bombshell." *New York Magazine*. http://nymag.com/news/features/lara-logan-cbs-news-2014-5/

Hellmueller, L. (2014). *The Washington, DC Media Corps in the 21st Century: The Source-Correspondent Relationship*. Palgrave Macmillan.

Hellmueller, L., Vos, T. P., & Poepsel, M. A. (2013). "Shifting journalistic capital? Transparency and objectivity in the twenty-first century." *Journalism Studies*, 14(3): 287–304.

Henningham, J. (1985). "Journalism as a profession: A reexamination." *Australian Journal of Communication*, 8(1): 1–17.

Herbst, S. (2010). *Rude Democracy: Civility and Incivility in American Politics*. Philadelphia, PA: Temple University Press.

H. G. (2014). "Oversight Online: Comment Section Conundrums." *The Economist*, January 30. http://www.economist.com/blogs/babbage/2014/01/oversight-online

Hindman, E. B. (2005). "Jayson Blair, The *New York Times*, and Paradigm Repair." *Journal of Communication* 55(2): 225–241.

Holton, A. E., & Molyneux, L. (2015 online). "Identity Lost? The Personal Impact of Brand Journalism." *Journalism*, Vol. 18, Is. 2. http://journals.sagepub.com/doi/abs/10.1177/1464884915608816

Holton, J. A. (2008). "Grounded Theory as a General Research Methodology." *Grounded Theory Review* 7(2). http://groundedtheoryreview.com/2008/06/30/grounded-theory-as-ageneral-research-methodology/

Hudak, J. (2016, 24 February). "Shining light on explanatory journalism's impact on media, democracy, and society." http://www.brookings.edu/blogs/fixgov/posts/2016/02/25-explanatory-journalism-project-media-democracy-hudak

Huddleston, Jr., T. (2016, 5 May). "Katie Couric Could be on Her Way Out at Yahoo." Fortune.com. http://fortune.com/2016/05/05/katie-couric-leaving-yahoo/

Hughes, J. (2012, March 6). "Sticks and stones: The case for civility in American political discourse." *Christian Science Monitor* (pp. 1–3). Retrieved from http://www.csmonitor.com/Commentary/John-Hughes/2012/0306/Sticks-and-stones-the-case-for-civility-in-Americanpolitical-discourse

Ingram, M. (2014). "Moot Is Right—We're a Lot Better Off with Online Anonymity Than We Would be without It." *Gigaom*, February 18. http://gigaom.com/2014/02/18/moot-isright-were-a-lot-better-off-with-online-anonymity-than-we-would-be-without-it/

Irwin, L. (2010a, December 2). "FCC Commissioner Blasts State of TV News." Studio Briefing. Retrieved from http://www.studiobriefing.net/2010/12/fcc-commissioner-blasts-state-of-tvnews/

Irwin, L. (2010b, December 3). "Tom Brokaw Decries Media's Divisive Dialogue. Studio Briefing." Retrieved from http://www.studiobriefing.net/2010/12/tom-brokaw-decries-mediasdivisive-dialogue/

Jacobs, R. N. (2017). "Journalism After Trump." *American Journal of Cultural Sociology*. doi:10.1057/s41290-017-0044-8.

Jacobs, R. N., & Townsley, E. (2011). *The Space of Opinion*. New York: Oxford University Press.

Jacobs, S., & Jackson, S. (1983). "Speech act structure in conversation: Rational aspects of pragmatic coherence." In R. T. Craig & K. Tracy (Eds.), *Conversational coherence: Form, structure, and strategy*. Beverly Hills, CA: Sage, 47–66.

Jaffer, J. (2017, 17 October). Tenth Annual Richard S. Salant Lecture on Freedom of the Press. Harvard Kennedy School Shorenstein Center on Media, Politics and Public Policy.

Jameson, F. (1983). "Postmodernism and Consumer Society." In Foster, H. (Ed.) *The anti-aesthetic: Essays in postmodern culture*. Bay Press, 11–125.

Jamieson, K. H. (2018). *Cyberwar: How Russian Hackers and Trolls Helped Elect a President: What We Don't, Can't, and Do Know*. New York: Oxford University Press.

Jamieson, K. H., & Capella, J. N. (2008). *Echo chamber: Rush Limbaugh and the conservative media establishment*. New York: Oxford University Press.

Jamieson, K. H., Fallis, T., & Darr, C. (2013). "Problematic congressional discourse." In C. Rountree (Ed.), *Venomous speech: Problems with American political discourse on the right and left*. Santa Barbara, CA: Praeger. Retrieved from http://ebooks.abc-clio.com/reader.aspx?isbn¼9780313398674&id¼A3642C-353

Jamieson, K. H., Hardy, B. W., & Romer, D. (2007). "The Effectiveness of the Press in serving the Needs of American Democracy." Edited by *The Annenberg Democracy*

Project. In *Institutions of American Democracy: A Republic Divided* (pp. 21–51). New York: Oxford University Press.

Janowitz, M. (1975, Winter). "Professional models in journalism: The gatekeeper and the advocate." *Journalism Quarterly*, 52, 618–626, 662.

Jarvis, S. E., & Han, S. (2018). *Votes that Count and Voters Who Don't: How Journalists Sideline Electoral Participation (Without Even Knowing It).* Penn State University Press.

Journalism That Matters. (2015). Experience engagement conference website. Retrieved from http://journalismthatmatters.org/experienceengagement/

Katz, E. (1996). "And deliver us from segmentation." *Annals of the American Academy of Political and Social Science*, 546, 22–33.

Katz, E. (2009). "The End of Television? Its Impact on the World (So Far)." *The Annals of the American Academy of Political and Social Science*, Vol. 625. Introduction (pp. 6–18). Sage Publications.

Kaufman, L. (1993). "The Right Stuff." *American Journalism Review*, December. http://ajrarchive.org/article_printable.asp?id=1395

Kennedy, D. (2012). "In New Haven, a Crisis of Confidence over User Comments." *Nieman Journalism Lab*. http://www.niemanlab.org/2012/02/in-new-haven-a-crisis-of-confidenceover-user-comments/

Kenski, K., Coe, K., & Rains, S. (2012). "Patterns and determinants of civility in online discussions: Final report to the National Institute for Civil Discourse." Retrieved from http://nicd.arizona.edu/research-report/patterns-and-determinants-civility

Keohane, J. (2017, 16 February). "What News-Writing Bots Mean for the Future of Journalism." Wired.com. https://www.wired.com/2017/02/robots-wrote-this-story/

Kirsner, S. (2014, 13 April). "Aereo's $97m question for the Supreme Court." *The Boston Globe*. http://www.bostonglobe.com/business/2014/04/12/aereo-streaming-service-presents-supreme-court-with-question/2JMRzN5DqKWzSautrnEmjK/story.html?s_campaign=8315

Kitch, C. (2003). "Generational identity and memory in American newsmagazines." *Journalism*, 4:185–202.

Klaidman, S., & Beauchamp, T. (1987). *The Virtuous Journalist*. New York: Oxford University Press.

Kline, D., & Burstein, D. (2005). *Blog! How the Newest Media Revolution Is Changing Politics, Business and Culture* (New York: CDS Books).

Knowledge Management Culture. (2015). "KM best practices." Retrieved from http://www.kmbestpractices.com/km-culture.html

Koblin, J. (2017, 31 May). "Megyn Kelly, on NBC with New Shows, Moves Past Trump Turmoil." *New York Times*. https://www.nytimes.com/2017/05/31/business/media/megyn-kelly-nbc.html?ribbon-ad-idx=4&rref=business/media&module=Ribbon&version=context&region=Header&action=click&contentCollection=Media&pgtype=article

Koblin, J., & Rutenberg, J. (2017, 30 May). "Scott Pelley Said to Be Leaving Post as 'CBS Evening News' Anchor." *New York Times*. https://www.nytimes.com/2017/05/30/

business/media/scott-pelley-cbs-evening-news.html?mabReward=A5&recp=0&moduleDetail=recommendations-0&action=click&contentCollection=Media&region=Footer&module=WhatsNext&version=WhatsNext&contentID=WhatsNext&src=recg&pgtype=article

Koppel, T. (2010, 14 November). "Olbermann, O'Reilly and the death of real news." *The Washington Post.*

Kosoff, M. (2016, 15 September). "How Facebook Says It's Fixing Its Fake-News Problem." *Vanity Fair.* http://www.vanityfair.com/news/2016/09/how-facebook-says-its-fixing-its-fake-news-problem

KPBS. (2013, 16 February). "Out of Order: Civility in Politics." http://www.kpbs.org/news/2013/feb/11/out-order-civility-politics/

Ksiazek, T. B. (2015) "Civil Interactivity: How News Organizations' Commenting Policies Explain Civility and Hostility in User Comments." *Journal of Broadcasting & Electronic Media*, Vol. 59, Is. 4, pp. 556–573.

Ksiazek, T. B. (2016, 2 August). "Commenting on the News: Explaining the degree and quality of user comments on news websites." *Journalism Studies.* http://dx.doi.org/10.1080/1461670X.2016.1209977

Kunkel, T. (2004). "Fade Out." *American Journalism Review.* August/September. http://ajrarchive.org/Article.asp?id=3710

Lampe, C., Zube, P., Lee, J., Hyun Park, C., & Johnston, E. (2014). "Crowdsourcing Civility: A Natural Experiment Examining the Effects of Distributed Moderation in Online Forums." *Government Information Quarterly* 31(2): 317–326.

Lave, J., & Wenger, E. (1991). *Situated learning: Legitimate peripheral participation.* Cambridge, England: Cambridge University Press.

Lawson, R. (2016, 7 April). "Gloria Vanderbilt Documentary *Nothing Left Unsaid* Doesn't Say Enough." *Vanity Fair.* http://www.vanityfair.com/hollywood/2016/04/nothing-left-unsaid-gloria-vanderbilt-anderson-cooper-hbo-review#2

Lee, J. (2015, May). "The Double-Edged Sword: The Effects of Journalists' Social Media Activities on Audience Perceptions of Journalists and Their News Products." *Journal of Computer-Mediated Communication.* Vol. 20. http://onlinelibrary.wiley.com/doi/10.1111/jcc4.12113/full

Levy, Steven. (2012, 24 April). "Can an Algorithm Write a Better News Story Than a Human Reporter?" *Wired.* http://www.wired.com/gadgetlab/2012/04/can-an-algorithm-write-a-better-news-story-than-a-human-reporter/

Lewis, S. C. (2012). "The Tension between Professional Control and Open Participation: Journalism and its Boundaries." *Information, Communication & Society*, Vol. 15, Is. 6, pp. 836–866.

Lynch, D. (2015). "Above & beyond: Looking at the future of journalism education." Retrieved from http://knightfoundation.org/features/je-the-state-of-american journalism/

Lindlof, T. R. (1988). "Media audiences as interpretive communities." *Communication Yearbook*, 11, 81–107.

Lindlof, T. R., & Taylor, B. C. (2011). *Qualitative Communication Research Methods.* 3rd ed. Thousand Oaks, CA: Sage.

Liu, E. (2012). "Viewpoint: Civility Is Overrated: Politics Doesn't Need to be More Nice; it Needs to be More Real." *Time*. http://ideas.time.com/2012/10/16/civility-in-elections-isoverrated/

Loke, J. (2012). "Old Turf, New Neighbors: Journalists' Perspectives on Their New Shared Space." *Journalism Practice* 6:233–249.

Lule, J. (2001). *Daily News, Eternal Stories: The Mythological Role of Journalism*. The Guilford Press.

Macaulay, C. (1999). "Inscribing the palimpsest: Information sources in the newsroom." In K. Buckner (Ed.), *Esprit i3 workshop on ethnographic studies in real and virtual environments: Inhabited information spaces and connected communities* (pp. 42–52). Edinburgh, Scotland: Queen Margaret College.

Macy, B. (2008). "Language Barriers." *American Journalism Review*, October/November. http://ajrarchive.org/Article.asp?id=4609

Manga, J. (2003). *Talking Trash: The Cultural Politics of Daytime TV Talk*. NYU Press.

Marcus, J. (2009). "Sticks and Stones." *Columbia Journalism Review*. http://www.cjr.org/critical_eye/sticks_and_stones_1.php?page=all#sthash.bGEcr52r.dpuf.

Martel, N. (2012, 8 April). "Cable Talkers' Latest Status Symbol: A Studio At Home." *The Washington Post*. https://www.washingtonpost.com/lifestyle/style/cable-talkers-latest-status-symbol-a-studio-at-home/2012/04/08/gIQALioc4S_story.html?utm_term=.6979e5afb738

Marx, G. (2010). "Embrace the Wonk." *Columbia Journalism Review*. http://www.cjr.org/feature/embrace_the_wonk_1.php?page=all

Massing, M. (2015, 25 June). "Digital Journalism: Next Generation." *The New York Review*, pp. 42–44.

Matsaganis, M. D., & Katz, V. S. (2013). "How ethnic media producers constitute their communities of practice: An ecological approach." *Journalism*, 15(7): 926–944.

McChesney, R., & Nichols, J. (2010). *The death and life of American journalism: The media revolution that will begin the World again*. New York: Nation Books.

McChesney, R., & Pickard, V. (Eds.). (2011). *Will the last reporter please turn out the lights: The collapse of journalism and what can be done to fix it*. New York: The New Press.

McCoy, T. (2015, 11 February). "Why Jon Stewart and Brian Williams should just switch jobs." *The Washington Post*. https://www.washingtonpost.com/news/morning-mix/wp/2015/02/11/why-jon-stewart-and-brian-williams-should-just-switch-jobs/?utm_term=.8dbe6ed5fcb4

McElroy, K. (2013). "Where Old (Gatekeepers) Meets New (Media)." *Journalism Practice* 7(6): 755–771.

Meares, J. (2011). "Giffords Analysis Machine in Overdrive." *Columbia Journalism Review*. http://www.cjr.org/campaign_desk/giffords_analysis_machine_in_o.php?page=all

The Media Insight Project (2018). "Americans and the News Media: What they do—and don't—understand about each other." https://www.americanpressinstitute.org/publications/reports/survey-research/americans-and-the-news-media/

Meltzer, K. (2011). "Comparing Theories of Repair across Communication Research." *Journal of Communications Media Studies* 3(1): 10–25.

Meltzer, K. (2003). "There's No Such Thing as an 'All-News Network,'" presented at the Annual American Culture Association/Popular Culture Association Conference, New Orleans, LA, April 16–19.

Meltzer, K., & Hoover, J. D. (2014). "Civility in News Discourse: The Case of PBS' Brooks and Shields." *Electronic News*, December.

Meltzer, K., & Martik, E. (2017). "Journalists as Communities of Practice: Advancing a theoretical framework for understanding journalism." *Journal of Communication Inquiry*. July 2017, 41(3): 207–226.

Meltzer, K. (2010). *TV News Anchors and Journalistic Tradition: How Journalists Adapt to Technology*. New York: Peter Lang Publishing.

Merritt, D. (1999). "Public journalism and public life: Why telling the news is not enough." In H. Tumber (Ed.), *News: A reader* (pp. 365–378). Oxford, England: Oxford University Press.

Meyer, H. K., & Carey, M. C. (2014). "In Moderation: Examining How Journalists' Attitudes toward Online Comments Affect the Creation of Community." *Journalism Practice* 8(2): 213–228.

Meyers, O. (2003). "Israeli journalists as an interpretive memory community: The case study of Haolam Hazeh" (Doctoral dissertation). The Annenberg School for Communication, University of Pennsylvania, Philadelphia, PA.

Meyers, O., & Davidson, R. (2016, June). "Conceptualizing Journalistic Careers: Between Interpretive Community and Tribes of Professionalism." *Sociology Compass*, Vol. 10, Is. 6, pp. 419–431.

Mirkinson, J. (2013, 22 June). "'Rock Center' Airs Last Show; Brian Williams Reportedly 'Insulted' By NBC Cancellation." http://www.huffingtonpost.com/2013/06/22/rock-center-last-show-brian-williams-insulted-nbc_n_3482998.html?utm_hp_ref=media

Mirkinson, J. (2013, 11 May). "Brian Williams On 'Rock Center' Cancellation: 'I'm So Proud Of The Work We Did.'" *Huffington Post*. http://www.huffingtonpost.com/2013/05/11/brian-williams-rock-center-cancellation-nbc_n_3259278.html

Mitchell, A., Gottfried, J., Barthel, M., & Shearer, E. (2016, 7 July). "The Modern News Consumer." 1. *Pathways to News*. Pew Research Center. http://www.journalism.org/2016/07/07/pathways-to-news/

Mitchell, A., Jurkowitz, M., Holcomb, J., Enda, J. & Anderson, M. (2013, 10 June). "Nonprofit Journalism: A Growing but Fragile Part of the U.S. News System." http://www.journalism.org/2013/06/10/nonprofit-journalism/

Moos, J. (2012). "Hoyer: Today's Journalists 'See Their Job Not to Inform but to Incite.'" *Poynter*, September 21. http://www.poynter.org/mediawire/top-stories/189207/hoyertodays-journalists-see-their-job-not-to-inform-but-to-incite/

Moy, P., M. A. Xenos, & V. K. Hess. (2005). "Communication and citizenship: Mapping the political effects of infotainment." *Mass Communication & Society*, Vol. 8, Is. 2.

Moyer, J. W. (2016, 3 March). "Trump inspires gloomy Ted Koppel to scold Bill O'Reilly over the state of TV news." *The Washington Post*. https://www.washingtonpost.

com/news/morning-mix/wp/2016/03/03/trump-inspires-gloomy-ted-koppel-to-scold-bill-oreilly-over-the-state-of-tv-news/?hpid=hp_no_name_morning-mix-story-f%3Ahomepage%2Fstory

Muddiman, A. (2014a). "Instability of Incivility: How Partisanship and Individual Differences Shape Perceptions and News Coverage of Political Incivility." Paper presented to the Political Communication Division of the National Communication Association, Chicago, November.

Muddiman, A. (2014b). "Two-Dimensional Political Incivility: Clarifying Incivility Using News Frames and Individuals' Judgments." Paper presented to the Political Communication Division of the National Communication Association, Chicago, November.

Muddiman, A., & J. Pond-Cobb. (2015, 21 November). "Interacting with Incivility: How Citizens Engage with Incivility in the News." National Communication Association 101st Annual Convention, Las Vegas, Nevada.

Mutz, D. C. (2015). *In Your Face Politics: The Consequences of Uncivil Media*. Princeton, NJ: Princeton University Press.

Mutz, D. C. (2007, November). "Effects of 'In-Your-Face' Television Discourse on Perceptions of a Legitimate Opposition." *American Political Science Review* 101(4): 621–635.

Mutz, D. C., & Reeves, B. (2005, February). "The New Videomalaise: Effects of Televised Incivility on Political Trust." *American Political Science Review* 99(1): 1–15.

Mutz, D. (2006). *Hearing the other side: Deliberative versus participatory democracy*. New York: Cambridge University Press.

Mutz, D. C. (2002). "The consequences of cross-cutting networks for political participation." *American Journal of Political Science*, 46, 838–855.

Mutz, D. C., & Martin, P. S. (2001). "Facilitating communication across lines of political difference: The role of mass media." *American Political Science Review*, 95, 97–114.

Myers, S. (2011, 20 September). "Ira Glass: Commentary Is Trouncing Fact-based Reporting because of Its Down-to-Earth Style." *Poynter*. http://www.poynter.org/mediawire/topstories/146547/ira-glass-commentary-is-trouncing-fact-based-reporting-because-of-itsdown-to-earth-style/

Nerone, J. (2013). "The historical roots of the normative model of journalism." *Journalism*, 14, 446–458. doi: 10.1177/1464884912464177.

Ng, E. W. J., & Detenber, B. H. (2005). "The Impact of Synchronicity and Civility in Online Political Discussions on Perceptions and Intentions to Participate." *Journal of Computer-Mediated Communication* 10 (3). doi: 10.1111/j.1083-6101.2005.tb00252.x.

Nielsen, C. E. (2014). "Coproduction or Cohabitation: Are Anonymous Online Comments on Newspaper Websites Shaping News Content?" *New Media & Society* 16(3): 470–487.

Nyhan, B. (2014). "Political Science and Journalism: BFFs?" *Columbia Journalism Review*. http://www.cjr.org/united_states_project/nyhan_reflections_political_science_and_journalism.php?page=all

Olmstead, K., Mitchell, A., Holcomb, J., & Vogt, N. (2014). Pew State of the Media 2014 Report. http://www.journalism.org/2014/03/26/news-video-on-the-web/ and http://www.journalism.org/2014/03/26/developments-in-online-news-video-content/

Ordway, D. M. (2016). "Journalism branding: Impact on reporters' personal identities." Journalist's Resource. https://journalistsresource.org/studies/society/news-media/brand-journalism-impact-reporter-personal-identity

Ornebring, H. (Speaker) (2008). The two professionalisms of journalism: Updating journalism research for the 21st century. International Communication Association Annual Meeting, Quebec, Canada.

Pagano, P. (1993). "Public Perspectives on the Press." *American Journalism Review*, December. http://ajrarchive.org/article_printable.asp?id=1482

Papacharissi, Z. (2004). "Democracy Online: Civility, Politeness, and the Democratic Potential of Online Political Discussion Groups." *New Media & Society* 6(2): 259–283.

Parker, K. (2015, 10 February). "Why did Brian Williams do it?" *The Washington Post*. https://www.washingtonpost.com/opinions/for-brian-williams-will-close-enough-amount-to-good-enough/2015/02/10/a5d0ebdc-b151-11e4-854b-a38d13486ba1_story.html?utm_term=.d02b4e14c015

Partsch, F. (2011). "Civility Project Proposal." *Association of Opinion Journalists*, March 20, 2014. http://www.opinionjournalists.org/aboutncew/an-aoj-project/

Pauly, J. J. (1990). "The politics of the new journalism." In N. Sims (Ed.), *Literary journalism in the twentieth century* (pp. 110–129). New York: Oxford University Press.

PBS. (2013). "PBS and member stations mark 10 years as America's most trusted institution and an 'excellent' use of tax dollars." Retrieved from http://www.pbs.org/about/news/archive/2013/pbs-most-trusted/

PBS NewsHour. (2012). Transcripts and broadcasts from the following dates are quoted from throughout the article: January 6, January 13, January 20, January 31, February 3, February 10, February 28, March 2, March 9, March 16, March 23, March 30, April 13, April 20, April 27, May 18, June 8, June 22, July 27, August 3, September 28, October 5, October 12, October 19, October 26, November 2. Retrieved from http://www.pbs.org/about/news/archive/2013/pbs-most-trusted/

Peters, J. (2010). "Trust Falls: Lessons from St. Louis on Authority, Credibility, and Online Communications." *Columbia Journalism Review*. http://www.cjr.org/the_news_frontier/trust_falls.php?page=all

Pew Research Center for the People & the Press. (2010). *Fewer Journalists Stand Out in Fragmented News Universe*. http://www.people-press.org/2010/10/14/fewer-journalistsstand-out-in-fragmented-news-universe/

Pew Research Center for the People & the Press. (2012). *Further Decline in Credibility Ratings for Most News Organizations*. http://www.people-press.org/2012/08/16/further-decline-incredibility-ratings-for-most-news-organizations/

Pew Research Center's Project for Excellence in Journalism. (2012). "The State of the News Media 2012." Retrieved from http://stateofthemedia.org/2012/network-news-the-pace-ofchange-accelerates/

Pew Research Center's Project for Excellence in Journalism. (2013). "The State of the News Media 2013." Retrieved from http://stateofthemedia.org/2013/network-news-a-year-ofchange-and-challenge-at-nbc/

The Pew Research Center's Project for Excellence in Journalism (2013). "The State of the News Media 2013." http://stateofthemedia.org/2013/special-reports-landing-page/the-changing-tv-news-landscape/

Phelps, A. (2011, 7 November). "RE: FW: NewsWorks: Back-to-the-Future Community News." *Nieman Lab.* http://www.niemanlab.org/2011/11/re-fw-newsworks-back-to-thefuture-community-news/

Pickard, V. (2010, December). "Forgotten lessons for journalism's future." *Communication Currents*, 5(6). Retrieved from http://www.natcom.org/CommCurrentsArticle.aspx?id¼1006

Pickard, V. (2015). *America's Battle for Media Democracy: The Triumph of Corporate Libertarianism and the Future of Media Reform*. New York: Cambridge University Press.

Pompeo, J. (2018, 4 December). "Everyone's For Sale: A Generation of Digital-Media Darlings Prepares for a Frigid Winter." *Vanity Fair.* https://www.vanityfair.com/news/2018/12/a-generation-of-digital-media-darlings-prepares-for-a-frigid-winter

Poniewozik, J. (2010, 16 November). "Olbermann Jousts Koppel in battle of high horses." Tuned In blog on Time.com.

Porter, E. (2017, 21 October). Presentation at 2017 Journalism/Interactive conference on panel, "Research Misinformation." Philip Merrill College of Journalism, University of Maryland.

Powell, T. (2012, 24 October). "As 4 Stations Cancel His Show, Is Tavis Smiley's Advocacy Journalism too Political for Public Radio?" *Poynter.* http://www.poynter.org/mediawire/making-sense-of-news/192366/is-tavis-smiley-too-political-for-public-radio/

Prior, M. (2003). "Any good news in soft news? The impact of soft news preference on political knowledge." *Political Communication*, Vol. 20, Is. 2.

Prochazka, F. Weber, P., & Schweiger, W. (2016, 22 March). "Effects of civility and reasoning in user comments on perceived journalistic quality." *Journalism Studies.* https://doi.org/10.1080/1461670X.2016.1161497

PRRI/Brookings (2014). What Americans Want from Immigration Reform in 2014: Findings from the PRRI/Brookings Religion, Values and Immigration Reform Survey, Panel Call Back. https://www.brookings.edu/wp-content/uploads/2016/06/FinalImmigrationSurvey-2.pdf

Reader, B. (2012). "Free Press vs. Free Speech? The Rhetoric of "Civility." In Regard to Anonymous Online Comments." *Journalism & Mass Communication Quarterly* 89(3): 495–513.

Reese, S. D. (1990). "The News Paradigm and the Ideology of Objectivity: A Socialist at the *Wall Street Journal.*" Special theories of journalism issue. *Critical Studies in Mass Communication* 7(4): 390–409.

Roig-Franzia, M., Higham, S., & Brittain, A. (2015, 15 February). "Williams undone by his gift for storytelling." *The Washington Post.* A1.

Romenesko, J. (2013). "Columbia Journalism Review Hears from Readers Upset about The F-Word on the Cover." http://jimromenesko.com/2013/11/06/cjr-hears-from-readersupset-about-the-f-word-on-the-cover/

Rose, A. (2008). "Louts Out." Currents section. *Columbia Journalism Review* 30:10–11. http://www.cjr.org/currents/louts_out.php

Rosen, J. (2005, 21 January). "Bloggers vs. Journalists is Over," *PressThink*. http://journalism.nyu.edu/pubzone/weblogs/pressthink

Rosenstiel, T. (2015). Democracy Fund workshop, October 2015, Washington, DC. Also see: Kovach, B. & Rosenstiel, T. (2001). *The Elements of Journalism: What Newspeople Should Know and the Public Should Expect.* New York: Three Rivers Press. https://www.americanpressinstitute.org/journalism-essentials/what-is-journalism/elements-journalism/

Rosenstiel, T. (2016, 20 December). "What the post-Trump debate over journalism gets wrong: We don't need journalists to hold fast or change everything, but a little of both." Brookings. https://www.brookings.edu/research/what-the-debate-over-journalism-post-trump-gets-wrong/

Roth, W., & Lee, Y. (2006). "Contradictions in theorizing and implementing communities in education." *Educational Research Review*, 1(1): 27–40.

Rountree, C. (Ed.). (2013). *Venomous speech: Problems with American political discourse on the right and left.* Santa Barbara, CA: Praeger.

Santana, A. D. (2014). "Virtuous or Vitriolic." *Journalism Practice* 8(1): 18–33.

Sblendorio, P. (2016, 20 May). "Kelly Ripa is ABC's new bachelorette: A breakdown of her inaugural co-hosts on 'Live,' including Jimmy Kimmel and Jussie Smollett." *NY Daily News*. http://www.nydailynews.com/entertainment/kelly-ripa-abc-bachelorette-meet-eligible-live-co-hosts-article-1.2643871

Scarborough, J. (2016, 18 April) "Megyn Kelly, Fox News, and the curse of Glenn Beck." *The Washington Post*. http://wpo.st/l_bV1

Schudson, M. (1982). "The politics of narrative form: The emergence of news conventions in print and television." *Daedalus*, 111, 97–112.

Scott, G. (2008). *The Talk Show Revolution: How TV and Radio Talk Shows Have Changed America.* iUniverse.

Serazio, M. (2014). "The New Media Designs of Political Consultants: Campaign Production in a Fragmented Era." *Journal of Communication* 64 (2014) 743–763.

Shafer, J. (2015, 6 February). "Brian Williams' Slow Jam." *Politico*. http://www.politico.com/magazine/story/2015/02/brian-williamss-jack-shafer-114974

Shattuc, J. M. (1997). *The Talking Cure: TV Talk Shows and Women.* New York: Routledge.

Sherman, G. (2017, 18 January). "CNN's Jeff Zucker on Covering Donald Trump—Past, Present, and Future." http://nymag.com/daily/intelligencer/2017/01/cnns-zucker-on-covering-trump-past-present-and-future.html

Shiver, J., Jr. (2010). "Embracing Original Content." *American Journalism Review*, September. http://ajrarchive.org/Article.asp?id=4903

Siguenza, S. (2014, 7 April). "Secrets from snow fall: Rough sketches, best practices and more." *American Journalism Review*. Retrieved from http://ajr.org/2014/04/07/secretssnow-fall-rough-sketches-best-practices/

Sobieraj, S., & Berry, J. M. (2011). "From incivility to outrage: Political discourse in blogs, talk radio, and cable news." *Political Communication*, 28(1): 19–41.

Sonderman, J. (2012, 28 November). " 'Just the facts' isn't good enough for journalists anymore, says Tow Center's journalism manifesto." The Poynter Institute. http://www.poynter.org/2012/just-the-facts-isnt-good-enough-for-journalists-anymore-says-tow-centers-journalism-manifesto/196457/

St. John III, B., & Johnson, K. A. (Eds.) (2012). *News with a View: Essays on the Eclipse of Objectivity in Modern Journalism.* Jefferson, NC: McFarland & Co. Inc.

Steinberg, B. (2013, 19 November). "CNN to Use Erin Burnett Maternity Leave to Give Spotlight to Others." *Variety.*

Steinberg, B. (2014, 9 January). "CNN Eyes Primetime Shake-up: Who's In and Who's Out?" *Variety.*

Steinberg, D. (2017, 19 October). "Lindsay Czarniak on leaving ESPN, Jemele Hill and what comes next." *The Washington Post.* https://www.washingtonpost.com/news/dc-sports-bog/wp/2017/10/19/lindsay-czarniak-on-leaving-espn-jemele-hill-and-what-comes-next/?utm_term=.6411cc8b2035

Steinberg, J. (2015a, 5 October). "MSNBC to Undergo More Changes, NBC News Chief Andrew Lack Says." *Variety.* http://variety.com/2015/tv/news/msnbc-changes-news-chief-andrew-lack-1201610162/

Steinberg, J. (2015b, 6 March). "Andrew Lack Returns to NBC as News Chief, Will Face Challenges Restoring Credibility." *Variety.* http://variety.com/2015/tv/news/andrew-lack-will-face-challenges-in-return-to-nbcu-as-news-chief-1201447765/

Steiner, L. (2012). "Failed Theories: Explaining Gender Difference in Journalism." *Review of Communication*, Vol. 12, Issue 3, pp. 201–223. https://doi.org/10.1080/15358593.2012.666559

Stelter, B. (2014, 10 April). "CNN announces new prime time lineup." http://money.cnn.com/2014/04/10/news/cnn-upfronts/index.html?iid=HP_River

Stelter, B. (2014, 6 July). "Shakeup at ABC News: What's the real story?" CNN "Reliable Sources." http://reliablesources.blogs.cnn.com/2014/07/06/shakeup-at-abc-news-what-is-the-real-story/

Stiff, J. B., & Mongeau, P. (2003). *Persuasive Communication.* 2nd ed. New York: Guilford Press.

Stranahan, S. Q. (2004). "Assembling All the Pieces." *Columbia Journalism Review.* http://www.cjr.org/politics/assembling_all_the_pieces.php?page=all&print=true

Stroud, N. J. (2011). *Niche news: The politics of news choice.* New York: Oxford University Press.

Stroud, N. (2013). *Engaging News Project.* The Annette Strauss Institute for Civic Life. http://engagingnewsproject.org/

Stryker, R., Conway, B., & Danielson, T. (2014). *What Is Political Incivility?* http://nicd.arizona.edu/research-report/what-political-incivility.

Sullivan, M. (2017a, 27 March). "Scott Pelley is pulling no punches on the nightly news—and people are taking notice." *The Washington Post.* https://www.washingtonpost.com/lifestyle/style/scott-pelley-is-pulling-no-punches-on-the-nightly-news--and-people-are-taking-notice/2017/03/26/9763bf7c-0e4a-11e7-9d5a-a83e627dc120_story.html?utm_term=.499a9615a6e2

Sullivan, M. (2017b, 8 January). "It's time to retire the tainted term 'fake news.'" *The Washington Post*. https://www.washingtonpost.com/lifestyle/style/its-time-to-retire-the-tainted-term-fake-news/2017/01/06/a5a7516c-d375-11e6-945a76f69a399dd5_story.html?utm_term=.5172768d8f1c

Sullivan, M. (2017c, 29 January). "More facts, fewer pundits: Here's how the media can regain the public's trust." *The Washington Post*. https://www.washingtonpost.com/lifestyle/style/more-facts-fewer-pundits-heres-how-the-media-can-regain-the-publics-trust/2017/01/29/9c0232ba-e4a7-11e6-a453-19ec4b3d09ba_story.html?utm_term=.0f164a42febb

Suls, R. (2014, 9 January). "Who is this man? Many Americans don't recognize top news anchor." Pew Research Center. http://www.pewresearch.org/fact-tank/2014/01/09/who-is-this-man-many-americans-dont-recognize-top-news-anchor/

Tandoc Jr., E. C., Hellmueller, L., & Vos, T. P. (2013). "Mind the gap: Between journalistic role conception and role enactment." *Journalism Practice*, 7(5): 539–554.

Tannen, Deborah. (1998). *The Argument Culture*. New York: Random House.

Tarde, G. (1989). "Opinion and conversation" (J. Ruth, Trans.). (Unpublished translation of "L'opinion et la conversation" [Opinion and conversation]). In G. Tarde (Ed.), L'opinion et la foule [Mass opinion]. Paris: Presses Universitaires de France (Original work published 1899).

Taylor, J. B. (2017). "The Educative Effects of Extreme Television Media." *American Politics Research*. Vol. 45, Is. 1, 2017.

Tenenboim-Weinblatt, K. (2009). "Jester, Fake Journalist, or the New Walter Lippmann? Recognition Processes of Jon Stewart by the U.S. Journalistic Community." *International Journal of Communication* [S.l.], 3: 416–439.

The Daily Show (2012). "Civil Disservice." http://thedailyshow.cc.com/videos/slfmox/civildisservice

Thornborrow, J., & Montgomery, M. (2010). "Special issue on personalization in the broadcast news interview." *Discourse & Communication*, 4(2): 99–104. http://journals.sagepub.com/doi/pdf/10.1177/1750481310364332

Timberg, B. M., Erler, R. J., & Newcomb, H. (2002). *Television Talk: A History of the TV Talk Show* (Texas Film and Media Studies Series). University of Texas Press.

Todd, C. (2017, 22 January). "Conway: Press Secretary Gave 'Alternative Facts.'" NBC News "Meet the Press." http://www.nbcnews.com/meet-the-press/video/conway-press-secretary-gave-alternative-facts-860142147643

Tow Center for Digital Journalism. (2014, 13 November). *Sensor Journalism: Communities of Practice*. Retrieved from http://towcenter.org/sensor-journalism-communities-of-practice/

Tsukayama, H. (2014a, 2 April). "With Fire TV, Amazon joins growing battle among tech giants to reinvent TV watching." *The Washington Post*. https://www.washingtonpost.com/business/economy/with-fire-tv-amazon-joins-growing-battle-among-tech-giants-to-reinvent-tv-watching/2014/04/02/5d57f0b4ba9711e3-96ae-f2c36d2b1245_story.html?utm_term=.58ffda1f20aa

Tsukayama, H. (2014b, 2 April). "Why Amazon wants to rule your television." *The Washington Post*. http://www.washingtonpost.com/blogs/the-switch/wp/2014/04/02/why-amazon-wants-to-rule-your-television/

Tuchman, G. (1978). *Making News*. New York: Free Press.
Tunstall, J. (1971). *Journalists at Work; Specialist Correspondents: Their News Organizations, News Sources, and Competitor-Colleagues*. Beverly Hills, CA: Sage Publications.
Tugend, A. (2002). "Maybe Not." *American Journalism Review*, May. http://ajrarchive.org/article_printable.asp?id=2521
Tumber, H. (1999). *News: A Reader*. Oxford: Oxford University Press.
Underwood, D., & Stamm, K. (2001). "Are journalists really irreligious? A multidimensional analysis." *Journalism & Mass Communication Quarterly*, 78(4): 771.
Usher, N. (2012). "Reshaping the Public Radio Newsroom for the Digital Future." *Radio Journal*. 11(1): 65–79.
Usher, N. (2012b). "Going Web-First at the Christian Science Monitor: A three-part study of change." *International Journal of Communication*, 6, 1898–1917.
Usher, N. (2010). "Goodbye to the news: How out-of-work journalists assess enduring news values and the new media landscape." *New Media and Society*, 12(6): 911–928.
Usher, N. (2016). *Interactive Journalism: Hackers, Data, and Code*. Champaign: University of Illinois Press.
Usher, N., Holcomb, J., and Littman, J. (2018). "Twitter Makes It Worse: Political Journalists, Gendered Echo Chambers, and the Amplification of Gender Bias." *The International Journal of Press/Politics*, Vol. 23, Issue 3. https://doi.org/10.1177/1940161218781254
Vaughn, S. L. (Ed.). (2008). *Encyclopedia of American journalism* (p. 443). New York: Taylor & Francis Group.
Vraga, E. K., Edgerly, S., Bode, L., Carr, D. J., Bard, M., Johnson, C., Kim, Y. M., & Shah, D. V. (2012). "The correspondent, the comic, and the combatant: The consequences of host style in political talk shows." *Journalism and Mass Communication Quarterly*, 89, 1, 5–22.
Wahl-Jorgensen, K. (2004). "A 'Legitimate Beef' Or 'Raw Meat?' Civility, Multiculturalism, and Letters to the Editor." *Communication Review* 7(1): 89–105.
Walker, T. (2013, September 20). "Perks for employees and how Google changed the way we work (while waiting in line)." *The Independent*. Retrieved from http://www.independent.co.uk/news/world/americas/perks-for-employees-and-how-google-changedthe-way-we-work-while-waiting-in-line-8830243.html
Wallace, B. (2011). "NewsTrust Baltimore: An Experiment in Civility." *Columbia Journalism Review*. http://www.cjr.org/the_news_frontier/newstrust_baltimore_an_experim.php?page=all.
Wallenstein, A. (2012, 29 November). "Zucker aims to broaden focus of CNN." *Variety*. http://variety.com/2012/tv/news/zucker-aims-to-broaden-focus-of-cnn-1118062853/
Wallenstein, A. (2013). "Katie Couric's Bad Bet: Leaving ABC News for Yahoo." *Variety*. http://variety.com/2013/digital/news/katie-courics-bad-bet-leaving-abc-news-for-yahoo-1200870428/
Wallenstein, A. (2016, 25 July). "Where Yahoo Stars Like Katie Couric Could Fit in Verizon's Content Universe." *Variety*. http://variety.com/2016/digital/news/where-yahoo-stars-like-katie-couric-could-fit-in-verizons-content-universe-1201820625/

Wang, A. B. (2016, 16 November). "'Post-truth' named 2016 word of the year by Oxford Dictionaries." *The Washington Post*. https://www.washingtonpost.com/news/the-fix/wp/2016/11/16/post-truth-named-2016-word-of-the-year-by-oxford-dictionaries/?utm_term=.c7a3d1d2b9d8

Ward, B. (2007, 9 April). "Don Imus and the State of Public Discourse." *Poynter*. http://www.poynter.org/latest-news/everyday-ethics/81668/don-imus-and-the-state-of-public-discourse/

Wardle, C. (2016a). "[M/D]isinformation Reading List." First Draft News. https://firstdraftnews.com/misinformation-reading-list

Wardle, C. (2016b). "6 types of misinformation circulated this election season." *Columbia Journalism Review*. https://www.cjr.org/tow_center/6_types_election_fake_news.php

Wardle, C. (2017, 1 February). American Heritage lecture at Marymount University, Arlington, VA.

Weaver, D., & Wilhoit, G. (1986). *The American journalist: A portrait of U.S. news people and their work*. Bloomington: Indiana University Press.

Weber, M. (1947). *The theory of social and economic organization*. New York: Free Press.

Weber Shandwick, Powell Tate, & KRC Research. (2013). *Civility in America*. http://www.webershandwick.com/uploads/news/files/Civility_in_America_2013_Exec_Summary.pd

Weiss, A., & Domingo, D. (2010). "Innovation processes in online newsrooms as actor networks and communities of practice." *New Media & Society*, 12, 1156–1171.

Wemple, E. (2012, 22 June). "Politico Suspends Reporter." *The Washington Post*. http://www.washingtonpost.com/blogs/erik-wemple/post/politico-suspends-reporter/2012/06/22/ gJQAvvf8uV_blog.html

Wemple, E. (2013, 27 March). "Fox News all day: Hard, and conservative." Washington Post.com. http://www.washingtonpost.com/blogs/erik-wemple/wp/2013/03/27/fox-news-all-day-hard-and-conservative/?hpid=z4

Wemple, E. (2015, 19 November). "CNN correspondent suspended over tweet about House vote." *The Washington Post*. https://www.washingtonpost.com/blogs/erik-wemple/wp/2015/11/19/dear-cnn-are-you-biased/?postshare=3741448033902145&tid=ss_mail

Wemple, E. (2015b, 2 September). "CNN shops again at Politico, picking up media reporter Dylan Byers." *The Washington Post*. https://www.washingtonpost.com/blogs/erik-wemple/wp/2015/09/02/cnn-shops-again-at-politico-picking-up-media-reporter-dylan-byers/?utm_term=.a7e91ef7cecb

Wenger, E. (1998). *Communities of practice: Learning, meaning, and identity*. Cambridge, UK: Cambridge University Press.

Wenger, E. (2006, June). "Communities of practice: A brief introduction." Retrieved from http://www.ewenger.com/theory/index.htm

Wenger, E. (2012). "Communities of practice and social learning systems: The career of a concept." Retrieved from http://wenger-trayner.com/wp-content/uploads/2012/01/09-10-27-CoPs-and-systems-v2.01.pdf

Wenger, E., & McDermott, R. (2002). *Cultivating communities of practice: A guide to managing knowledge*. Boston, MA: Harvard Business School Press.

West, D. M., & Stone, B. (2014). *Nudging News Producers and Consumers toward More Thoughtful, Less Polarized Discourse.* Brookings Institution. http://www.brookings.edu/research/papers/2014/02/05-news-media-polarization-democracy-west-stone

White, D. M. (1950). "The gatekeeper: A case study in the selection of news." In H. Tumber (Ed.), *News: A reader* (pp. 66–72). Oxford, England: Oxford University Press.

Wihbey, J. (2013). *Interrogating the Network: The Year in Social Media Research.* http://www.niemanlab.org/2013/12/interrogating-the-network-the-year-in-social-media-research/

Wihbey, J. (2014). *What's New in Digital and Social Media Research: Linking Helps Save Newspapers and How Multitasking Spikes Arousal.* http://www.niemanlab.org/2014/01/whats-new-in-digital-and-social-media-research-linking-helps-save-newspapers-and-howmultitasking-spikes-arousal/

Williams, B., & Delli Carpini, M. X. (2011). *After Broadcast News: Media Regimes, Democracy, and the New Information Environment.* Cambridge, UK: Cambridge University Press.

Winter, W. L. (2012, 22 March). *RIP, American Press Institute.* Retrieved from http://jimromenesko.com/2012/03/22/rip-american-press-institute/

Wood, H. (2009). *Talking with Television: Women, Talk Shows, and Modern Self-Reflexivity (Feminist Studies and Media Culture).* University of Illinois Press.

Wyatt, W. (2012). "Blame narratives and the news: An ethical analysis." *Journalism & Communication Monographs*, 14, 153–208.

Yahr, E. (2014, 23 February). "Piers Morgan's CNN Show will be canceled." *The Washington Post.*

Yahr, E. (2016, 20 September). "How Anthony Bourdain went from CNN's biggest risk to its most unexpected star." *The Washington Post.* https://www.washingtonpost.com/lifestyle/food/how-anthony-bourdain-went-from-cnns-biggest-risk-to-its-most-unexpected-star/2016/09/19/e0baf73a-7b06-11e6-bd86-b7bbd53d2b5d_story.html?utm_term=.a540ba212492

York, C. (2013). "Cultivating Political Incivility: Cable News, Network News, and Public Perceptions." *Electronic News* 7(3): 107–125.

Zelizer, B. (1992). "CNN, the Gulf War, and journalistic practice." *Journal of Communication*, 42(1), 66–81.

Zelizer, B. (1993). "Journalists as Interpretive Communities." *Critical Studies in Mass Communication*, 10, pp. 219–237.

Zelizer, B. (1997, 17 February). "Journalism in the mirror." *The Nation*, p. 10.

Zelizer, B. (2012, 27 November). "On the shelf life of democracy in journalism scholarship." *Journalism*, 14, 459–473. doi: 10.1177/1464884912464179.

Index

ABC television; news, 40, 102, 143, 165, 168, 172, 178, 200, 201, 202
accountability, 15, 68, 96, 127, 193
accuracy, 10, 29, 122, 123
adversarial journalism, 28, 46
advocacy, 7, 28, 79, 88, 155
Ailes, Roger, 46, 103, 183, 191
AJR (*American Journalism Review*), 82–84, 86, 88, 90, 146, 148, 218, 219
algorithms, xi, 9
Allegheny College Prize for Civility in Public Life, 155, 219
Allen, Jon, 39, 40, 45, 46, 68, 69, 117, 118, 143, 173, 179, 186, 198, 217
"alternative facts," 4
Altman, Josh, 32, 52, 117, 202
Amanpour, Christiane, 4, 5
Amazon, 9, 195
anonymity (online), 52, 80, 84, 90, 126, 128
anonymous sources, 29
anonymous reader comments, 79, 88, 126–129
AOP (Association of Opinion Journalists), 24, 93
Associated Press, The, 28, 76

Baron, Marty, 4
Bartiromo, Maria, 57, 64, 65, 132, 134, 192, 199
Bashir, Martin, 76, 88
Beck, Glenn, 174

Benedetto, Richard, 33, 45–48, 89, 109, 113, 114, 131, 144, 151, 194
Benghazi, 65, 116
Bernstein, Carl, 69
Bezos, Jeff, 5, 205
Bias; biased, 3, 10, 32, 47, 57, 87, 89, 107, 110, 132, 143, 218
biases, 59, 132
"Blackfish," 60
Bloomberg News, 7, 39, 40, 69, 117, 143, 198, 217
boundary work, journalistic, 13, 16–18, 20, 92
Bourdain, Anthony, 59, 60, 61, 63, 64
branding, 43, 67–69, 73, 151, 191
brands, 68, 69, 175, 196, 207
Brazile, Donna, 31
Brokaw, Tom, 76
Brookings Institution, 89, 102, 207, 210
Brooks, David, xiv, 155, 157–165, 211, 212
Burnett, Erin, 59, 111

Calderone, Michael, 32, 51, 67, 89, 98, 115–117, 144–146, 149, 150, 201, 212
Carlson, Tucker, 8
Carville, James, 30
Carvin, Andy, 24, 89
CBS, 3, 40, 45, 102, 136, 139, 140, 167–169, 178, 186, 191, 198, 200, 201, 202
celebrity, 10, 24, 38, 172, 174, 175

Index

censor; censoring, 81, 92, 130
censorship, 140
Civilitas, 83
civility, 2, 3, 8, 31, 75–88, 90–93, 95–97, 105, 109, 113, 118, 122, 123, 126–128, 130, 131, 154, 155, 157, 159, 163–165, 183, 212–214, 218, 219
CJR (Columbia Journalism Review), 82, 85, 86, 88, 89, 93, 218, 219
Clark, Roy Peter, 81, 83, 86
CNBC, 134, 141, 198
CNN, xii, 4, 6, 27, 29, 30, 31, 34–36, 39, 46, 50, 58–66, 73, 97, 101–103, 106, 107, 110–112, 116, 133, 137, 140–144, 150, 167, 168, 171, 177, 178, 184, 186, 191, 192, 194, 196–198, 201, 203–205, 207, 210
Colbert Report, 8, 76
Colmes, Alan, 211, 212
Columbia Journalism Review, 12, 82, 145
Committee to Protect Journalists, 5
Community of practice, 13–26, 145, 154, 215
Conway, Kellyanne, 4
Cooper, Anderson, xiv, 59, 60, 168–173, 175, 176, 192, 212
Copps, Michael, 12, 76
Couric, Katie, xiv, 59, 168–170, 172, 173, 175–179, 212
Couric-Yahoo, 178
credibility, 11, 79, 80, 92, 199, 210
Cronkite, Walter, 169
crosstalk, political, 156, 158
C-SPAN, 151, 197
Czarniak, Lindsay, 183

Data-driven storytelling, 10
deliberative democracy; discourse, 79, 156, 157
dialogical news, xiii, 32, 96
dialogue, 72, 76, 115, 218
disinformation, 7, 11
Dowd, Maureen, 59, 191

echo-chamber, 10, 115, 116

enterprise story (journalism), 41
explanatory journalism, 70, 149, 150, 207

Facebook, 41, 42, 53, 67, 72, 89, 90, 127, 128, 153, 181, 187, 209, 214
fact-based reporting, 6, 86, 107
fact-checking, 11, 37, 96, 104, 214
Farhi, Paul, 6, 27, 30, 36, 37, 40, 41, 43, 65, 71, 72, 76, 106, 107, 123, 124, 126–128, 144–146, 170, 185, 187–190
Farrow, Ronan, 65
FCC, 8, 12, 215, 219
First Amendment, 1, 4, 92
FiveThirtyEight, 66
Fox, 2, 27, 33, 35, 36, 39, 40, 45, 46, 50, 51, 57, 58, 60, 62, 63, 65, 66, 98, 101–103, 105, 111–116, 119, 122, 131–133, 136, 141, 143, 174, 177, 183, 186, 191, 192, 198, 201–203, 211

Gannett, 90, 206, 219
gatekeeper, 53, 54; gatekeeping, 96
Gawker Media, 90
Giffords, Gabrielle, 8, 76, 85
Glass, Ira, 86
Gregory, David, 30, 141

Hannity, Sean, 104, 141, 177, 211, 212
Harris-Perry, Melissa, 65, 66
Henderson, Jim, 55, 56, 97, 99, 100, 103, 104, 111, 112, 125, 126, 185, 197, 205
Huffington Post; HuffPost 9, 33, 35, 52, 58, 88, 128, 131, 144, 149, 151, 198
Hutchins Commission, 217
Hybrid; hybridity; hybridization, 10, 29, 59, 149, 165, 168, 169, 170, 212
hyper-fragmentation, 11

identity (journalistic, occupational), 17, 18, 21, 22
ideological, 6, 36, 37, 84, 116, 117, 118, 121, 130, 132, 185, 191, 219
ideology, political, 48, 123, 160
Ifill, Gwen, 158

inaccuracy, 32, 78, 122
incivility, xiii, xiv, 1, 10, 73, 75–85,
  87–89, 91–93, 95–99, 101, 103, 105,
  107, 109–111, 113, 115, 117–127,
  129–131, 133, 135, 137, 139, 141, 143,
  145, 147, 149, 151, 153–155, 157, 159,
  161, 163, 165, 210–213, 217
infotainment, 170, 212
Infowars, 6
interpretive communities, journalists as,
  12–14, 16–21, 25, 26, 81
interpretive news, 32, 34, 35, 96
investigative reporting, journalism, 28,
  54, 108, 214, 215
iReport, CNN, 39, 110

Jones, Alex, 6
journalists-turned-academics, 83, 218

Keane, Angela Greiling, 7
Kelly, Megyn, 2, 66, 174, 177, 191, 192
Kinja, 90
Klein, Ezra, 66, 69, 105, 149
Koppel, Ted, 2, 76, 87, 119
Krauthammer, Charles, 165
Kurtz, Howard, 145, 146

Lambidakis, Stephanie, 136–138, 139,
  140, 198, 199
Lehrer, Jim, 164
Lemon, Don, 59, 184
Limbaugh, Rush, 48, 76
literacy, news media, 10, 123, 209, 213,
  214
literary journalism, 28, 79

Maddow, Rachel, 103, 141
Massimo, Rick, 44, 45, 49, 89, 122, 123
Mastio, Dave, 32, 39, 45, 50, 52, 70,
  97, 104, 112, 128, 130, 132, 135, 153,
  154, 175, 204, 218, 219
Matalin, Mary, 30
Matthews, Chris, 30, 151
McCurry, Mike, 7
McLaughlin Group, 119, 129, 165

media regime, 29, 213
media-tized; mediatization, xiii, 32
metajournalistic discourse, 13, 20, 21
misinformation, 7, 11, 219
Morgan, Piers, 59
MSNBC, 3, 27, 31, 33–36, 40, 45, 46,
  51, 58, 63–66, 76, 88, 101–103, 105,
  111–116, 118, 119, 131, 132, 137, 140,
  141, 177, 186, 191, 192, 198, 203
Muir, David, 172, 184
Mundy, Liza, 35, 49, 70, 108, 124, 125,
  134, 144, 190, 218
Murdoch, Rupert, 103, 122, 206

NBC network, 6, 36, 40, 66, 102, 141,
  165, 168, 174, 176, 178, 179, 186,
  191, 192, 199, 202, 217
NBCnews.com, 202
NCEW (National Conference of
  Editorial Writers), 84
New York Times, The, 9, 35, 40, 54, 66,
  69, 71, 90, 101, 105, 106, 113, 116,
  127, 128, 130, 132, 137, 141, 144,
  145, 149–151, 171, 186, 189, 190, 199,
  200, 217
Nieman Journalism Lab, 82, 89, 90, 218
nonprofit media, 7, 89, 91, 108, 214
NPR, 4, 10, 31, 86

Obama, President Barack, 1, 3, 57, 59,
  60, 76, 87, 98, 116, 125, 138, 142,
  158, 160–162, 194, 215
objective journalism, xiii, xiv, 2, 28, 29,
  37, 38, 47, 54, 67, 69, 79, 111, 117,
  132, 133, 143, 145, 146, 148, 152,
  156, 174, 187, 207, 209
objectivity (in news), 10, 27–29, 106,
  108, 132, 141, 156
Olbermann, Keith, 76
Omidyar, Pierre, 189
op-ed, 76, 103, 104, 113, 141, 154, 155
Oprah Winfrey, 8, 167, 168, 176, 177
O'Brien, Conan, 177, 180
O'Reilly, Bill; "The O'Reilly Factor," 2, 30,
  51, 59, 87, 88, 119, 132, 179, 185, 191

Palin, Sarah, 30, 76
parasocial interaction; parasocial relationship, 171, 195
participatory democracy, 156
partisan news; partisan press, 6, 10, 28–31, 40, 47, 59, 76, 77, 79, 96, 98, 117, 121, 134, 143, 149, 154, 165, 187, 211, 217
PBS, xiv, 83, 86, 155, 157–165, 211; "Newshour," 155, 157–165, 211
Pelley, Scott, 3, 191
Perlmutter, Bruce, 52, 62, 89, 105, 113, 139, 140, 174, 196
personality-driven news, 62, 172, 210
Pew Research Center, xiii, 9, 31, 32, 38, 66, 75, 80, 86, 98, 102, 192, 211, 214, 218
Phillips, Amber, 27, 54, 67, 98, 101, 111, 120, 142, 152, 153, 187, 191, 196, 197, 206, 207
point-of-view journalism, 63, 67, 98, 103, 106, 114, 115, 132, 140, 141, 144, 211
polarization, political, 10, 29, 56, 57, 115, 118, 210, 218
Politico, 7, 69, 88, 144, 146, 150, 151, 179, 197
post-truth, 4
Poynter Institute, 81–83, 87, 89, 218
ProPublica, 108, 189
pundit, 30–32, 86, 116
punditry, 27, 28, 31

quasi-journalist, 30, 88

Reuters, 146
Rieder, Rem, 34, 41, 42, 53, 57, 58, 64, 107, 108, 115, 117, 120, 121, 126, 134, 135, 143–146, 148, 206
"Rock Center," 87, 167, 168, 174–177
Romenesko, Jim, 93, 145
Romney, Mitt, 88, 116, 158–162
Rosen, Jay, 141, 145, 150
Rosenstiel, Tom, 145, 210, 214
RTDNA, 24

RTNDA, 25
Ryan, Paul, 163

Satullo, Chris, 6, 7, 214
Sawyer, Diane, 172
Scarborough, Joe, 3, 174
Schieffer, Bob, 83
selective exposure, 10, 110, 117, 190
self-branding, journalistic, 67, 70, 71, 73, 210
Sesno, Frank, 35, 58, 59, 100, 121, 140, 141, 144, 173, 178, 191, 193, 204
Shafer, Jack, 38, 40, 70, 122, 130, 139, 144–148, 169, 177, 179, 180, 200, 217
Shaw, Bernard, 64
Shields, Mark, xiv, 155, 157–165, 211, 212
Shorenstein Center on Media, Politics, and Public Policy, 89
Silver, Nate, 66
Smiley, Tavis, 88
solutions journalism, 7
Stelter, Brian, 57, 63, 97, 101, 103, 104, 106, 114, 115, 117, 132, 140, 141, 144–146, 150, 167, 171–173, 176, 184, 192, 198
Stephanopoulos, George, 8, 171, 172
Stewart, Jon, 38, 76, 88, 123, 136, 168, 180, 181
Sullivan, Andrew, 8, 110, 191 66, 70
Sullivan, Margaret, 3, 4, 31, 32, 145

Todd, Chuck, 136, 141
Tow Center for Digital Journalism, 9, 22, 89
transparency (in journalism), 10, 29, 165, 186, 210
Trump, President Donald; administration, 1–8, 27, 28, 31, 215
Twitter, 2, 41–43, 51, 53, 67, 69, 72, 88, 90, 98, 106, 110, 117, 118, 137, 153, 181, 196, 197, 200, 203, 209, 218

USA Today, 39, 41, 50, 71, 90, 97, 99, 100, 104, 112, 128, 144, 153, 154, 219 user-generated content, 9, 194

Vandehei, Jim, 69
Van Susteren, Greta, 8, 87, 191
Vice News, 202
Vox, 39, 66, 207

Washington Post, The, 2–5, 9, 27, 31, 35–37, 40, 54, 58, 66, 67, 71, 72, 76, 89, 106, 111, 127, 137, 144, 145, 149, 150, 153, 180, 186, 189, 201, 205, 218
watchdog role of journalism, xiv, 31, 32, 48
Watergate, 28, 48, 69

Wemple, Erik, 37, 38, 40, 59, 67, 68, 75, 88, 102, 103, 118, 119, 129, 144–147, 150, 151, 173, 175, 177, 202
Williams, Brian, xiv, 36, 38, 66, 167, 168, 170, 172–176, 179–181, 184, 192, 212
Woodruff, Judy, 158, 163, 164
Woodward, Bob, 69

Yahoo, 72, 90, 168, 178

Zelizer, Barbie, 12, 17, 18, 19, 20, 29, 81, 89, 92, 93
Zucker, Jeff, 4, 6, 59, 60, 62, 65, 210
Zuckerberg, Mark, 209

www.ingramcontent.com/pod-product-compliance
Lightning Source LLC
Chambersburg PA
CBHW020644230426
43665CB00008B/309